Least of the Apostles

Least of the Apostles

Paul and His Legacies in Earliest Christianity

Brendan W. Case
and William Glass

Foreword by Douglas A. Campbell

◆PICKWICK *Publications* • Eugene, Oregon

LEAST OF THE APOSTLES
Paul and His Legacies in Earliest Christianity

Copyright © 2022 Brendan W. Case and William Glass. All rights reserved. Except for brief quotations in critical publications or reviews, no part of this book may be reproduced in any manner without prior written permission from the publisher. Write: Permissions, Wipf and Stock Publishers, 199 W. 8th Ave., Suite 3, Eugene, OR 97401.

Pickwick Publications
An Imprint of Wipf and Stock Publishers
199 W. 8th Ave., Suite 3
Eugene, OR 97401

www.wipfandstock.com

PAPERBACK ISBN: 978-1-6667-3133-0
HARDCOVER ISBN: 978-1-6667-2372-4
EBOOK ISBN: 978-1-6667-2373-1

Cataloguing-in-Publication data:

Names: Case, Brendan [author]. | Glass, William [author]

Title: Least of the apostles : Paul and his legacies in earliest Christianity / Brendan W. Case and William Glass.

Description: Eugene, OR: Pickwick Publications, 2022 | Includes bibliographical references and index.

Identifiers: ISBN 978-1-6667-3133-0 (paperback) | ISBN 978-1-6667-2372-4 (hardcover) | ISBN 978-1-6667-2373-1 (ebook)

Subjects: LCSH: Paul, the Apostle, Saint | Bible—Epistles of Paul—Criticism, interpretation, etc. | Bible.—James—Criticism, interpretation, etc. | Bible.—Gospels—Criticism, interpretation, etc. | Bible.—Hebrews—Criticism, interpretation, etc. | History of biblical events

Classification: BS2506.3 C37 2022 (print) | BS2506.3 (ebook)

05/13/22

Scripture quotations marked (RSV) are taken from Revised Standard Version of the Bible, copyright © 1946, 1952, and 1971 National Council of the Churches of Christ in the United States of America. Used by permission. All rights reserved worldwide.

For Alissa and Ana

Contents

Foreword by Douglas A. Campbell | ix
Acknowledgments | xiii

Introduction: Crooked Lines through Pauline Scholarship | 1

Paul among the Apostles

1. James as the Origin of Pauline Justification | 13
2. The Immoral Brother and the Apostolic Decree: The Ethics of 1 Corinthians | 47
3. Pauline Evidence for Markan Posteriority | 69

The Legacies of Paul

4. Apollos and the Pauline Influence on Hebrews: A Proposal of Origin and Occasion | 93
5. "What Is Born of Spirit Is Spirit": Paul's "Spiritual Body" in Luke and John | 126
6. In Memoriam: The Influence of Paul and Peter on the New Testament and the Early Church | 146

Conclusion: Prolegomena to Any Future New Testament Theology | 183

Bibliography | 199
Scripture Index | 213
Ancient Authors Index | 225
Keywords and Modern Authors Index | 227

Foreword

Douglas A. Campbell

As Brendan Case and William Glass both well know, much Pauline analysis today is still shaped by the paradigmatic views of F. C. Baur. Moreover, much analysis is then shaped in turn by the explanation of Paul principally constructed by J. B. Lightfoot in opposition to the views of Baur and the so-called "Tübingen School." Indeed, these two paradigms stand opposing one another like superpowers, while later scholars scurry to and fro across the contested Pauline terrain between them on expeditions and sorties whose basic terms have already been set.

Baur's vision of Paul and his relationship with the rest of the early church was Hegelian and dialectical. It took conflict to be the key feature of the church, with Paul's position being stringently opposed by an antithetical Jewish Christian view of the gospel. The book of Acts then reflects a later, more pacific, and more domesticated age. Acts's portrayal of the harmony in the early church is consequently somewhat disingenuous, as are the names attached to many of the NT's documents; these later texts paper over the original all-important conflict. By way of contrast, Lightfoot offered a much more urbane vision of the church that was rightly ordered, ultimately in rather episcopal terms. He used later

Christian literature, including an edited collection of writings not found in the canon, "the Apostolic Fathers," to suggest that the early church was very much as Acts depicted it—unfolding in a largely harmonious way under the authorized direction of its appointed leaders, and ultimately tending towards the organization that Ignatius would shortly recommend, namely, bishops.

After the advent of these two early schools of Pauline interpretation, scholars invariably face the questions they posed—not to mention, the powerful answers they articulated—as they try to grasp the apostle Paul's life and legacy. To what extent *was* conflict a feature of his life and work, and how important was conflict for what actually happened in the development of the early church? Was this conflict, if it took place, critical *for* the subsequent development of the Jesus movement into the Christian church?! Hence, was the leadership of the early church *fundamentally* riven apart by key differences of opinion about salvation and ethics in relation to Jewish concerns, or were the differences in question resolved over the course of a long journey that fundamentally tended toward reconciliation and agreement? Moreover, to what extent are the NT texts, both Pauline and non-Pauline, embedded *directly* in this journey, authored by its participants as they work through their differences, as against created to impart a later viewpoint resulting from one faction's triumph and consequent partial rewriting of that journey in more acceptable and irenic terms? History, after all, is generally written by its victors.

The paradigms of Baur and of Lightfoot continue to pose these questions to all scholars of Paul, and ultimately to all NT work, because Paul is here seen to be, in some sense, the fundamental and ground-breaking figure and so the key to the whole. And Brendan Case and William Glass in full appreciation of this agenda offer here their own set of answers by pressing an important although under-utilized method, and showing how it leads to rather unexpected insights. The result is a highly creative, synthetic, and ultimately rather fascinating collection of judgments.

Correctly taking Paul to be the key, they begin their distinctive work by following the dictum of John Knox that Paul's own authentic letters *must* be privileged initially over all other sources because they are incontestably primary data, deriving from an eyewitness, and all other texts and data are contestable and/or secondary. Paul's data must therefore control the introduction of other evidence, although it is a great gift to modern scholars seeking to trace a way through this complex material that it can act in this way. Paul's first-hand data must be pressed hard, and the trail followed where it leads—and this is where the work of Case and Glass becomes so interesting.

They argue that a lot of scholars have been unduly influenced by Baur's overarching solution, not to mention by his suspicions and skepticism, and so have failed to grasp how Paul's data points toward many of Lightfoot's explanations, or at least, to explanations sharing his more catholic viewpoint. Baur is not left behind. But the conflicts that are found and traced through Paul's life and work are not as extensive or fundamental as Baur's original thesis suggested. A picture emerges rather of early church leaders working through their differences, and ultimately together, and this picture allows many of the more skeptical judgments made by modern scholars treading in Baur's dialectical footsteps concerning authorship to be challenged in turn. In essence, a synthetic account of the early church emerges from their careful, critical reading of Paul, along with a corresponding set of judgments about the authorship and import of various NT texts that can be shown—at least arguably—to integrate with this basic picture. So it makes sense, for example, for James to have written James, and to have written it in the way he has, without suggesting thereby that a conflict with Paul and with Paul's views is irreconcilable. (And so on.)

One of the great joys in life as a teacher is seeing brilliant students learn what they need to learn and then go on to find dazzling new applications and insights of their own. It is therefore a very great joy for me to be able to indicate here just how interesting the insights of Brendan Case and William Glass are—and to acknowledge in the same breath just how inappropriate it would be to continue to call them students. My students are now my teachers. Having said this, I wager that I will not be the only person who is now taught by them when it comes to explaining that perenially fascinating, critical, and difficult figure, the apostle Paul, along with his impact on his fellow leaders in the early church, not to mention on those writings in the NT that do not bear his name but that seem to have been written with his views and influence very much in mind. *Tolle lege.*

Acknowledgments

I (Brendan) must first thank William, not least for convincing me to embark on this (frankly) hare-brained enterprise, and for the countless ways in which he has improved my own contributions. Above all, though, I'm grateful for the gift of his friendship; my life would be much poorer (and my calendar much emptier!) without our many running discussions and disagreements, which are among my great joys and consolations.

Next, I must thank my family, beginning with my dear wife, Alissa, and our four children, Amelia, Estelle, Teddy, and Eloise. You are all so kind, funny, intelligent, and sweet, and I feel keenly how little I deserve a life with you. I'm also so grateful for my mom, Susan, for holding our family together with both hands, and for my sister, Lizzy, for her friendship and encouragement.

I would also like to thank my teachers, especially Douglas Campbell, whose work on Paul initially inspired this project, and my doctor-father, Paul Griffiths, who taught me to read and think. Richard Hays provided helpful comments on an early draft of the "spiritual bodies" chapter, and the members of the 2014–2015 New Testament Colloquium at Duke Divinity School offered trenchant comments on and criticism of an early version of the chapter on Synoptic traditions in Paul. Needless to say, all remaining errors are my own.

I (William) must say, to Brendan, on all fronts, ditto. Brendan is, and has always been, *il miglior fabbro*. It is worth acknowledging, in part, because this project will remove all doubt about it. But having him as a friend is more than enough consolation for losing one argument after another for nigh on ten years now. Brendan belongs to that rare class of friends whose ideas have so profoundly shaped mine that I can no longer tell when I'm just stealing them from him.

To Damaris, Dan, Karis, Ron, Susie, Joy, Jon-Karl, Alicia, Chelsea, Mom: unending gratitude.

To Audrey, Grant, Katrina, Johnny, Amber, Matt, Liam, Ezra, Theo, and Annabelle: finishing my part of this project would not have happened if you all had not kept me alive and well during these plague-ridden times. This project will not measure up to the debt I owe you, but I offer it anyway.

To Douglas Campbell, on whose shoulders Brendan and I have stood (and from whose shoulders we have no doubt too often fallen), thank you for a vision of Paul that is worthy of the Gospel he preached.

And to Ana (and *Cafecita*), no words are sufficient. Only a whole life offered will do.

Introduction

Crooked Lines through Pauline Scholarship

WILLIAM GLASS

The Bible tells us to love our neighbors, and also to love our enemies; probably because generally these are the same people.
—G. K. CHESTERTON, *Illustrated London News*, July 16, 1910

IN THE UNITED STATES, there is still a sufficient crumb of faith left in the general public that one can witness an extremely odd thing in the world: an informal discussion of the New Testament by people who do not specialize in studying it. Such discussions are exciting, partly for the passion with which they are pursued and partly for the window they provide into the relationship between specialist research and the filtering of that research into the common gloss. A few years ago, at a gathering of friends from one of our churches, one friend advocated in the strongest possible terms that Paul worried her because he denigrated the human body in favor of spiritual realities. Another responded that the bodily resurrection of Jesus was the "center" of Pauline thought. He then proceeded to give a precise description of the resurrection body based on the fact that the marks from the crucifixion were still in Jesus' hands when he was resurrected. In response, the first friend queried, stumping the resurrection enthusiast, what right he had to assume Paul knew about the wounds in Jesus' hands after the resurrection: after all, Paul explicitly claims no such knowledge.

Another friend insisted that the heart of Paul, the New Testament, and the whole of Scripture, was the justification of sinners by grace through faith; a person does not even begin to understand Paul, he continued, until she believes this. During the remainder of that evening, in fits and starts, discussion circulated around modern ethics and sexuality, slavery and modern issues of race, Pauline psychology ("he was a genius and deeply troubled with his own self-discovery"), the question of whether he authored all the letters attributed to him (and what that would mean), and whether Paul's mission would have made sense to the historical Jesus. Someone brought up, as evidence that he probably would not, a then-recent movie about Paul written by Robert Orlando, *A Polite Bribe*, in which Orlando contests that the historical Jesus, had he known Paul, would probably have had a difficult time recognizing him as a legitimate disciple; this was certainly the case with Jesus's chosen Twelve.

We are aware that the above report may seem rather like a Platonic dialogue in modern dress. How convenient that the writers of a book on Paul should have so many discussions with non-experts that just *happen* to revolve around current (and former) Pauline debates! We trust, however, that those who have involved themselves in the American religious scene will recognize this episode from their own experience. And we think there is great profit to be had, as this book will show, in surrounding NT scholarship with a cloud of witnesses different from those to whom we most often look. As I (William) witnessed this discussion unfolding, it occurred to me that in an SBL meeting, these conversations would probably all occur in separate rooms. This is not a problem, necessarily; specialty requires focus and when it comes to scholarly insight, as often as not, the riches are in the niches. But specialization can also reify existing scotoses, with few avenues for a check on blind spots. The persistent difficulties in the study of Paul are as much sociological, scholastic even, as they are ideological.

Introduction 3

I. Do We Need Another Genealogy of Pauline Studies?

In short, probably not. We have written this book to make a constructive proposal to the study of the apostle to the gentiles. We have to say where we think our study fits, but we are painfully aware (having studied most of them) of the accelerated proliferation of door-stopping Paul books, with their enormous diagnoses of "where it all went wrong."[1] Our approach is modest; let a thousand flowers bloom! If Paul is difficult enough that the Prince of the Apostles had a hard time with him (2 Pet 3:15), we should not hope to get along with less than the entire Pauline enterprise. As the following will show, we have learned much from every stream of thought: Catholic and Protestant, "apocalyptic" and "salvation-historical," perspectives old, new, and otherwise, covenant (and new covenant) theology, and even the work of analytic philosophers (gasp!) has illuminated our endeavor to understand the great missionary of Tarsus. But it seems these days that any Paul book must justify itself by appeal to some sweeping systemic problem with the discipline as a whole. In contrast, the rationale for our book is simply that the essays within it have something to add to the conversation.

But taken together, they do offer a modest contribution to the scholarly habits of New Testament scholars. What emerges from the essays below is a Paul who is, first and foremost, an apostle of Jesus, a witness of the Lord's resurrection who, by that fact, was deputized and authorized with a message for the world. That message and office were not Paul's alone but were held in common between himself and a handful of confreres whose names appear both within and outside the Pauline corpus. The office Paul held and the trust that accompanied it were public; as he himself (probably) said, "this was not done in a corner" (Acts 26:26). Crucial to understanding Paul, as the essays below will contend, is the relationship that he himself had with others of those who were also apostles. And that relationship thus illuminates the rest of the New Testament.

The difficult, hard-won unity of mission and purpose that Paul and the other apostles maintained is so commonly attested to and reflected upon within the New Testament that one is astonished to see how rare

---

1. Or book-length surveys of the discipline as companion volumes to such works (see Wright, *Paul and His Recent Interpreters*). Wright's book begins with Baur and the Tübingen hypothesis and does a masterful job tracing the through-lines in subsequent movements in the study of Paul. It is also among the more entertaining contributions to the discussion; what could we hope to add?

discussions of it are within the study of his thought and work. There are scores of books that attempt to situate Paul in his relationships to Judaism, to philosophy, to the political realities of his day, or even to all of them![2] But the corpus of literature explicitly addressing Paul's relationships to the Twelve and to the communities they founded is vanishingly small, even if there are plenty of reproduced assumptions at work in the rest of the guild. This is where we raise our ragged sail. Paul is not merely an apostle but one *of the apostles*, albeit in his own words, the least of them. And the essays below, which attempt to mine that insight for all it's worth, contribute what we take to be a cleaner, straighter line from Pentecost to Polycarp, from the life of Jesus of Nazareth to the powerful bishoprics of the early Church.

It is hard to know why Pauline scholarship so rarely explores the effects on Paul's thought of the relationships with those who were the first to lay claim to an office he came to share in. Part of the problem, we suspect, is the legacy of F. C. Baur, who both contemplated deeply the importance of Paul's relationship to the other apostles and (so many now agree) overcooked his evidence a bit to overstate the conflict between them. Very few scholars still preserve Baur's restriction of the Pauline canon to include only Galatians, Romans, and the Corinthian letters. Nor will many maintain his Hegelian account of the early Church's resolution of Judaism and Hellenism into something called "early catholicism." As Wright notes, quite correctly, "Baur's categories do not in fact correspond to, or well describe, any actual phenomena in the first century or the centuries on either side."[3] Still, in a curious display of scholarly fashion, the revision of most of Baur's conclusions has at the same time reified a lot of his approach to, among other things, questions of authenticity and pseudepigraphy, the history of religions, and even the life of Jesus! But perhaps nowhere is Baur's continuing influence more readily felt than in the assumption of veracity for conflict-driven accounts of the New Testament Church. As the essays below will show, scholars have taken as axiomatic that the communities whose existence is revealed in the New Testament documents are relatively isolated and, to the extent that they are aware of other communities, rivalrous. To the extent that anything

---

2. E.g., Engberg-Pedersen, *Cosmology and Self in the Apostle Paul*; Engberg-Pedersen, *Paul and the Stoics*; Horsley, *Paul and Empire*; Sanders, *Paul and Palestinian Judaism*. Wright, *Paul and the Faithfulness of God*, is so enormous in large part because he tries to situate Paul conclusively among all these differing worlds.

3. Wright, *Paul and His Recent Interpreters*, 16.

in the New Testament appears to say otherwise, it is largely held to be a product of the second generation. This narrative is for the most part a figment of scholarly imagination and it requires skipping over a large amount of evidence both in the New Testament and elsewhere. But it rests, like a concealed foundation, beneath a large network of assumptions about the meanings of the documents within the New Testament.

The materials we do have testify, instead, to a hard-won collegiality, maintained at great personal and corporate cost, between the Apostle to the gentiles, the followers of the Jewish Messiah, and the communities they each founded. These people knew one another and, at the command of their Teacher and Lord, loved one another—even when they did not like each other that much. None of this is to deny the existence of real conflict; the New Testament simply will not allow that conclusion. But that conflict was nestled, we will argue, within a larger commitment to fellowship and unity of message and purpose. The constant repetition of a few names within the New Testament gives literary witness to the fact that the lives and work of the earliest Christian missionaries were mutually entangled. We recall the wry observation of Richard Bauckham that Tübingen-influenced accounts of the formation of the gospels seem to rest on an assumption that all those who knew Jesus in his life simply died and went to heaven after the resurrection![4] Our proposal concerning the entanglement of life and work among those called apostles will have, we hope, an equally powerful if opposite hermeneutical significance.

II. Our Modest New Proposal

The various studies that follow amount to a piecemeal but serious engagement with conflict-driven narratives of the early church. They accomplish that work by a deep meditation on the life and impact of Paul the Apostle. The work gathers into two sections, with the first exploring Paul's relationship to the other apostles and eyewitnesses of the Lord, while the second attempts to evaluate Paul's legacy in the early church. The first chapter begins from the observation that, as interpretations of one another, the epistle of James and the letters of Paul leave a great deal to be desired. To alleviate such obvious misreadings, scholars have tended to interpose the agency of various intermediaries between Paul and James, irresponsible, antinomian interpreters of Paul whose abuses the letter aims to correct. Such imagined

---

4. Bauckham, *Jesus and the Eyewitnesses*, 7.

communities, we argue, provide a faulty background for the letter in that (a) there is no evidence in James or in Paul's letters where James is in view that such people exist, and (b) James shows no knowledge whatsoever of the key Pauline polemics (e.g., circumcision, food laws, table fellowship, assembly). On the other hand, Gal 2 does witness to people who came from James and who, if Paul represents them fairly (cf. Acts 15:1), seemed to emphasize works of Torah as preconditions for membership in the church and salvation by Jesus. We then argue a reconfigured version of the "intermediary" hypothesis, in which the epistle to James comes first and is subsequently adapted, prior to the Jerusalem Council, by some Christians loyal to James in an effort to counter the Pauline Torah-free (or "Torah-light") mission. Their adaptation of James involves a profound transformation of the letter itself; James's works of charity and justice are replaced by an emphasis on obedience to parts of the Torah designed to cordon off Jews from gentiles, most importantly circumcision. The emergence of this new doctrine in his churches, then, is the origin of the Pauline doctrine of justification. By it, he intends to counteract the work of Jewish Christian missionary interlopers on his gentile congregations.

The second chapter picks up on the other side of the Council, with Paul attempting to bring gentile churches into compliance with a Decree from the epicenter of Jewish Christianity. It begins by noting the oddity of Paul's excommunication of the immoral brother in 1 Cor 5:1. Given the pervasiveness of all sorts of grievous sin at Corinth, why does Paul order the excommunication only of the brother who is sleeping with his father's wife? Theological and sociological reasons are canvassed, each proving unsatisfactory for the same reason: whatever principle would justify the removal of the brother in 5:1 would also compel the removal of others who are not forced to leave. In the absence of principled judgments, a contingent, pastoral reason is desired and found in the apostolic decree recorded in Acts 15 and alluded to in Gal 2. The presence of so clear an example of lawlessness in the gentile churches might endanger the deal Paul has just struck at Jerusalem, which had at last granted legitimacy to the Torah-free (uncircumcised) gentile mission. It is no coincidence, we argue, that a letter written with that event in mind should also contain an extended and complicated argument for abstinence, by and large, from known consumption of idol-meat. Paul's difficulty in that section arises, we argue (following John Hurd's 1965 proposal), from the fact that Paul's own previous teaching and practice among the Corinthians had given no sign that idol-meat was a problem for Christians who know there is one God, one Lord Jesus

Christ, and hence that an idol is nothing. Implied in this reading of 1 Corinthians, we conclude, is a Paul who is much more zealous for unity with the Jerusalem church than is commonly thought. We analyze the reasons for that in terms of Paul's "body of Christ" ecclesiology.

On the strength of the two chapters above, we begin to glimpse a much closer relationship between the apostles than had previously been thought to be the case. Chapter 3 demonstrates that Paul, far from being only distantly interested in the words of the Lord, was instead deeply influenced by the traditions that came to reside in Matthew and Luke. Moreover, this Matthean or Lukan influence is evident even in Paul's quotations from or allusions to pericopes which also appear in the Gospel of Mark. This influence suggests, we think, that what some have called "the one absolutely assured result" of Synoptic studies—Markan Priority—is ripe for reexamination. If the argument here is correct, it suggests that Paul is a crucial figure for understanding not only the church of the first generation and its expansion throughout the Mediterranean but also how the life of Jesus was remembered and how traditions about him were gathered together and passed on. This chapter pushes the gospels and Paul close together, creating just such a picture of their relationships as one might gather from holding Gal 2 and 1 Cor 15 together.

Part II (chapter 4) commences with a discussion of Hebrews as an early installment in the remembrance of Paul. Written (we argue) by Apollos in the early 60s, to the Jews in the Roman congregation, the letter addresses the problem of recent imprisonment of gentile believers for gathering an illegal assembly. Although the Jewish brothers might be tempted to abandon those who were in prison as though they were not in one body with them, and to forsake the gathering of themselves together, Apollos warns them that to turn away from their gentile brothers would be tantamount to crucifying again the Lord Jesus. Apollos, onetime acquaintance of Paul and partner in a complicated cooperation with the church at Corinth, performs a delicate rendition of Paul's epistolary voice (rhetor that he is) to a congregation that was both familiar with that voice and aware that Paul had died, in order to remind them of the thing for which Paul had died. Paul, like his associate Timothy just freed from prison (Heb 13:23), had suffered and (in Paul's case) died for the unity of Jew and gentile in one body of Christ. Apollos's rhetorical *imitatio Pauli* is thus a dramatic remembrance of the Jewish apostle to the gentiles who was willing to sacrifice so many of his own prerogatives, indeed his own life, if it meant Jewish and gentile Christians could each recognize one another in the ecclesial body of Jesus.

Chapter 5 explores the reception of the Pauline epistles in the Gospels of Luke and John by examining what appear to be two different responses to Paul's teaching that the dead rise in a "spiritual body," since "flesh and blood cannot inherit the kingdom of God" (1 Cor 15:45, 50). This teaching seems to have provoked a decidedly anxious reaction from Luke, who reports the resurrected Jesus as pointing to his hands and feet and insisting that "a spirit does not have flesh and blood" (Luke 24:39). John, by contrast, seems to have been fascinated by Paul's portrayal of the resurrected body. Indeed, the Gospel appears to allude to 1 Cor 15:35–50 in discussions of Christ's descent from heaven, of the resurrection which transfigures his corruptible flesh into a glorious Spirit-giver, and of the new birth "by water and the Spirit," which assimilates humanity to him. If we are right to see in the fourth gospel a sustained interest in Paul's groundbreaking ideas about the resurrection, then the fourth evangelist would seem to be not an isolated sectarian but a participant in the complicated theater of Paul's missionary activity.

Chapter 6 examines the role of Peter and Paul as initial guarantors of the trans-local unity that would later be the charge of the church's first bishops. Although this chapter would just as appropriately have fit into Section I's discussion of the relation of Paul to the apostles, it is the legacy of the relationship between these two giants, as well as Peter's attempt to reckon with Paul's writings, that provides the argumentative entrée into the question of their relationship as living apostles. Additionally, it is the legacy of the interpretation of their relationship in the modern period that gave thematic rise to this book in the first place. It thus seemed appropriate to place it here, giving us the additional benefit of dramatizing the inherent artificiality of any distinction between the apostles and their legacies. The apostolic church left us two indivisibly distinct inheritances: the New Testament and the second-century church. We begin from the modern scholarly image of a lifelong rivalry between Peter and Paul, each one claiming to be a legitimate apostle and casting doubt upon the legitimacy of the other. In the minds of scholars who subscribe to this view, the friendlier narrative of Acts is seen as at best pious fiction and at worst deliberate misinformation. Of course the image of Peter and Paul in perpetual conflict relies exegetically, we argue, upon a strong, permanent reading of Gal 2:11–16 and not much else. Noting that other passages in Paul seem to suggest that Gal 2 may not testify to a permanent state of affairs, we turn to the absolute consensus, in the hundred years after they died, that Peter and Paul labored together to maintain a difficult and hard-won unity of message and mission. We argue that Acts presents a more balanced picture of conflict and resolution than scholars in Baur's wake often allowed. Noting Baur's observation that Acts makes Peter look more like Paul and Paul more like Peter, we demonstrate from Paul's letters that there are places where he makes *himself* look like Peter (and the Jerusalem church). We likewise show from Peter's letters (making the case *en route* for the authenticity of both 1 and 2 Peter), that there are Pauline moments to be had in there as well. Thus, if Acts is involved in a whitewash, it is a whitewash of which Peter and Paul must themselves be guilty as well. We conclude, therefore, that although the NT documents themselves reveal a difficult relationship between the two men, both Peter and Paul worked hard at a unity not only between their churches but between one another as witnesses to the events concerning Christ. The traditions concerning their death within short proximity of one another reveal two apostles whose apprehensions and difficulties with one another found expression not in bitter rivalry but in patient endurance and Christ-like suffering grace.

A concluding chapter draws these threads together in a discussion both of what we see this project to have accomplished and where we hope to see it go. An implication of the engagements chronicled here, between Paul and the other apostles, and between all of them and their successors, is that they not only created a shared culture of worship, thought, practice, and mission, but they knew themselves to be doing so. And they recognized one another as valid and necessary players in that enterprise. The literary form of that recognition is what Brevard Childs calls "canon consciousness," an awareness that a body of work is being formed that will always speak best when its components speak together. We are only just beginning to make suggestions on this score; we trust that more discoveries will complicate and illuminate the picture in even more mysterious and beautiful ways. But an implication of the work gathered here is that, in the face of doubt, where one New Testament document appears to illuminate the other, it is best to assume that it does until proven otherwise.

Baur's reading of early Christianity is too simple; as we have already noted, it obscures the complicated nature of the early church's conflicts. There were multiple parties to the conflicts over gentile inclusion in the people of the Jewish Messiah; what was needed therefore was not Hegelian synthesis but an ecumenical council. The agents of the conflict seen in the pages of the New Testament were *also* the agents of reconciliation; love of neighbor, in the early church, meant just as often love of enemies. Their relationships, complicated, costly, and fraught at times with suspicion, were nevertheless borne of repeated engagement with one another—in person, in writing, and by delegation. The roads between earliest Christian communities, conceptually and literally, were quite well-traveled. This implies that the encounters between the apostles in the NT are snapshots, not time-elapsed photos. They witness a moment, preceded and followed by other moments, in which the message of Christ was proclaimed again (or not) in the welcome of his disciples for one another. The Paul whom we see publicly shaming Peter in the flashback of Gal 2:11–16 is the same Paul who honors Peter as the first to see the risen Lord in 1 Cor 15:5. And the canon witnesses to this kind of complexity of social movement, the inhale and exhale of the body of Christ, as those who deal pain later apply the balm: *simul iustus et peccator*.

The continuity that draws Paul's entire story together in the context of the NT is thus a *narrative* continuity. And it is not for no reason, then, that the epistles first circulated under the cover of a narrative introduction in the book of Acts. We concur with a scholarly judgment that resists seeing in Luke's sequel a simple chronological tale of the growth of the early church. Evidence both internal and external calls that tale deeply into question. But we would also emphasize that as the present book took shape, every time we threw Acts out and resolved to work as faithfully as possible with the "first-hand" materials of the New Testament, Acts was waiting at the conclusion of those labors. Acts would predispose a reader to seeing a fundamental (narrative) continuity between James and Paul. Acts carefully and faithfully reports the significant distinctions in the roles of Paul and Peter (see ch. 6 below) while insisting that we see them as two men engaged in the service of one Lord. Acts identifies Apollos as a source of great encouragement to the church and also as a person who might cause occasional problems. And Acts, most importantly, testifies to a narrative coherence for the rest of the NT: a narrative that begins with shepherds and ends with Paul and Peter watching over their flocks by night—that begins with magi from the east and ends with the nations gathered to God. It is a narrative that begins with a Pharisee on the make, chasing Jewish Christians all over Palestine and Syria to imprison them, and ends with the least of the apostles, chasing gentiles to the corners of the world to release them from their chains.

Paul among the Apostles

1

James as the Origin of Pauline Justification

BRENDAN CASE

HOW DOES THE JUSTIFICATION material in the Epistle of James relate to justification in Paul's epistles? This is one of the great puzzles of New Testament studies, but at least since the Reformers placed justification at the center of Pauline interpretation,[1] the vast majority of commentators have offered variations on a single solution to it, taking James as derivative from and somehow responsive to Paul. Taking the form of an extended thought-experiment, this chapter entertains and develops a rival thesis, which was first sketched in just a few lines by J. A. T. Robinson, who suggested that Romans 4's discussion of Abraham is perhaps "a reply, not to James, but to the use made of him by Judaizers in a subtly different context (that of the basis of salvation for Gentiles)."[2] Far from being dependent on Paul, James might represent the earliest extant installment of justification discourse, which was relayed to Paul by "the Teachers,"[3]

---

1. As the "*articulus stantis et cadentis ecclesiae*"; cf. McGrath, *Iustitia Dei*, 189; cf. also Jüngel, *Justification*, 17n4.

2. Robinson, *Redating the New Testament*, 128.

3. As we will call them, following Martyn, *Theological Issues*, 9.

a group of Jewish-Christian missionaries closely linked with James and Jerusalem, who adapted James's discourse for a Law-observant mission to the gentiles, and so provoked a dramatic rejoinder from Paul in the Letter to the Galatians.

William Wrede and Abraham Schweitzer suggested long ago that justification is a polemical "subsidiary crater," conceptually isolated from Paul's primary account of salvation as participation in Christ.[4] Later still, J. Louis Martyn and Douglas Campbell developed this thesis by proposing that Paul's bitter controversy with the Teachers can account for the origin of this polemical discourse; this chapter extends that line of thought, by supposing that the Teachers did not originate justification discourse, but rather adapted it from the teachings of James, the brother of Jesus. This sketch of justification's development, proceeding from James to the Teachers to Paul, might prove capable of resolving the difficulties that have dogged earlier accounts.

James and the Justification of Jewish Christians

The modern debates over the origins and aims of James are vast, and nothing approaching a comprehensive treatment is possible here. In keeping with the chapter's speculative register, this section generally follows Richard Bauckham's treatment of the justification material in Jas 2:14–26 as fully independent of Paul, with the aim of demonstrating its plausibility and openness to accommodating our revisionist account of James' relation to Paul.

The Question of Authorship

As Bauckham correctly insists, the letter undoubtedly styles itself as authored by James the Just, the eldest brother of Jesus (Mark 6:7), the only James in the earliest church who needed no appositional modifier to distinguish him.[5] Elsewhere in the New Testament, a solitary "James" is always the Lord's brother (Acts 12:17; 15:13; Gal 2:9; cf. Jude 1), and so it

---

4. See especially Campbell, *The Deliverance of God*; Martyn, *Theological Issues*; Martyn, *Galatians*. William Wrede calls justification Paul's "polemical doctrine" (Wrede, *Paul*, 123); Albert Schweitzer refers to it as a "subsidiary crater" (Schweitzer, *Mysticism of Paul*, 225).

5. Cf. Matt 10:3; Mark 1:19; 15:40.

must be here.⁶ Further, James gives every indication of being a document written from Judea pre-70 CE to the worldwide community of *Jews*. It is addressed to "the twelve tribes of the Diaspora" (Jas 1:1), which, as Bauckham observes, refers straightforwardly to ethnic Israel.⁷ James's remark about the readers' "*synagogē*" (Jas 2:2) is likewise revealing; an "*ekklēsia*" wholly separate from the synagogue is presumably not in view here.⁸ Since it addresses the Diaspora generally, the letter's implied point of origin might well be Palestine, and likely Jerusalem.⁹

Bauckham terms the letter a "paraenetic encyclical," since it offers general, hypothetical exhortations to the global community of Jewish Christians.¹⁰ Early Jewish letters from Jerusalem to the Diaspora have a ready parallel in Jer 29:1–28,¹¹ and such a letter could easily have come from James, the undisputed leader of the Jerusalem church. Indeed, in

---

6. Cf. Martin Dibelius: "Our sources know only *one* person of reputation in primitive Christianity who could have been suggested by the way in which his name appears in the prescript of our letter: *James, the brother of Jesus*" (Dibelius, *James*, 12).

7. Bauckham, *James*, 14. Joel Marcus has proposed instead that James understands the ten "lost tribes" as converted gentiles (among whom the lost tribes had been assimilated centuries before) (Marcus, "The Twelve Tribes," 433–47). While he's surely right that the invocation of the Twelve Tribes reflects a belief in the eschatological ingathering of all Israel (cf. also Matt 19:28; Rev 7:4–8), the body of the epistle offers no indications that its intended audience includes gentiles; indeed, as we'll see below it repeatedly confounds such an expectation. First Peter 1:1 might initially seem to count against Bauckham's view, since 1 Pet 1:18 strongly suggests that the greeting "to the elect exiles of the diaspora" is actually addressed, not to Jews, but to converted *gentiles*. However, the comparison with 1 Peter actually seems to me to *confirm* the Jewish audience of James—throughout his first epistle, Peter uses forms of address that *prima facie* suggest a Jewish audience as a way of dramatizing his central concern to insist that his gentile readers have been incorporated into Israel *as gentiles* (cf. also 1 Pet 1:12–13; 2:5–12).

8. Jas 5:14 complicates this picture, but the basic point still likely stands. Cf. Witherington III, *Letters and Homilies for Early Jewish Christians*, 398.

9. Bauckham, *James*, 16.

10. Bauckham, *James*, 16. Martin Dibelius, like so many commentators, therefore simply misses the point when he observes, "There are no indications of an epistolary situation in Jas, there are also no *epistolary remarks* of any sort.... All these observations make it impossible to consider Jas an actual letter" (Dibelius, *James*, 2). There are no indications of a particular occasion for James because it, unlike a Pauline epistle, is not a writing evoked by a particular crisis or concern in a particular community; it is an encyclical, meant for the edification of all who might read it.

11. Bauckham, *James*, 20. Bauckham also catalogues a number of letters preserved in the Mishnah which seem to have been sent by Jerusalem priests to the Diaspora, advising communities there regarding cultic matters (Bauckham, *James*, 19).

Acts James proposes sending a similar encyclical to the global community of gentile Christians (Acts 15:20).

Of course, there is a common set of objections to James's authenticity that turns on a sharp distinction between "Hellenized" Diaspora Judaism and "Hebraic" Palestinian Judaism, but this distinction has been helpfully complicated (if not simply confounded) by Martin Hengel.[12] As he demonstrates, all first century Judaism, including that in Palestine, was at least partly Hellenized.[13] In his *Paulus und Jakobus*, Hengel observes that fully a third of the local inscriptions in and around Jerusalem during the Second Temple period are in Greek.[14] He goes on to summarize a set of twentieth century studies of the Epistle's rhetorical and stylistic features with this comment: "All that could indicate that it was written by a Greek-educated Palestinian Jew who knew both the Old Testament-Jewish Wisdom tradition and the basics of rhetoric (*die Grundbegriffe der Rhetorik*)."[15]

Was James Literate?

Hengel's judgment, however, raises a question pressed forcefully by Bart Ehrman: is it credible to think that James could have known Greek, much less have known even the basics of rhetorical composition? Relying on recent studies that place literacy in first-century Palestine at about 3 percent of the population, Ehrman concludes that it is highly unlikely that the son of an artisan (cf. Mark 6:3) would have had the ability even to read Greek, much less to compose in it with some sophistication.[16]

The first of Ehrman's claims that we ought to examine is that James could not have been literate, and certainly not in Greek. The most obvious argument against James's illiteracy is Jesus' literacy (Luke 4:16–17; cf. also his general facility with the Scriptures presupposed everywhere in the Gospels); Ehrman acknowledges this point, but doesn't reckon adequately with it.[17] If Jesus knew how to read (Hebrew, perhaps Aramaic), then he must have learned how to read. And any circumstance in which Jesus

---

12. Dibelius is representative: "Nor does the language of our text point to an author who spent his life as a Jew in Palestine. The author writes Greek as his mother tongue.... Furthermore, he uses the Greek Bible" (Dibelius, *James*, 17).

13. Hengel, *Judaism and Hellenism*; cf. Bauckham, *James*, 22.

14. Hengel, *Paulus und Jakobus*, 521.

15. Hengel, *Paulus und Jakobus*, 517.

16. Ehrman, *Forgery and Counterforgery*, 246–47, 286–87.

17. Ehrman, *Forgery and Counterforgery*, 286.

learned how to read is, *prima facie*, a circumstance in which James also could have learned to read. Further yet, there is no great reason to suppose that James would have known no Greek. It is altogether likely that Jesus' family would have spent time in the comparatively cosmopolitan towns of Sepphoris and Tiberias, which were only a few miles away from Nazareth, and where spoken Greek would've been relatively common.[18]

Further, both Hengel and Ehrman arguably exaggerate the extent of literary skill required of the author of the Epistle of James. After all, Randy Richards has shown that professional scribes, who were a ubiquitous, but often unnamed, feature of ancient letter writing,[19] could play an active role in determining the form of a letter. At times, argues Richards, "the form, syntax, vocabulary and style as well as specific pieces of content were contributed by the secretary, who was usually more experienced in epistolary expression, while the general content and perhaps argumentation remained the author's."[20] We know that even so competent a writer as Josephus relied on scribes to clean up his Greek;[21] perhaps James availed himself of similar help on a much more modest scale. In this case, nothing about the Epistle of James requires that its author himself have been a formally educated author; a literate, Greek-speaking Jew familiar with the Old Testament and with access to competent scribes would have sufficed.

Ehrman is quite critical of Richards on this score, however, arguing that the vast evidence for stylistic interventions in short, stereotyped letters is not relevant data, given the length and intricacy of NT epistles, and that the more relevant example of Cicero's scribe Tiro is too isolated and too removed from the apostles' experiences to be helpful.[22] Both

---

18. Cf. Crossan, *The Historical Jesus*, 19. Even the skeptical Dale Allison offers a far more temperate view of the problem than does Ehrman: "Given what we now know about the nature of first century Judaism, it would be imprudent to insist that James of Jerusalem could not have composed a letter in Greek. Greek was spoken—and not just in upper circles—in Jewish Palestine, Nazareth was close to Sepphoris and its Greek culture, and there were Greek-speaking Jews in Jerusalem from whom James, when he resided there, could have learned much were he so motivated" (Allison, *Epistle of James*, 25).

19. Richards, *Paul and First Century Letter Writing*, 60–64.

20. Richards, *Paul and First Century Letter Writing*, 65. Cf. also: "Most typical letter writers from Paul's day did not have the educational training to compose a pleasing letter. These less literate writers likely wanted the secretary to improve the grammar, etc." (Richards, *Paul and First Century Letter Writing*, 75).

21. Josephus, *Ag. Ap.* 1.50.

22. Ehrman, *Forgery and Counterforgery*, 218–22.

Ehrman and Richards alike, however, seem to me to neglect a key datum closer to Paul than Cicero. Origen famously hypothesized that the Epistle to the Hebrews had to have come from another hand than Paul's, given its clear stylistic departures from the Apostle's other letters.[23] However, he regularly referred to that letter as Pauline,[24] and even explicitly included it in a fourteen letter Pauline canon.[25] In the fragment preserved by Eusebius, Origen offers his preferred explanation for these seemingly incompatible data: "But as for myself, if I were to state my own opinion, I should say that the thoughts are the apostle's, but that the style and composition belonged to one who called to mind the apostle's teachings and, as it were, made short notes of what his master said."[26] Taken in light of his statements here and elsewhere in favor of Pauline authorship, it is clear that Origen believed it perfectly reasonable to credit Paul with the authorship of a letter whose specific wording was supplied by a more competent Greek stylist.[27]

Additionally, Ehrman seems to me to leave aside some crucial and unimpeachable data regarding the life of James and the earliest Church. We know that James (along with Peter and John) were leaders within a growing international movement in the first century (Gal 2:10), and that he was recognized as a prominent religious leader in Jerusalem by the high priest, Ananus, who had him executed as a "breaker of the Law."[28] We know that Peter, along with Jesus' other brothers, traveled throughout these scattered communities as itinerant missionaries (1 Cor 9:5). We know that another such missionary, Paul, regularly wrote letters to congregations identified with the Church. Our earliest sources regarding this movement presuppose that members in one place were involved and interested in the lives of members who lived vast distances away (cf.

---

23. Eusebius, *Hist. Eccl.* 6.25.11–13. I'm grateful to William for pointing out this material.

24. Origen, *De Principiis* 3.2.4: "And the apostle Paul warns us [Heb 2:1]: "Therefore we ought to give the more earnest heed to the things which we have heard, lest perhaps we should let them slip." Cf. also Origen, *De Principiis* 4.1.13; 4.1.24; 2.3.5; 2.7.7; 3.1.10; Origen, *Contra Celsum* 3.52; 7.29; Origen, *To Africanus* 9.

25. Origen, "Seventh Homily on Joshua," in *Homilies on Joshua*.

26. Eusebius, *Hist. Eccl.* 6.25.11–13.

27. As William argues in chapter 4, Origen was mistaken about the authorship of Hebrews, but more important than that for my purposes here is simply the fact that Origen viewed this mode of composition as a live option, not merely for ancient letter writers in general, but specifically for early Christians such as Paul.

28. Josephus, *Ant.* 20.9.1.

Acts 11:29-30; 15:1-29; Rom 16:1-16; 1 Cor 16:15; 1 Thess 1:7-8). More controversial, but still altogether probable, is this: James lived for almost thirty years in Jerusalem, where perhaps as much as a fifth of the population were native Greek speakers,[29] and which swelled several times a year with a massive influx of Greek-speaking pilgrims. Acts suggests that preaching to these pilgrims was a major focus of the earliest Church (cf. Acts 2:5-14), and that many of the converts in Jerusalem spoke Greek ("the Hellenists," cf. Acts 6:1).

In that situation, there is nothing at all surprising about the notion that a key leader such as James would not only have spoken Greek and been familiar with the Greek Bible, but would also have sent a letter to far-flung Greek-speaking churches; indeed, denying the possibility of any of this strikes me as tantamount to denying that he could have functioned as the sort of leader Paul and Acts clearly insist that he was. And if James did not actually fill that role, who did? (Perhaps Bruno Bauer was right, and Christianity really was the invention of the cultured Seneca!)[30]

Ehrman's rhetorically brilliant discussion presupposes at every point a view of James as an ordinary Galilean peasant, the sort of person who could not have composed a paragraph in Greek had his life depended on it. But the very fact that Ehrman is discussing James two millenia after his death means that he very likely was no ordinary peasant. Ordinary peasants certainly did not turn to scribes for help in composing their encyclicals; but then, ordinary peasants did not have crucified and resurrected Messiahs for brothers, nor did they come to head an international network of communities with a rapidly-multiplying membership. Ehrman is right to consider that the circumstances under which an authentic James could have been written would have been strange indeed; but they are no stranger than the undisputed circumstances of James's career in the altogether improbable community that was the early Church.

Ehrman's arguments about the impossibility of James' having written his Epistle are interestingly parallel to arguments made in the 19th century about the impossibility of Frederick Douglass's having written his *Narrative of the Life of Frederick Douglass*.[31] For instance, an A. C. C. Thompson objected that it was far more likely that Douglass was lying, and that an educated white man or woman had written the polished

---

29. Cf. Hengel, *The 'Hellenization' of Judea*, 10, cited in Bauckham, *James*, 24.

30. Cf. the discussion of Bauer's *Christ and the Caesars: How Christianity Originated from Graeco-Roman Civilization* (1877) in Powell, *Jesus as a Figure in History*, 252.

31. I'm grateful to Brandon Walsh for this insightful observation.

autobiography published under his name.[32] Nonetheless, unlikely though it was, Douglass had in fact learned to write while enslaved, and not merely to write, but to compose intricate and elevated prose.[33] Strange things sometimes happen—and the stranger they are, the more likely they are to excite the interest and commentary of historians like Ehrman.

An Aramaic Epistle?

A further potential cultural-linguistic challenge is the paucity of literature written from Palestine in Greek in this period; surely, some might think, the historical James would have written in his native Aramaic. However, in the first century, a letter written to Jews anywhere in the Mediterranean basin was almost bound to be written in that region's *lingua franca*, Greek. We find an important (if not exact) parallel to this situation in the works of Josephus, a Palestinian Jew and likely Aramaic speaker who (with scribal assistance, as we noted above) wrote his *Antiquities of the Jews* in Greek, so as to reach a Roman audience.

Nonetheless, it's worth briefly considering another possibility (introduced here only as a prompt to further reflection and research): perhaps James *was* composed in Aramaic and then translated into Greek. Josephus again furnishes a possible parallel; he introduces his first work, *The Jewish War*, by observing that he originally wrote it "for the 'upper Barbarians'[34] in my mother-tongue (*tois anō Barbarois tē patriō*)," presumably Aramaic, and then subsequently "translated it into Greek for the subjects of the Roman Empire."[35] Strikingly, as Thackeray notes in his introduction to the Loeb translation of *The Jewish War*, its Greek version

---

32. "I indulge no animosity against the fabricators and circulators of the Narrative, neither do I know them, but I positively declare the whole to be a bucket of falsehoods, from beginning to end. 1st. The identity of the author. About eight years ago I knew this recreant slave by the name of Frederick Bailey, (instead of Douglass.) He then lived with Mr. Edward Covy, and was an unlearned, and rather an ordinary negro, and am confident he was not capable of writing the Narrative alluded to; for none but an educated man, and one who had some knowledge of the rules of grammar, could write so correctly" (Thompson, "Refuge of Oppression").

33. For an account of Douglass's covert education, first in the Baltimore home of the Auld family, and then among poor white boys on the city's streets, cf. Blight, *Frederick Douglass*, 35–47.

34. He goes on to clarify that he has in mind the peoples of Parthia, Arabia, and Edessa (Josephus, *J.W.* 1.2).

35. Josephus, *J.W.* 1.1.

"shows no trace whatever of Semitic phraseology";³⁶ if Josephus hadn't told us that it was originally written in Aramaic, we'd have no way of finding this out for ourselves, given the current state of the evidence.

That James was composed in similar circumstance is a possibility worth considering, because there are in fact some internal indicators of a Semitic source-text. First and least determinative are the Semitisms which crop up in the epistle (e.g., "double-minded [*dipsychos*]" in 1:8 and 4:8;³⁷ "preferentiality [*prosōpolepsia*]" in 2:1³⁸). But more significant are the textual variations in the surviving versions of the letter, some of which might plausibly be explained as resulting from independent (and variously competent) translations of an Aramaic Vorlage.

Particularly important in this regard is Jas 2:19. Most versions include the phrase "*heis estin ho theos*," or its close equivalent, "*ho theos heis estin*," but the surviving mss. include a bewildering variety of alternatives, including:

> *heis estin theos*—945, 1241, 1739
> *heis theos estin*—B, 614, 630, 1505, 2412, 2495
> *heis ho estin theos*—C, 33, 81, 2992, syrh
> *theos heis estin*—330, 451, 2127
> *heis ho theos*—Cyril.³⁹

The profusion of alternatives to the majority reading, and particularly the barbaric variants which include an anarticular "god (*theos*)," are something of a puzzle, particularly in view of the fact that this exact phrase ("God is one [*heis estin ho theos*]") appears in Rom 3:30 with no attested variants at all—why did the scribes suddenly get itchy fingers when they arrived at Jas 2:19?⁴⁰

---

36. Josephus, *J.W.*, ix-x.

37. This word seems to be a translation of the Semitic idiom "double-hearted" (Heb., "*lev wa-lev*," Aram., "*levav wa-levav*")—Ps 12:3; 1 Chr 12:33; 1QH 12.4.14; 4Q542 1.1)—the Hebrew phrase also seems to stand behind Sirach's "with a double heart (*en kardia dissē*)" (1:28) (cf. List, "Δίψυχος," 95).

38. For this as a Semitism, cf. BDAG *ad loc*. It also appears several times in Paul's epistles (Rom 2:11; Eph 6:9; Col 3:25), although, as we'll consider below, this is possibly under the influence of James himself!

39. These variants (drawn from the apparatus of the NA-27) are helpfully tabulated here: https://en.wikipedia.org/wiki/Textual_variants_in_the_Epistle_of_James.

40. It seems reasonable to assume that accidental textual variants (caused by, e.g., omission or metathesis) should be roughly normally distributed across occurrences of a given phrase.

An Aramaic source-text provides a simple explanation for this confusion: perhaps they reflect independent translations of the Aramaic expression *"chad haw a'laha."* Unlike Greek and Hebrew, but like Latin, Aramaic lacks even a definite article, which means that expressions such as this one will offer standing temptations to the inexperienced translator to produce nonsense of the sort catalogued in the variants above. And strikingly, the Syriac (E. Aramaic) Peshitta version includes this precise reading of Jas 2:19—"God is one (*chad haw a'laha*)."

There are other instances in James in which textual variation might plausibly be traced to an Aramaic original (e.g., the confusion between *"katabainon"* and *"katerchomenon"* or *apo* and *para* in 1:17; the absence of articles for *"pneuma"* and *"ergon"* in some mss. of 2:26), but considering them in detail would take us too far afield here. Suffice it to say that the language in which the Epistle of James was composed ought to be investigated more vigorously than it seems to have been heretofore. If the Aramaic-hypothesis proved plausible, it would significantly lower the bar for the authenticity of James (Aramaic literacy being a more plausible aspiration for a first-century Galilean than Greek literacy), and would itself constitute indirect evidence for a relatively early date of composition for this Epistle.

Apart from linguistic considerations, the other common set of arguments for treating the Epistle of James as a forgery rely heavily on a seeming dependence of James upon Paul's thinking about justification.[41] The relevant passage (Jas 2:14–26) is considered in detail below, so it will suffice for now to observe that ruling out the Epistle's authenticity on the basis of its relation to Paul begs significant questions that remain to be addressed. To this point, then, nothing prevents us from adopting, as a first stage in our working hypothesis, Bauckham's proposal that the Epistle is an authentic letter of James the brother of Jesus.

Justification in Jas 2:14–26

The single passage in the Epistle of James in which justification discourse appears is a dialogue aimed at an inadequate account of the relation of

---

41. So, Dibelius: "The author, indeed, does stand within an early Christian development which does not directly derive from Paul . . . *but his remarks in 2:14ff are still inconceivable unless Paul had previously set for the slogan, 'faith, not works'*" (Dibelius, *James*, 179).

faith to works (Jas 2:14, 20).[42] Whether the interlocutor is an actual rival teacher (e.g., Paul or a disciple), or merely a literary *construct* used as a foil is debatable,[43] but the fact that the letter is likely a general and hortatory *encyclical* makes the latter hypothesis especially plausible.[44] Anyway, the position James opposes is clear enough: whoever says that his faith is separable from works is confused about their proper relation (Jas 2:18), which is like that of spirit to body—without works, faith is dead (Jas 2:17; cf. 2:26). In particular, James seems to imagine someone who claims that confession of the *Shema* (Jas 2:19; cf. Deut 6:4) offers special privileges before God independent of faithful obedience expressed in works of charity, such as feeding the hungry or clothing the naked (Jas 2:15-16). James's opponent even seems to think that "faith alone" might be enough to be justified before God (Jas 2:24).

Criticizing his (imagined?) interlocutor's complacency, James draws on the figure of Abraham, who was "justified by his works," in his obedient offering of Isaac (Jas 2:21; cf. Gen 22:1-18). James reads Gen 15:6, which describes the justification of Abraham by his faith, as a prophecy fulfilled in the Akedah (Jas 2:23). His reading of this verse in light of Gen 22 also shows his careful attention to a puzzling feature of the Abrahamic narrative: the trust which "was reckoned to him for righteousness (*elogisthē autō eis dikaiosunēn*)" (Gen 15:6 LXX) was offered in response to a promise given by God in Gen 15:5,[45] but in Gen 22, this promise reappears, this time given on the basis of Abraham's obedience in the Akedah.[46] Highlighting this intertextual relationship allows James to illustrate the interpenetration of faith and works—for Abraham, these were but two ways of picking out a single reality of trust that stakes its commitment even to the most trying obedience.[47] And, as Bauckham

---

42. Cf. Bauckham, *James*, 125; Dibelius: "One discerns in [Jas 2:1—3:12] the style of the diatribe... as it is known especially from Epictetus" (Debelius, *James*, 1). Cf. also Witherington, *Letters and Homilies*, 471.

43. Cf. Bauckham, *James*, 125. Scott McKnight calls the figure lampooned here a "universal person" (McKnight, *The Letter of James*, 227).

44. This would also parallel many other seemingly hypothetical scenarios in the letter: Jas 2:2; 3:14; 4:11; 5:14.

45. "Number the stars (*tous asteras*), if you can number them. And he said, 'Thus will be your seed (*to sperma sou*)'" (Gen 15:5 LXX).

46. "Because (*hou eineken*) you have done this thing,... I will surely multiply your seed (*to sperma sou*) as the stars (*hōs asteras*] of heaven" (Gen 22:16-17 LXX).

47. Cf. Bauckham, *James*, 122-24. Hengel rightly observes, "James's conception of faith (*Glaubensbegriff*) is fundamentally that of Judaism, in which faith could be understood as a work or a virtue" (Hengel, *Paulus und Jakobus*, 528).

notes, this reading of Abraham strongly echoes post-exilic texts such as 1 Macc 2:51–52: "Remember also the works (*ta erga*) of the fathers, which they did in their generations, and receive great glory and an eternal name. Was not Abraham found faithful (pistos) in the temptation, and it was reckoned to him as righteousness (*dikaiosunēn*)?"[48]

As early as 1 Maccabees, then, it was possible to treat the intertextual connection between Abraham's being found righteous in Gen 15 and his "testing" in the Akedah as picking out the interpenetration of faith and works; Paul's treatment of this passage in Gal 3 or Rom 4 has no explanatory advantages regarding the genesis of James over more traditional texts such as this one. Indeed, as a Christian, but still highly traditional interpretation of the significance of Abraham's faith and works for his righteousness, James more readily makes sense as an "intermediate" form between the post-exilic literature and justification discourse in Paul than vice versa.

An Anti-Pauline Polemic?

Bauckham illuminates a widely recognized feature of Jas 2: notwithstanding Martin Hengel's claims to the contrary, it is not particularly persuasive as anti-Pauline polemic.[49] The justification material, which the reader encounters as but one short subsection among many, is easily construed as a counterfactual meditation on an improper way of relating (the individual's) faith to "works," without any clear reference to an actual opponent. Further, this material reads most naturally as marking out proper conduct for law observant Jews; it gives no indication of controversies surrounding gentile inclusion, and so reads quite intelligibly as an installment in an intramural Jewish-Christian conversation about the conduct befitting a member of Israel.

The possibility that this discussion is merely a hypothetical reflection aimed at an all-Jewish audience is reinforced by the fact that in

---

48. Cf. Bauckham, *James*, 123; cf. also Sir 44:20.

49. Martin Hengel's proposal that Jas 2:8–13 already betrays an anti-Pauline edge simply does violence to the text (Hengel, *Paulus und Jakobus*, 527n46); the passage's clearest intertextual resonances are with Jesus' teaching on the "Greatest Commandment" in the Gospels (Matt 22:36–40), and, far from sounding anti-Pauline, its reading of that teaching itself echoes a key Pauline claim (cf. Gal 5:15; Jas 2:8). Bauckham correctly observes, "If James 2:14–26 is opposing Paul's understanding of justification by faith, it misses its target by a long way" (Bauckham, *James*, 128).

James the opposition between *erga* and *pistis* is not, as in Paul's writings, linked tightly by context to those acts which most clearly mark out Jews as separate from gentiles (i.e., dietary laws and circumcision).[50] In James, this question is *nowhere* in view. Rather, James treats "works" as acts of charity generically considered as the Law's sum and goal. These works, we must add, presumably include various cultic statutes (cf. Jas 2.8–10). Werner Georg Kümmel's assertion that the historical James would not have mentioned the Torah without adverting to the ritual and purity law would only follow if the letter were written in a polemical context in which the inviolability of those statutes had been called into question by a Torah-free mission to the gentiles;[51] in fact, the absence of such claims supports the opposite thesis to Kümmel's, namely, that James had no need to mention something he assumed all his readers took for granted (circumcision, kosher, and Sabbath).[52]

But if we abandon Paul as a foil for James's justification discourse, what are we to posit as background for its (at least imagined) opposition of faith to works? It might be enough to note, with Bauckham, that "people who profess religious belief while neglecting their charitable duties to those in need are too common a phenomenon to require any special explanation in this case."[53] For instance, such "hypocrites" seem to have figured prominently in the Matthean Jesus's polemics against the Pharisees: "So practice and observe whatever they tell you, but not what they do (*ta erga autōn*); for they preach, but do not practice" (Matt 23:3). The Pharisees, we might say, have faith, but not works.

However, Bauckham goes on to suggest that the hypocrisy James pillories might be situated against the background not only of widespread attacks in the Old Testament on treating Jewish cultic distinctives as a ground for boasting (i.e., Isa 58:1–8; Jer 7:1–7; Ezek 33:3–32), but

---

50. E.g., Gal 2:2–9, 12–16; 5:6; Phil 3:2–3; Rom 2:25–29; 3:28–30; 4:10–13; the absence of such concerns makes James's use of the generic "works" in place of Paul's "works of the Law" (Gal 2:16) all the more significant (cf. Bauckham, *James*, 128). We should also observe that in other first- and second-century texts, Jewish anxiety about the Torah-free mission is clearly linked to circumcision (cf. Acts 21:21; Justin Martyr, *Dial. Try.* 10). I am grateful to Joe Longarino for pointing out the passage in Justin.

51. Kümmel, *Introduction to the New Testament*, 413.

52. The situation is parallel to one E. P. Sanders notes: "Although the word 'covenant' has thus far not occurred in Sifre, it is clear that the entirety of Sifre Num. 1 presupposes a firm belief in a covenant between God and Israel" (Sanders, *Paul and Palestinian Judaism*, 84).

53. Bauckham, *James*, 126.

also of Second Temple texts that specifically highlight Jewish belief in and worship of the one true God as a source of merit and a ground for boasting (e.g., *Liber Antiquitatum Biblicarum* 23:12; 4 Ezra 3:31–32).[54] As N. T. Wright observes, "The *Shema* . . . was burned into the consciousness of Judaism in the first century. It was not the result of speculative metaphysical enquiry, but the battle cry of the nation that believed its god to be the only god, supreme in heaven and on earth."[55] These texts show that first century Jews might conceivably have treated the *Shema* as grounds for distinction from and privilege among the gentiles, and so as replacing acts of charity exactly as fasting or the Temple was envisioned to do in Isa 58 or Jer 7. In this section, then, James might raise that possibility, flesh it out argumentatively using a rhetorical foil, and reject it as inconsistent with authentic Jewish piety.

Many exegetes, keenly aware of James's defects as Pauline polemic but still keener to maintain its dependence on Paul, posit some second stage in the controversy which, falling between Paul and James, sufficiently distorts the teaching of the former to account for the latter's polemical stance. If Jas 2:14–26 is a reaction to Paul, then there are essentially two ways to account for a distorted version of Paul's teaching having reached its author: if the author was James himself, then it could have come by way of hazy oral reports, perhaps regarding Paul's early mission in the periods between his first and second Jerusalem visits (cf. Gal 1:18; 2:1), which confused some of his claims.[56] Or, if the Epistle of James is a forgery, then the letter's opponents might be later Paulinists whose enthusiasm for "faith alone" has taken Paul's actual teachings to new extremes.[57]

---

54. Bauckham, *James*, 126.

55. Wright, *The New Testament and the People of God*, 248. Cf. Ps 96:5, 10.

56. This approach is defended by Scott McKnight, Douglas Moo, and even Hengel. McKnight writes, "My conclusion is that James is responding either to Paul in the flesh, or, which is slightly more likely, to the early Paul or to early followers of Paul who had embraced his message and driven it to some distortions" (McKnight, *The Letter of James*, 263). Similarly, Douglas Moo holds, "It is not at all improbable that some Christians who had been exposed to Paul's argument may have—intentionally or not—converted it into an argument for spiritual passivity" (Moo, *James*, 28). Finally, Hengel judges that James has merely "oral knowledge (*mündliche Kentnisse*) of Pauline theology" (Hengel, *Paulus und Jakobus*, 528).

57. This position is endorsed by Kümmel: "The debate in 2:14 with a misunderstood secondary stage of Pauline theology not only presupposes a considerable chronological distance from Paul, . . . but also betrays a complete ignorance of the polemical intent of the Pauline theology" (Kümmel, *Introduction to the New Testament*,

However, both of these proposals suffer from two serious weaknesses. First, in both cases, these distorting mediators are always *posited*, rather than *discovered*. And second, both require significant distortion: particularly if the author of James is taken to be a Jewish-Christian Torah rigorist who criticizes Paul for (apparently) displacing the Law from its central place in the economy of salvation, it is hard to imagine how he could have eliminated the centrality of gentiles and circumcision to Paul's teaching on justification, no matter how garbled or malicious its transmission to him had been. We might anachronistically imagine the Epistle's author as something like Pelagius *avant la lettre*, advocating a strict moralism completely disjoined from any interest in Jewish cultic practice, but as this only would seem to generate more pressing historical difficulties than those it is meant to solve, the Jewish-Christian thesis seemingly must stand.

There is, however, an important recent treatment of James that calls into question its anti-Paulinist origins. In *Not by Paul Alone*, David Nienhuis argues that James was composed in the late second century, as the frontispiece for the Catholic Epistles collection, which was designed to provide an anti-Marcionite counterbalance to the Pauline letters.[58] Nienhuis's argument depends upon his claim that James is unattested in the patristic literature prior to Origen; he takes this thesis as the basis for a revisionist proposal that sees James as a "canon-conscious pseudepigrah" written to bind together the nascent Catholic epistles.[59]

There is not space here to engage Nienhuis fully, but a few comments are in order. First, his argument for patristic silence depends on an exceptionally high standard for attestation: unless patristic material can *only* be explained by appeal to James, he will not acknowledge its presence. By this standard, every known second-century source is indeed

---

413). So too, Udo Schnelle writes, "Perhaps [the author] knew Galatians and Romans only indirectly, through oral or written intermediaries unknown to us. He is possibly arguing against Christians who practiced a faith without works, and who appealed to Paul to justify their practice" (Schnelle, *The Theology of the New Testament*, 625). Likewise, Rudolf Bultmann suggests, "The fact that the author polemizes against the proposition that Abraham was justified by faith alone makes it likely that the point of view is supposed to be Paul's, or that of some group claiming Paul as its authority. If so, Paul's concept of faith is thereby utterly misunderstood" (Bultmann, *Theology of the New Testament*, 163).

58. Nienhuis, *Not by Paul Alone*, 22–28.

59. Nienhuis, *Not by Paul Alone*, 29–98, 163–232.

silent regarding James.[60] However, Nienhuis's standard is too exacting. For instance, Irenaeus's reference to Abraham as "a friend of God" seems *prima facie* to be dependent on Jas 2:23,[61] and Nienhuis's suggestion that it might be dependent instead on an earlier Jewish tradition that also used this phrase—either a known source, or some now-lost common tradition—is needlessly skeptical.[62]

And Nienhuis's attempt to read James as a response to Marcion is more incredible still, as James betrays no awareness of any key Marcionite claims—there is no hint of Marcion's "stranger God," nor of his abrogation of the OT.[63] As Joel Marcus observed in reviewing Nienhuis's work, "If [James] is anti-Marcionite polemic, it is subtle indeed."[64] In fact, we should go further even than Marcus. Not only is James no anti-Marcionite polemic; it is a gift to Marcion. As Nienhuis shows, the great Catholic opponents of Marcion—Irenaeus and Tertullian and Clement, i.a.—all take pains to emphasize the harmony of Paul's gospel and mission with that of the Jerusalem "pillars," Peter, James, and John.[65] But they likely addressed this because of Marcion's insistence that Paul's gospel was fundamentally opposed to that of the too-Jewish Jerusalem apostles. Given that polemical setting, James would have been a bruised reed for Catholics to lean on, for, with its seeming reversal of Paul's doctrine of justification, it is all-too-easily read as a direct attack on Paul's gospel by James himself. But once we notice how awkward a text James would have been in the context of anti-Marcionite polemic, an alternate account of the patristic silence Nienhius catalogues presents itself. Why do none of the second century fathers explicitly quote from James? Perhaps because they feared it to be a stumbling block in the fight against Marcionism, insofar as it undermined claims for a fundamental continuity between Paul and Jerusalem.

The problems inherent in either the "later Paulinists" or "distorted Paul" strategy for reading James as dependent on Paul commend our

---

60. Nienhuis, *Not by Paul Alone*, 34–55.

61. Irenaeus, *Adv. Haer.* 4.16.2.

62. Nienhuis, *Not by Paul Alone*, 36.

63. There's no equivalent in James to 1 Timothy's criticism of "antitheses of falsely so-called knowledge" (6:20), which might reasonably be read as alluding to Marcion's work of biblical criticism, "The Antitheses." For a reading of 1 Timothy along these lines, cf. Campbell, *Framing Paul*, 364–66.

64. Marcus, Review, 385.

65. Nienhuis, *Not by Paul Alone*, 37–43.

openness to alternative solutions. Bauckham's own is that James and Paul each developed their particular variety of justification discourse independently, from a common tradition of exegesis (perhaps, though he doesn't explicitly say this, such as the tradition evident in 1 Macc 2:51–52).[66] However, this proposal, while avoiding the problem of Pauline distortion besetting the two above, does not take seriously enough the density of verbal and thematic linkages that bind together James and Paul on justification; the two are not simply drawing on common motifs or tropes, but are our only extant installments in a highly developed exegetical discourse, each with more in common with one another than with earlier texts such as 1 Maccabees (for instance, each includes verbal, rather than nominative forms of *dikaiō-* roots). If neither depends on the other, then the similarity of James to Galatians or Romans is difficult to account for.

The Teachers and the Problem of Gentile-Inclusion

Fortunately, we can now sketch a fresh alternative, by pairing Bauckham's account of James with the highly occasional reading of justification in Paul developed by J. Louis Martyn and Douglas Campbell. On this interpretation, the Epistle of James is our earliest extant entry in the literature of justification, a traditional account of the relative operation of faith and works in God's covenant with Israel. This teaching is mediated to Paul by a group of Jewish-Christian missionaries whom we (following Martyn) will call the "Teachers."[67] These missionaries adapted justification discourse for preaching to unconverted gentiles, a transformation that, while retaining the three central semantic strands of James's teaching (*pist-*, *dikaiō-*, and *erg-* roots) and its focus on Abraham,[68] shifted the discourse markedly to address the nature of gentile inclusion in the covenant, and particularly their relation to the "works" that most clearly distinguished gentiles from Jews, namely circumcision, dietary laws, and Sabbath.[69] Narrated this way, the transformation of justification discourse

---

66. Bauckham, *James*, 131; cf. Witherington, *Letters and Homilies*, 479–80.

67. Martyn, *Theological Issues*, 9.

68. Campbell himself brushes up against this insight: "It is hard to the avoid the detection in [Rom 2:]13 of a slogan from the Teacher himself (*if not from James*)—the oft-repeated adage that the truly righteous must be 'doers of the word, and not merely hearers who deceive themselves' (Jas 1:22)" (Campbell, *Deliverance*, 582, my emphasis).

69. Martyn puts this with particular clarity: "As missionaries to Gentiles, the Teachers hear the Jewish-Christian tradition in a new context in which observance of

between James and Paul is entirely explicable—the changes we witness are exactly those we would expect from an attempt to apply James's intra-Jewish discussion to a gentile audience.

This narration of justification's history retains two key elements of earlier accounts. First, it posits a lineal relationship between James and Paul's epistles, but saves James from a gross misreading of Paul by insisting that he wrote *prior to* Paul's polemical adoption of justification. And second, it posits a distorting mediator to stand between James and Paul, but finds this mediator plainly evident in the pages of Acts and Galatians. In the following pages, I sketch the key developments in this account's rendition of the Teachers' controversy with Paul, and then consider the theological and exegetical dispute on display in the Pauline epistles. As with the section above on James, the burden of this section is not to vindicate Martyn's and Campbell's work definitively from all challenges, but rather to demonstrate their interpretations' plausibility and openness to inclusion in this revisionist account of James's relation to Paul.

Justification Discourse as a Pauline "Polemical Doctrine"

Is it plausible, however, to treat justification as merely a polemical discourse in Paul's letters? What grounds are there for treating justification discourse as anything other than Paul's deeply personal distillation of the lessons learned on the Damascus Road? First, we should note that Paul only deploys it in three of the undisputed letters, extensively in Galatians and Romans, and briefly in Phil 3:9.[70] We'll see below that Paul's opponents in Galatians are Jewish-Christian missionaries who insist that gentiles take up full law-observance; and, as Douglas Campbell suggests, there are clear indications in Philippians, and strong hints in Romans, that the same opponents are view there as well.[71] The sole burst of justification discourse in Philippians (at 3:9) is enclosed by Paul's dire warnings regarding opponents whose opposition to Paul apparently centers on the merits of Jewish identity, particularly in relation to circumcision

---

the Law is not—and cannot be—taken for granted. And because they carry out their mission by inviting Gentiles to *enter* the people of Israel, they necessarily posit an explicit relation between rectification and observance of the Law" (Martyn, *Theological Issues*, 148).

70. Eph 2:8–9 and Tit 3:5–9 offer less-developed forms of justification discourse, but both letters also suggest a concern about gentile inclusion (Eph 2:11–19; Tit 1:10, 14).

71. Campbell, *Deliverance*, 505.

and dietary laws (Phil 3:2-8, 18-19). And, as Campbell observes, Paul describes the false teachers opposed in both Romans and Philippians as servants of their "belly" (Rom 16:18; Phil 3:19).[72] Add to that the profound argumentative overlap between Romans and Galatians,[73] along with Campbell's argument that much of Rom 1–4 reads most intelligibly as Paul's *reductio ad absurdum* of the Teachers' own views,[74] and Romans likewise might be neatly fitted in place as a further installment in Paul's "judaizing correspondence."

Justification discourse is not only limited to Paul's controversies with the Teachers, but Paul's most important soteriological categories (which Campbell calls a "pneumatologically participatory, matyrological eschatology") largely float free of it.[75] Paul's characteristic slogan for redeemed existence is life "in Christ,"[76] whose definitive marker is not an interior conversion from works-righteousness to humble faith, but rather the sacramental death-and-resurrection of baptism.[77] Further, Paul's frequent discussions of the human act of "*pistis*" lack any clear indication that it is a uniquely determinative condition of salvation,[78] and the binary opposition that seems to drive Paul's thinking is not that between faith and works, but rather between the flesh and the Spirit.[79] Finally, an exegetical interest in Abraham as a paragon of faith is nowhere in view outside the justification texts; elsewhere, Paul's most common appeal to the Abrahamic narrative (here in striking agreement with James!) is by way of allusions to Abraham's offering of Isaac as a type of God the Father's handing his beloved Son over to death.[80]

---

72. Campbell, *Deliverance*, 505.

73. Rom 3:20-22/Gal 2:16; Rom 4:1-25/Gal 3:6-16; Rom 7, 9-11/Gal 3:17-25; Rom 3:8; 6:1/Gal 5:13.

74. Esp. Rom 2:1—3:18; cf. Campbell, *Deliverance*, 547-83.

75. Campbell, *The Quest for Paul's Gospel*, 57-59.

76. Rom 8:1, 39; 12:5; 16:7; 1 Cor 1:2, 30; 3:1; 4:10; 2 Cor 2:17; cf. Campbell, *Deliverance*, 64.

77. Rom 6:3-4; 1 Cor 12:13; Gal 3:27-28; Eph 4:5; Col 2:12; cf. Campbell, *Deliverance*, 64.

78. Faith is a crucial virtue, but in coordination with hope and love (1 Cor 13:13; Gal 5:6; Col 1:4-5; 1 Thess 1:3; 5:8; 2 Thess 1:3); cf. Campbell, *Deliverance*, 67-68.

79. Rom 8:1-13; 1 Cor 5:5; 2 Cor 3:6; Gal 5:17; Eph 6:12; Col 2:5. These distinctions coincide at Phil 3:3 and Rom 2:28-29, but the general point stands—the "flesh/Spirit" opposition does more work in Paul's thought than does the "faith/works" opposition.

80. Rom 5:10; 8:3, 29, 32; Gal 4:4; Col 1:13; 1 Thess 1:10. Cf. Campbell, *Deliverance*, 63.

These observations support Wrede's proposal that justification discourse is Paul's "polemical doctrine,"[81] a self-contained exegetical and theological engagement deployed against a particular Jewish-Christian insistence on gentile Torah-observance. But justification discourse's isolation within Paul's larger corpus makes it all the more plausible that the distinctive features of this discourse might prove not to be devised by Paul at all, but rather to be aspects of his opponents' thought, which he must adapt in order to refute. Put more simply, if justification were really Paul's native account of his Torah-free mission to the gentiles, why do we see no hint of that discourse in his letters to the Torah-free congregations in Thessalonikē, Corinth,[82] or Colossae? Why does the discourse *only* appear when Paul has the Teachers in his sights? If it appeared there because it is particularly adapted to them, then Paul's discussions of justification would be a rich vein for mining the Teachers' own views, a task to which we can now turn.

What the Teachers Did

Acts suggests that Paul's first engagement with Jewish-Christian (and Jerusalemite) advocates of gentile circumcision occurs in Antioch (Acts 15:1–2), and Paul's account in Galatians of a similar controversy over Torah-observance with Jewish Christians in Antioch links his opponents explicitly with James (Gal 2:12).[83] The controversy there is sufficiently severe that the church sends a delegation to Jerusalem to resolve the matter (Acts 15:2), where "false brothers" (Gal 2:4), who resemble the "circumcision party" in Antioch,[84] again oppose Paul, though he is eventually recognized by the Jerusalem "pillars" as bearing a unique apostolate to the gentiles (Gal 2:9). The Jerusalem pillars also ask Paul to "remember the poor in Jerusalem" (Gal 2:10), a request he honored by initiating a monetary collection among his far-flung churches; we can track the

81. Wrede, *Paul*, 123.

82. 2 Cor 3 provides a partial and illuminating exception—we'll return to it below.

83. The plotline of this controversy is simplified considerably if we identify Gal 2:11–14 with Acts 15:1–4, and take it that Paul has reversed the story's ordering for rhetorical reasons; but regardless, the connections of the opponents in Acts 15 with Jerusalem make a link of some sort with James almost unavoidable.

84. Again, this depends on identifying the Jerusalem conferences of Gal 2 and Acts 15, and then identifying the "false brothers" of Gal 2:4 with the Pharisaic Christians of Acts 15:5, a decision justified not least by the resulting simplification of the overall narrative.

James as the Origin of Pauline Justification 33

progress of this project through (in order) 1 Cor 16:1–4, 2 Cor 8–9, and Rom 15:25–32.

Sometime later, though, Paul learns that some of his predominantly gentile congregations—certainly in Galatia, but likely also in Corinth—founded during earlier missionary journeys, are being "evangelized" by a rival group of Jewish-Christian missionaries (the Teachers, as Martyn termed them, or the "super-apostles," as Paul mockingly calls them in 2 Cor 11:5) demanding that all gentile Christians take up full law observance (Gal 4:10; 6:13). Galatians 1:6–7 and 2 Cor 11:4 suggest that they are Christian missionaries (they seem to refer to their teaching as a "gospel"), while Gal 5:12, 6:13, and 2 Cor 11:22 suggest that they are Jewish.[85] In their advocacy of gentile law-observance, these Jewish-Christian missionaries are linked to the faction in Antioch which Acts 15:1 associates with Jerusalem, and Gal 2:12 links to James.[86]

Martyn has further argued that Gal 4:26 hints that the Teachers also laid claim to the authority of the Jerusalem church,[87] a possibility

---

85. Cf. Martyn, *Theological Issues*, 13; cf. also Barclay, "Mirror-Reading," 86. Given the likely priority of 2 Corinthians to Galatians (for this point, and for the unity of 2 Corinthians, see Campbell, *Framing Paul*, 98–121), an identification of the "super apostles" (2 Cor 11:5) with the Teachers would mean that 2 Corinthians marked their first appearance under Paul's pen. The overlaps between the Teachers of Galatians and the super-apostles of 2 Corinthians seems to me to counsel against Campbell's suggestion that the super-apostles might in fact be "Apollos and his colleagues," who were active in Corinth, and with whom Paul clearly had a somewhat rocky relationship (cf. 1 Cor 1:12; 3:4–6; 16:12) (Campbell, *Framing Paul*, 96). In any case, as we'll see below, one of Paul's key strategies for responding to the super-apostles—the distinction between the killing letter and the life-giving Spirit (2 Cor 3:6)—is taken up and expanded in his response to the Teachers in Rom 2 and 7–8 in particular. Whether these opponents belong to a single group, *Paul* evidently linked them in his own mind.

86. Cf. Campbell, *Deliverance*, 506; cf. also Martyn, *Theological Issues*, 28–32.

87. Martyn argues that Gal 4:21–30 betrays Paul's fears concerning the Jerusalem church's relation to the Teachers at the time he wrote Galatians (Martyn, *Galatians*, 440). In this "allegory," he insinuates that Genesis itself figures the persecution of the freeborn, Torah-free churches by the enslaved Torah-observant churches (Gal 4:21–30). But as Martyn suggests, the best explanation for Paul's linking the enslaved "present Jerusalem" with the persecuting Law-observant churches (Gal 4:29) is precisely that the Teachers themselves rather plausibly claimed to represent the authority of the "mother Church" in Jerusalem (cf. Gal 4:26). Paul's churches have no need for the "present Jerusalem, in slavery with her children" (Gal 4:25) but rather look to the "heavenly Jerusalem" of their eschatological hope. This allegory deftly gives Paul the exegetical high ground within the Abrahamic narrative, and offers a swift jab at the Teachers' connection to "the present Jerusalem," which—it seems that Paul fears—may be irreconcilably given over to the Teachers' heresy.

strengthened by their apparent appeal among the Corinthians to "letters of recommendation" on their behalf (2 Cor 3:1). The prime candidates for the authors of these letters are surely the apostles associated with Jerusalem, notably Peter and "the brothers of the Lord" to whose reputation Paul himself appealed in 1 Cor 9:5. And finally, *Paul* links these three groups simply by writing as though what happened in Antioch, and even more so his relationship with the Jerusalem church, is somehow bound up with the arrival of these Jewish-Christian missionaries in Galatia. This explicit linking, combined with the resemblances among Paul's opponents in Jerusalem, Antioch, and Galatia, suggest that they are, if not the same individuals, at least members of a common movement, centered on Jerusalem and James.[88]

It is unclear how much control James had over this Torah-observant mission to the gentiles that emerged from his orbit. However, both Acts and Galatians agree that James came to accept the legitimacy of Paul's Torah-free mission.[89] So, prima facie, we should construe the Teachers' subversion of Paul's gospel in the post-conference period as in opposition to James' own views, at least as they were expressed to and interpreted by the broader church.[90] But this does not, of course, rule out the possibility that James was at this point covertly encouraging the Teachers, something Paul at least seems to have considered likely.[91]

Before we turn to what the Teachers taught, we should take a moment to descend into the weeds of Pauline chronology; it will pay dividends below in our account of Paul's response to the Teachers. There are several indications that Galatians fits squarely within the period of the collection defined by 1 Corinthians, 2 Corinthians, and Romans. As we noted, Gal 2:10 seems to refer to the beginning of this undertaking, and a

---

88. Cf. Longenecker, *Galatians*, xcv, 51.

89. Gal 2:9; Acts 15:19, though Acts suggests that James did insist on imposing some restrictions that might be considered "Torah-light" (15:20). Indeed, Paul's original mission itself arguably advocated "Torah-light" observance for gentiles, notably in the requirement of exclusive devotion to Israel's God. "Turning from idols to serve the true and living God" (1 Thess 1:9) is a decent summary of the first and second of the Ten Commandments, after all!

90. And broadly supporting this thesis is the fact that, as Hengel observes, James was eventually executed as a "Law-breaker," one who overturned the Mosaic covenant (Hengel, *Paulus und Jakobus*, 524; cf. Josephus, *Ant*. 18.20).

91. Cf. Martyn's reading of Gal 4:26 as a none-too-subtle criticism of the Jerusalem church itself, "in slavery with her children," namely, the Teachers (Martyn, *Galatians*, 440).

close comparison of Paul's descriptions of its progress seems to betray the outbreak of the crisis in Galatia which prompted the writing of Galatians. In 1 Cor 16:1, Paul refers to the Galatians as participants in the collection, alongside the Macedonians and Achaeans, but by the writing of Rom 15:26, only the Macedonians and Achaeans remain—the crisis reflected in Galatians seems to have arisen after the writing of 1 Corinthians, and to remain unresolved (or to have resolved unhappily) sometime before the writing of Romans.

How does Galatians relate to 2 Corinthians? The Teachers appear as threats in both, but it is striking that 2 Corinthians is the only Pauline letter aimed at them which lacks even a semblance of justification-discourse. I would hypothesize that 2 Corinthians marked Paul's earliest engagement with the Teachers, one which reflects a relatively sketchy understanding of their message; by the time Paul writes Galatians from Corinth,[92] however, he has learned a great deal more about their views, both from messengers arriving from Galatia, and also likely from informants on the ground in Corinth. What did he learn?

What the Teachers Taught

The prior section sketched Paul's struggle against a Jacobite Jewish-Christian mission to the gentiles; this section situates the origins of Paul's justification discourse within this controversy, arguing that the Teachers lifted justification from James's discussion of covenant-obligations for *Jews* and transformed it into an evangelistic description of the conditions for *gentile* entry into the covenant. Paul's writings on justification would then prove to have been his particular response to the Teachers, employing their key terms and textual strongholds to hoist them on their own petard.

As we saw above, Galatians sketches the Teachers in profile: they are a group of zealous Jewish-Christian missionaries with strong ties to James and Jerusalem, who quite plausibly claim to represent the "mother church" there (cf. Gal 2:12; 4:25–26; 5:13; cf. Acts 15:1). Whereas James, writing to the worldwide community of Jews, could assume that everyone he addresses was already part of God's covenant people (cf. Jas 1:1; 2:2), the Teachers, in extending justification discourse to gentiles,[93] press

---

92. On the likelihood of a Corinthian *Nebenaddressat* in Galatians, cf. Campbell, *Framing Paul*, 125–54.

93. We need not, of course, assume that they had access to a copy of James—the

the problem of election to the surface. If the God of Israel is calling all the nations to submit to the reign of his Messiah, do these gentile converts need to become Jewish, by bearing in their bodies the marks of Israel's national life (circumcision, kosher, Sabbath)? In Paul's terms, must they "judaize" (Gal 2:14)?[94]

Despite these clear lines of controversy, Martyn hastens to add that Paul and the Teachers likely share some basic doctrinal commitments, among them the importance of "faith" (*pistis*) in Christ as a virtue.[95] There is nothing surprising in the notion that an emphasis on human faith would have had a significant place in the Teachers' preaching,[96] since "*pist-*" terminology, used in reference to the individual's trust in God's gracious action in Christ, was a key element in all known early Christian proclamation, presumably even going back to Jesus.[97] Indeed, Paul's own use of "faith" terms is heavily weighted toward an anthropological (i.e., *fides qua creditur*) sense.[98]

---

teaching might equally have come from James to the Teachers orally, or in a different written form that no longer survives.

94. There is good reason to think that Paul himself engaged in just such a "Torah-observant" mission to the gentiles during at least the initial years following his call. To pieces of data are relevant here: first, Paul's claim that he is "not still preaching circumcision" (Gal 5:11), which, in the context of Galatians, clearly evokes a past mission in close continuity with the Teachers'. (Paula Fredriksen suggests that this refers to a mission to non-Christian Jews in the period *before* his call [Fredriksen, *When Christians Were Jews*, 151], but this is implausible—the verb "*kērussō*" appears sixteen times in the ten-letter Pauline canon, and twice more in the Pastorals, and in every other case, it indisputably refers to preaching the gospel). Second, and still more pressing, if Paul had in fact already adopted the "Torah-free" gospel by the time of his first post-call visit to Jerusalem (Gal 1:18), why didn't the controversy that eventually precipitated the "Jerusalem conference" fourteen years later (Gal 2:1–10) break out on that initial visit?

95. Martyn, *Theological Issues*, 142–47. Campbell's criticism of Martyn's form-critical approach is generally compelling, but does not touch the more moderate claim about "faith" defended here (Campbell, *Deliverance*, 846).

96. As Martyn rightly suggests, Paul is likely criticizing the Teachers at least in part for not taking seriously the full implications of this aspect of their shared beliefs (Martyn, *Theological Issues*, 141–49).

97. "Repent and believe (*pisteuete*) in the gospel" (Mark 1:15). "Faith" as the human act of trust in Christ is a key term in all three Synoptics (Matt 17:20; Mark 5:34; Luke 17:6), the Johannine literature (John 3:16; 20:31; 1 John 3:23), the Epistle to the Hebrews (11:6), 1 Peter (1:8), and Jude (1:5). And as Acts represents it, the apostles frequently exhorted their hearers to "*pistis*": Phillip (8:37), Peter (10:43), and Paul (19:2) all speak in these terms.

98. E.g., 1 Cor 2:5; 13:2, 13; 15:14, 17; 2 Cor 1:24; 4:13; 5:7; 8:7; 10:15; 1 Thess 1:2, 8; 3:2, 5–7, 10; 5:8; 2 Thess 1:3–4, 11; cf. Tit 1:1; 2:2. As Douglas Campbell observes,

Paul and the Teachers seem also to have shared a basic commitment to the importance of good "works" in the life of believers, and to a final judgment informed in some way by the whole shape of a person's life (cf. 1 Cor 3:13–15; 2 Cor 5:10; 9:8; Eph 2:10; Phil 2:12; Col 1:10; 1 Thess 1:3); this is particularly clear in Rom 2 (esp. 2:6, 13), to which we'll return shortly. Paul and the Teachers thus share a basic commitment to the importance of trust in Christ and of God's ultimate, impartial judgment of all humanity; they bitterly diverge, however, over whether believers in Christ must also take up full Torah-observance if they are to receive a favorable verdict at that final judgment.

Paul insists that, by the Spirit, a gentile can be incorporated into the Church precisely *as a gentile*, without first becoming a Jew (Gal 3:1–2). The Teachers might have viewed this proposal with grave doubts, perhaps rooted in a straightforward reading of passages such as Gen 17:13.[99] The Teachers' response to Paul's seeming antinomianism arguably included a number of elements that make excellent sense as a development of James, including an emphasis on the necessity of *erga* as a complement to *pistis*, with a strong moralizing as well as cultic bent; a prophetic reading of the Abrahamic narrative; and the use of Lev 18 as a key organizing proof text.

First, as Martyn and Campbell argue, we ought to read the "*erga / pistis*" opposition in passages such as Gal 2:16 to elaborate, not a necessary spiritual progression *within* Paul's own teaching,[100] but rather, a simple either/or contrast of two rival gospels.[101] On this reading, the Teachers insisted that a gentile too can be "justified" before God only by adopting the way of life described in the Law; Paul seems to summarize

---

Paul's radical commitment to "Christ's eschatological life [as] the critical disclosure of God's salvation" does not prevent him from, along with the rest of the early Church, insisting that "those who merely evidence trust in [Christ's resurrection from the dead and ascension to lordship], and in the God who acts through them, seem to be granted a future share in the events themselves" (Campbell, *Deliverance*, 810).

99. Cf. Dunn: "If an unbaptized Christian is for most of us a contradiction in terms, even more so was a Jew who did not practice the works of the law, circumcision, table regulations and Sabbath" (Dunn, *Jesus, Paul, and the Law*, 194). Cf. also Martyn, *Theological Issues*, 17.

100. As in "Justification Theory," cf. Campbell, *Deliverance*, 15–24.

101. Cf. Campbell, *Deliverance*, 844–46; Dunn confirms at least the oppositional relation: "Paul's point is precisely that these two are alternatives—justification by works of law and justification by faith in Jesus are *antithetical opposites*" (Dunn, *Jesus, Paul, and the Law*, 195).

their position (whether they did or not) with the slogan, "the works of the Law (*ta erga nomou*)."¹⁰²

And as Campbell has also argued, in their account of the "works" required by God, the Teachers might well also have appealed to Lev 18:5,¹⁰³ understood as a lens through which to view the whole Torah.¹⁰⁴ Campbell observes that Lev 18:5 is easily read as promising "eschatological life" to those who "do" the Law, and thereby receive a verdict of "righteous" on judgment day.¹⁰⁵ It is, in short, the perfect proof-text for this set of Torah-rigorist Jewish-Christian missionaries to the gentiles, and it seems plausible to think that it appears in Gal 3:12 and in Romans (quoted at 10:5, and alluded to at 2:26, 7:10), precisely because of the Teachers' use of this verse to summarize their gospel.

Reading the Teachers as developing the justification discourse found in James lends further plausibility to the notion that Lev 18:5 was one of their key texts, because Lev 17–19 seems to have been a critical text for James. For instance, he repeatedly appeals to Lev 19 in his epistle: Lev 19:12 (Jas 5:12), 19:13 (Jas 5:4), 19:15 (Jas 2:1, 9), 19:16 (Jas 4:11), 19:17b (Jas 5:20), 19:18a (Jas 5:9).¹⁰⁶ Further, in Acts 15:20, James relies on the Levitical guidelines for strangers in the land (Lev 17:10—18:30) in constructing the "Apostolic Decree." In keeping with the moral outlook of James, the Teachers thus might have claimed to be returning the Pauline churches' attention back to the one indispensable resource for holy living: the Torah.¹⁰⁷

Moreover, Paul's concern to rebut charges of libertinism in Rom 3:18, 6:1, and Gal 5:13, as well as his appeal to the Ninth Commandment in Rom 7:7, might also signal that the Teachers' gospel has a strong moralizing as well as cultic element. This suggests that their proclamation was continuous with the fundamentally ethical orientation of justification

---

102. As John Barclay puts it, "If Paul makes a denial [e.g., "No one is justified by works of the Law" (Gal 2:16)], we may assume that, *at least*, those whom he addresses may be prone to regard what he denies as true, and *at most*, someone has explicitly asserted it" (Barclay, "Mirror Reading," 84). Dunn also suggests that Paul's opponents taught in terms of "works of the Law" (Dunn, *The Theology of Paul the Apostle*, 359).

103. The slippage from the verb "*poieō*" to the noun "*ergon*" probably relates to the fact that the substantive of the former, "*poiema*," was relatively uncommon in Koiné (cf. Campbell, *Deliverance*, 787).

104. Gal 3:12; cf. Campbell, *Deliverance*, 585, 813.

105. Campbell, *Deliverance*, 813.

106. Bauckham tabulates these allusions (Bacukham, *James*, 143).

107. Cf. Jas 1:25; 2:8; cf. also Martyn, *Theological Issues*, 16–17.

discourse in James (e.g., 2:14–16), but added to it an explicit emphasis on the importance of biblical ritual practice (paradigmatically circumcision) in promoting righteousness. As J. Louis Martyn and Douglas Campbell have rightly emphasized, Paul's opponents seem to take it that fleshly Torah-observance constitutes a kind of spiritual surgery, amputating the sinful "desire of the flesh" (Gal 5:16), and so allowing them to fulfill the Law and secure a favorable judgment before God.[108]

The Teachers might also have defended their linking of faith and works by adapting James's exegesis of Gen 15:6 as a prophecy,[109] but now highlighting its intertextual relationship to Gen 17 (a suspicion warranted principally by Paul's lengthy engagement in Rom 4:9–25 with this text, seemingly so inhospitable to his message).[110] This shift in focus from James's interest in the Akedah of Gen 22 to circumcision would have made excellent rhetorical sense given their gentile audience, for whom circumcision would have been one of the most obvious markers of Jewish difference and distinction.[111] As the Teachers might have told the story, the Abrahamic covenant of land and descendants was *inaugurated* with faith, but its eternal *sign* is circumcision.[112] Like James, they present faith in Christ and obedience to the Law (now emphasized, for their gentile

---

108. This was a common theme in Second Temple Judaism, deriving ultimately from God's promise in Deuteronomy to "circumcise your heart and the heart of your offspring" (Deut 30:6). In the Dead Sea Scrolls, we read, "[No member of the community] shall walk in the stubbornness of his heart, so that he strays after his heart, after his eyes, and after the thought of his Impulse (*mahasebet yisro*). On the contrary, they shall circumcise in the community the foreskin of the Impulse (*'orlat yeser*)" (1QS 5:5, quoted in Martyn, *Theological Issues*, 254n8). And Paul's contemporary Philo of Alexandria advocated "a twofold circumcision . . . that which is of the flesh . . . and that which is of the male creature . . . in respect of his thoughts . . . since that which is, properly speaking, masculine in us is the intellect, the superfluous shoots of which it is necessary to prune away and to cast off, so that it, becoming clean and pure from all wickedness and vile, may worship God as his priest" (Philo, *Questions and Answers on Genesis* 3.46, quoted in Campbell, *Deliverance of God*, 566–67).

109. Cf. Martyn, *Theological Issues*, 87. The only alternative to this thesis is to suppose that James used this passage, and that Paul independently deployed it Christologically in his polemic against the Teachers.

110. Cf. Campbell, *Deliverance*, 733.

111. Campbell is illuminating in this regard: "It seems likely that the Teachers would appeal to Abraham . . . the pagan proselyte par excellence—as well as the father of Judaism" (Campbell, *Deliverance*, 722). The Teachers' interest in Abraham turned on his role as archetypal pagan proselyte; James's interest turned on Abraham's role as archetypal Jew.

112. Gal 3:6–8; cf. Gen 15:5, 7; 17:6–8, 11, 13.

hearers, in terms of circumcision) as two ways of picking out a single, inseparable reality. For the Teachers, then, Paul's gospel might have appeared to be not so much incorrect as radically incomplete.[113]

How Did Paul Respond to the Teachers?

This concluding section brings us once more to the surface of Paul's letters, and to its most controversial aspect, the doctrine of justification. Nothing approaching a full description of this feature of Paul's thought, much less its scholarly reception, can be attempted here.[114] Instead, I'll conclude by showing how our reconstruction of the Teacher's movements might illuminate Paul's famous appropriation of their native "justification discourse," in the teaching that "one is not *dikaio*-ed[115] by *erga nomou*, but by *pistis Christou*." What are we to make of the three controverted components of this teaching, in light of its hypothesized background in the Teachers' transformation of material preserved for us in the Epistle of James?

I argued above that 2 Corinthians represents Paul's earliest response to the Teachers. While this letter does not employ justification discourse, it does develop the crucial conceptual distinction which underlies Paul's subsequent development of that discourse, particularly in Romans. As we observed above, the Teachers seem to have impressed the Corinthians with "letters of recommendation" from leaders in the Jerusalem church (2 Cor 3:1). Paul confronts their request that he produce similar bona fides by insisting that *they* are his letter of recommendation (2 Cor 3:2), which establishes his qualification as a "minister of a new covenant, not of the letter, but of the spirit: for the letter kills, but the spirit gives life" (2 Cor 3:6).[116] I would suggest that this contrast is Paul's instinctive, if

---

113. Longenecker writes, "Probably, as well, [the opponents] claimed not to be opposing Paul, but to be completing his message" (Longenecker, *Galatians*, xcv).

114. A longer treatment of this issue can be found in chapter three of my book: Case, *The Accountable Animal*.

115. "Δικαιόω generally refers to the particular part of a judicial process when the presiding authority makes a critical decision, stating that someone is 'in the right' (or not), that is, rendering a verdict. So a judge or judges may uphold a charge against a person or exonerate that person of the charge, and so on" (Campbell, *The Deliverance of God*, 659). Cf. LSJ *ad loc.* A. III.

116. Paul here blends allusions to Ezek 37 with Ezek 36:22–38's earlier promise of a "new heart," and Jer 31's promise of a "new covenant." For Paul's allusive use of Ezek 36 and Jer 31 in 2 Cor 3, cf. esp. Richard Hays, *Echoes of Scripture in the Letters of Paul*,

elliptical, framing of the distinction he will later reformulate, using the Teachers' own categories, as that between "*erga nomou*" and "*pistis Christou*": we aren't justified through "what the Law does (*erga nomou*, construed as a subjective genitive),[117] because what the Law does is kill (Rom 7:11; 2 Cor 3:6). Rather, we are justified through the faithfulness of Christ (*pistis Christou*, also construed as a subjective genitive), because it is only through being conformed to Christ's faithful life, death, and resurrection by the outpouring of the Spirit that we are made righteous and so vindicated in the final judgment.

In Rom 2, Paul returns to the contrast between the Spirit and the letter, this time in the context of Paul's attempt to relativize the Teacher's claim to privilege, rooted in the possession of the Law, versus sinful gentiles in the face of God's impartial judgment (cf. Rom 2:6, 11).[118] Paul endorses this coming judgment as firmly as do the Teachers: the LORD, as Ps 72:12 insists, "will render to each according to his works" (Rom 2:6); he is impartial (Rom 2:11; cf. Jas 2:1), and so "not the hearers of the law are just before God, but the doers of the law shall be justified" (Rom 2:13; cf. Jas 1:23). The echoes of the Epistle of James are noisier here than anywhere else in Paul's works; whether he knows James directly or is aware of this material by way of the Teachers, it seems as though Paul is here emphasizing his agreement with some of his opponents' core convictions.[119]

122-53, as well as Pitre et al., *Paul*, loc. 3880-915. Hays rightly sees Ezek 37 as at least distantly evoked by Paul's network of allusions (Hays, *Echoes of Scripture in the Letters of Paul*, 129-30).

117. See below for further discussion of this interpretation, which has been defended by, e.g., Gaston, *Paul and the Torah*, 104-6; Owen, "Works of the Law," 554; Leithart, *Delivered from the Elements of the World*, 143. Parts of p. 41-45 are adapted, with permission, from Case, *The Accountable Animal*, 70-81.

118. The dominant approach is to see the interlocutor introduced in 2:1 as a "non-Christian Jewish man," who "stands in for the Jewish people as a whole" (cf. McFadden, *Judgment according to Works*, 58). Douglas Campbell, by contrast and (in my view) correctly, sees the interlocutor as a particular *Christian* Jew, who represents the Teachers (Campbell, *Deliverance of God*, 495-97).

119. Campbell is surely right that "it is hard to the avoid the detection in [Rom 2:]13 of a slogan from the Teacher himself (*if not from James*)—the oft-repeated adage that the truly righteous must be 'doers of the word, and not merely hearers who deceive themselves' (Jas 1:22)" (Campbell, *Deliverance of God*, 582, my emphasis). While I think Campbell goes too far in his proposed partition of the text into Pauline and non-Pauline speakers (Campbell, *The Deliverance of God*, 547-70), I am convinced by his broader proposal for the occasion of Romans, as a further intervention by Paul to stop the ongoing interference by the Teachers in churches planted by him. I take it,

The remainder of Rom 2, however, constitutes a *reductio ad absurdum* of the Teachers' insistence on pairing belief in an impartial judgment of *individuals* according to their works with *group* advantages for the Jewish people (defined by *halakah*) as a whole. Jews who commit flagrant sins, Paul insists, derive no benefit at the judgment from fleshly circumcision (Rom 2:17–25), while gentiles who "fulfill the Law" will be acquitted even without circumcision (Rom 2:26–29). These gentiles described in Rom 2:26–29 as "keeping the ordinances of the Law" (2:26) must be Christians—after all, they possess the Spirit (2:29)![120] But notice that he also describes them as possessing "the circumcision of the heart, in the Spirit, not the letter."[121] Paul alludes here to a distinction he develops extensively elsewhere: in itself, as a mere external letter, the Law kills (*grámma apokténnei*, 2 Cor 3:6), but as written on one's heart by the Spirit (2 Cor 3:3), it gives life (*pneûma zōopoieî*) (2 Cor 3:6).

As Gaston, Owen, and Leithart have argued, Paul's claims that "the letter kills" (2 Cor 3:6), or that "the Law works (*katergázetai*) wrath" (Rom 4:15) ought to be allowed to interpret his statements elsewhere about "the works of the Law." After all, it's quite natural to construe Paul's "works of the Law," not as an attributive genitive ("works in accord with the Law"), but instead as a *subjective* genitive, "the Law's works," or even "what the Law does."[122] And, as Gaston rightly emphasizes, Paul has a great deal to say just in Romans about what the Law does: it "closes every mouth and makes the whole world stand guilty (3:19) . . . brings knowledge of sin (3:20) . . . charges sin (5:13) . . . increases Adam's fault (5:20) . . . has authority over a human being (7:1) . . . provides an occasion for sin (7:8,

---

however, that Rom 2–4 does not reflect Paul's rejection of the premise that the doers of the Law will be justified, but rather that it constitutes his argument that, e.g., circumcision or kosher observance is irrelevant to gentiles' becoming such "doers" in the age of the Spirit's outpouring (see below).

120. Cf. Pitre et al., *Paul*, loc. 4009–20.

121. On the "circumcision of the heart" as baptism, cf. Col 2:11–12.

122. "The phrase would therefore denote the effects of the Law's activity among humankind. . . . Paul is prone to use this expression when the agency of the Law in effecting justification is the issue at stake. The emphasis in this turn of phrase would then lie not so much on human failure fully to obey the Law (though that is implied) as on the Law's own inability (owing to the gripping power of sin) to produce in people a righteousness that can survive before the bar of God's judgment" (Owen, "Works of the Law," 554). Cf. also Gaston, *Paul and the Torah*, 104–6; Leithart, *Delivered from the Elements of the World*, 143.

James as the Origin of Pauline Justification 43

9) . . . deceives (7:11) . . . causes death (7:10) . . . [and] kills (7:11)."[123] In this light, it's hardly shocking that "what the Law does" cannot justify us!

The problem, as Paul goes on to clarify, is not with the Law itself, which is "holy and just and good" (Rom 7:12), but with the "fleshly" persons, "sold under sin," to whom it is given (7:14).[124] "The letter kills" (2 Cor 3:6) only those who are in the flesh, and does so by raising sinful desires into consciousness, teaching them what it is to covet by its very command not to covet (Rom 7:7; cf. Exod 20:17).[125] Far from excising "the desire of the flesh" (cf. Gal 5:16), the sin-subjugated Law inadvertently kills its possessors by making sin exceedingly sinful (Rom 7:13).

In fact, the Law's own agency is what is at issue in Romans 3:20, where Paul maintains that "by works of the Law no flesh will be justified." Paul here emphasizes that the Law acts so as to shut every mouth (3:19) and to bring the knowledge of sin (3:20). Indeed, the content of "what the Law says" (3:19) seems to be given in the catena of biblical passages on human sinfulness set out in Rom 3:10–18.[126] But in that context, a sudden comment on "[human] legal works" would imply a change of subject twice in the span of two verses, from what the Law does (shut every mouth) to what we do ("works of the Law") back to what the Law does (introduce the knowledge of sin). By contrast, interpreting "érga nomoû" as "the Law's works" yields a single, seamless line of thought in Romans 3:19–20: the Law silences humanity in their sin and makes them liable before God (3:19), and so we aren't justified through what the Law does (3:20a), since the knowledge of sin is through the Law (3:20b).

If Rom 7 elaborates Paul's claim that "the letter kills," Romans 8 similarly expands on his parallel claim that "the Spirit gives life" (2 Cor 3:6), offering Paul's most extensive account of why the Teachers' (or James'!) "doer of the Law" must be "in the Spirit" rather than "in the letter" (cf. Rom 2:13, 29). In both 2 Cor 3 and Rom 8, Paul reflects on the promise of

---

123. Gaston, *Paul and the Torah*, 104.

124. It seems clear that Rom 7:7–25 is spoken in the voice of an unregenerate person (perhaps Paul himself prior to receiving the Spirit); where he was once "fleshly, sold under sin" (7:14), he has now been liberated by the Spirit "from the law of sin and death" (Rom 8:2). For this reading, cf. Campbell, *Deliverance of God*, 140–41; Schreiner, *Paul*, 132.

125. For this connection between 2 Cor 3 and Rom 7, cf. Origen, *Commentary on Romans* 2.13, 15–46; Augustine, *On the Spirit and the Letter* 1.13.21—25.42.

126. We should think as well of the "curse" which Paul warns is pronounced on those who "rely on works of the Law (*ex érgōn nómou*)" (Gal 3:10), and the catena of curses pronounced against covenant-breakers in Deut 27:15-26; 28:15-68.

Ezek 37:1–14, of Israel's resurrection by "the Spirit of life" (Ezek 37:5) to renewed obedience to and intimacy with God. Romans 8 opens by evoking Ezek 37 in the context of the present life: "For the law of the Spirit of life (*toû pneúmatos tēs zōēs*) in Christ Jesus freed me from the law of sin and death" (Rom 8:2).[127] "Those who walk according to the Spirit" can "fulfill the just requirement of the Law" (8:4), and so ultimately receive the vindicating resurrection from the dead (Rom 8:9–11), because the Law's command—paradigmatically, in Rom 7:7, "do not covet"—is itself spiritual (7:14).

Paul denies that our ultimate vindication comes from "what the Law does," and insists instead that it comes from (in effect) what the Spirit does—or rather, as he puts it in his developed version of justification discourse, "through Christ's fidelity (*pistis Christou*)."[128] In the resurrection, the Father overturns Jesus' death-sentence and so declares him, with the Roman centurion in Luke 23:47, "innocent (*dikaios*)." As Leithart puts it, "'Justification' is the liberating verdict that takes the form of resurrection." And this is why Paul (or his impersonator) writes, in 1 Timothy, that in the resurrection, Christ's faithfulness "was vindicated by the Spirit (*edikaiōthē en pneúmati*)" (3:16); in Rom 6:7, Paul makes the same point by insisting, "The one who died has been delivered from Sin (*ho apothanōn dedikaíōtai apò hamartías*)."[129]

127. Strikingly, the only other occurrence of this expression in the NT is an even noisier allusion to Ezek 37 than is Rom 8:2. Revelation 11:11's visionary says "after three and a half days, the Spirit of life (*pneûma zōēs*) from God entered in them [sc. the two slain witnesses], and they stood on their feet (*éstēsan epì toùs pódas autôn*)," a verse which, along with its echo of Ezek 37:5, also clearly echoes 37:10: "The Spirit entered into them and they lived and stood upon their feet (*éstēsan epì toùs pódas autôn*)."

128. In addition to Hays's classic treatment of this phrase (Hays, *The Faithfulness of Christ*), the most compelling datum favor of the subjective genitive reading is, as Douglas Campbell has particularly emphasized, the clear parallelism between "the coming of faith (*elthein tēn pistin*)" in Gal 3:23 and the coming of Christ in Gal 3:24, 4:3–4 (Campbell, *The Quest for Paul's Gospel*, 208–32). John Barclay makes a strong case for the objective genitive reading in *Paul and the Gift*, but the ability of the subjective genitive reading to explain this curious alternation between "*pistis*" and Christ is decisive, in my view.

129. "Rom. vi. 1—11 is concerned with the death of Christ and the participation of the believer in this death. By baptism the Christian is incorporated into that kind of death which Christ died, *tō homoiōmati toû thanátou autoû* [Rom 6:5]. Thus the most natural way of understanding verse 7 in its context is to see that the death spoken of is the death of Christ. It is this specific death which brings justification. *Ho apothanōn* does refer to the believer but only in so far as he has died with Christ in baptism" (Scroggs, "Romans VI. 7," 106). Scroggs does, however, miss the full force of this verse,

Christ is the paradigm of justification, the fully faithful one whose life is vindicated in his resurrection from the dead. And as Paul makes clear, this initial vindication is the engine of our coming vindication, for Christ himself is himself raised as a "life-giving Spirit" (1 Cor 15:45), and so is present and active even now in those who are "in the Spirit" (Rom 8:9–10) by virtue of the sacramental death-and-resurrection of baptism (cf. Rom 6:2–4; Gal 3:24–27). As John Henry Newman observes, this is why Paul insists that Christ "was . . . raised for our justification (*dià tēn dikaíōsin hēmōn*)" (Rom 4:25): in his resurrection, Christ is transfigured from flesh to Spirit (cf. 1 Cor 15:45, 50), and ascends so that he might "return to us invisibly in the attributes of a Spirit." Justification, then, is "through the faithfulness of Christ," because that faithfulness secured his resurrection and ascension, and the same faithfulness assures ours as well, insofar as we are conformed to it by the Spirit who makes Christ dwell in us.

Our interpretation of Paul's justification discourse has focused principally on its mature version in Romans, as interpreted through its earliest adumbration in 2 Cor 3. If we turn back to Galatians, however, with an eye on its "final draft" in Romans, it too offers several indications of Paul's concern to contrast the death-dealing Law with the life-giving Spirit. After describing how justification is not "through the Law's works" (Gal 2:16), he observes, "I died through the Law, to the Law, that I might live to God" (Gal 2:19). Here, then, is our grand theme from Rom 7. And now, Paul insists, "it is no longer I who live, but Christ who lives in me; and the life I now live in the flesh I live by the faithfulness of the Son of God" (Gal 2:20). Here too is the key theme of Rom 8 (cf. esp. 8:9–11): Christ's faithfulness is the cause of his indwelling the baptized by the Spirit, and so empowering them for a faithfulness to the Law which the Law itself was powerless to effect. Just as in Rom 7–8 and in 2 Cor 3:6, Gal 2:19–20 insists that the letter kills, but the Spirit gives life.

---

by reading "*dedikaíōtai*" in the middle voice, with the sense of "has atoned [for sin]," rather than in the passive ("has been delivered [from Sin]"). He thus takes the object of the verb to be those Christ saves, rather than Christ himself. However, as Douglas Campbell rightly emphasizes, "The presence of *apo* here is an especially strong indicator of Paul's fundamentally liberative meaning," which in this case can only be applied to "the one who died" himself, i.e., Jesus (Campbell, *The Deliverance of God*, 663).

Conclusion: Canonical and Hermeneutical Implications of an Historical Solution

By virtue of appearing to us only "in a glass, darkly," the Teachers are necessarily a more shadowy subject even than their sometime leader, James. What do we gain by so uncertain a rendition of justification's career? We certainly do not gain an unobjectionable historical account of this period; there is too little evidence, and that sifted too quickly, for certainty to be possible. Recall that this essay began by observing a set of interpretive problems that earlier treatments of James's relation to Paul consistently fall into. The principal goal of this thought-experiment has been to sketch a rendition of that relation that succumbs to none of those classic difficulties, by demonstrating that the Teachers movements and message can be plausibly read as recognizable developments of justification in James, and as plausible bearers of that discourse to Paul.

And if correct, this reading would have a twofold canonical payoff. First, it would correct the exegetical tendency to marginalize James in interpretations of justification in Paul: in point of fact, Paul's justification texts might derive from James, not vice versa. Second, notwithstanding Paul's suspicions to the contrary, this reading suggests that there is no reason to read Paul's polemic against the Teachers as having traction on James's earlier, Jewish-Christian discussion of justification. For Paul, the key is not to disavow works as such (cf. Gal 5:6), but rather to maintain that a life which God will ultimately vindicate in the resurrection is the product, not of the killing letter, but of the life-giving Spirit (2 Cor 3:6), not of "what the Law does," but rather "of the faithfulness of Christ." And on this point the evidence of Acts 15:13–21 suggests a James in agreement—however grudging—with Paul.

2

The Immoral Brother and the Apostolic Decree

The Ethics of 1 Corinthians

WILLIAM GLASS

PAUL'S COMMAND IN 1 COR 5:2–5 to expel the brother who is involved in sexual relations with his stepmother has baffled interpreters and elicited quite a diversity of interpretations.[1] Their puzzlement arises from the fact that most often in the Corinthian letters, Paul deals with sin in the church by exhorting the community to patience (1 Cor 7:20) and mutual accommodation (8:12). These exhortations are most clearly discernible in the case of the injustices at the Lord's Supper or the taking of brothers to court, for example, but it could be argued that even when Paul issues strong rebukes, he still seems to envision restoration of the sinner within the community. In the case of incest, however, Paul seems to command instant, decisive action. The two most popular interpretations attribute Paul's severity either (a) to the peculiar character of sexual sin or (b) to

---

1. Anthony Thiselton notes the tension that arises, asserting that "Paul expounds *both* an absolutist *and* a situational ethic. On the first he is unwilling to negotiate; on the second, negotiation, dialogue, and 'what if . . . ?' remain all-important, and Paul combines a situational ethic with pastoral judgment" (Thiselton, *First Epistle to the Corinthians*, 381–82).

concerns about community purity. But both of these explications leave Paul's argument conspicuously unaccounted for in places. This chapter will examine the flaws in each hypothesis, in order to make room for a third; for it is my thesis that, historically speaking, Paul's stringency owes to a concern for compliance by his predominantly gentile churches with the Decree issued at the Jerusalem council reported in Acts 15 and Gal 2. In this concern, I will argue, Paul acts out his conviction that the church's knowledge of God is expressed in self-giving love for all members of the Body of Christ, which makes unity in the Lord's *body* a necessary condition for knowing His *mind*.

I. Theology and Sexual Immorality

A large group of interpreters has explained the immediacy of Paul's response by arguing that Paul held sexual immorality to be chief in a theological hierarchy of sins. Chrysostom stands at the head of a long tradition when he explains Paul's stringency by the observation that "it was not possible to mention anything worse than fornication."[2] Among modern scholars, Conzelmann holds that Paul acts out of a theological conviction, "plainly taking his cue from a Jewish saying which describes fornication as the direst of sins."[3] Thiselton notes that the largest group of modern scholars understand "a qualitative difference in Paul's thinking, either in terms of (a) the destructiveness of [sexual immorality's] effects; or (b) in terms of its intrinsic sinfulness; or (c) its damaging effects specifically upon the self."[4] Among these scholars, the majority understand Paul's reaction to the instance of sexual immorality referenced in chapter five by reference to 6:18, and its seeming assertion that sexual sins are "against one's own body" rather than outside of it. For all of these interpreters, Paul sees in sexual immorality a particular viciousness necessitating immediate removal of the offender.

But this interpretation is not without its problems. First, Paul seems clearly to insist the Corinthian brothers and sisters are one body, such that if one member suffers, the others suffer with her (12:26). Although there may be sin against one's own body, no sin is *merely* so. Thus, if there

---

2. Quoted in Thiselton, *First Epistle to the Corinthians*, 471.

3. Conzelmann, *1 Corinthians*, 112.

4. Thiselton, *First Epistle to the Corinthians*, 472. He notes F. F. Bruce, Bruce N. Fisk, Kenneth Bailey, and H. A. W. Meyer.

is sin of some members of the body against others, that sin is also against one's own body, and vice versa. This logic would compel at least as drastic an action as that found in 1 Cor 5 in the case of, say, the believers who were taking others to court (1 Cor 6) and harming their own members. Secondly (and more importantly), Paul argues that each of the Corinthians' bodies is a "member" of Christ (6:15), such that, for example, sexual relations with a prostitute are a uniting of Christ's *own* body with that of the prostitute.[5] This logic intertwines the Corinthians' bodies with one another and with the body of Christ in such a way that it cannot be merely metaphor when Paul asserts that whoever takes the Eucharist unworthily, "will be guilty (*enochos*) of the body... of the Lord" (11:27). But although Paul warns the Corinthians that God will judge their sinfulness, he allows those members a place in the church. It seems quite strange that person A would be excommunicated for sinning against her own body but person B would not be excommunicated for sinning against the body of person A (and vice versa). Moreover, it is difficult to imagine in any case that a person's sin against her own body would compel Paul to excommunicate her while her sin against the *verum Corpus Christi* brings about no such reaction from Paul. Thus, it seems unlikely that "sin against one's own body" constitutes a rationale for excommunicating the immoral brother, and outside of that it is difficult to discern any other theological argument for the excommunication.

II. The Purity of the Congregation

Other commentators see in the background of the command to expel the immoral brother a concern motivated not by Proverbs and its hierarchy of sins but by the insistence upon purity in the face of possible contagions. Dale Martin, for example, has argued that Paul's excommunication of the man is motivated by a "primary concern [. . .] for the purity of the church, the body of Christ, and his anxieties center on the man as a potentially polluting agent within Christ's body, an agent whose presence threatens to pollute the entire body."[6] He reads Paul, that is, to be concerned about sex with *outsiders*. For Martin, Paul conceives of purity in the church along the lines of an actual body, and such intrusions as the immoral brother represent potentially fatal pathogens. And he marshals

---

5. See Martin, *Corinthian Body*, 178.
6. See Martin, *Corinthian Body*, 168.

an impressive array of medical texts to delineate two distinct patterns of speech about the body and its relationship to the world. Noting the presence of both patterns of speech in the Corinthian letters (one of which Paul promotes and the other of which he rejects), Martin concludes that Paul's wide-ranging discourse is united by the presence of two differing species of body logic.[7]

The second of those two, which Martin associates with the "weak" at Corinth, understands the body to be unstable and susceptible at all times to pollution. The "strong" at Corinth hold to a conception of the body as an agent in the world, able to affect the *cosmos*.[8] On this construal, Martin thinks he can account not only for the immoral brother's behavior in Corinth but the Corinthians' boasting in it (1 Cor 5:2). While the strong, he thinks, were probably ascetic in their sexual mores, they were probably also unconcerned with the behavior of the lower classes, having already decided that they are unavoidably lecherous.[9] Martin thus takes Paul to be rebuking both the action of the immoral brother in having illicit sex with an outsider, and hence subjecting the body to corruption, as well as the failure of the community to see themselves as compromised by his actions. For Martin, Paul intends that the "strong" at Corinth should see themselves as one (vulnerable) body with the weak. He rebukes the strong even as he pronounces judgment on the immoral brother.

In many ways, this is a perfectly plausible reading, and I will later argue that Paul is indeed eager that the Corinthians should see themselves as one body. But as Martin himself admits, his reading sits in deep tension with some parts of 1 Corinthians: "It is hard to see how Paul can insist that sexual intercourse between a Christian man and a prostitute pollutes the *pneuma* of Christ[10] . . . and simultaneously argue that the holiness of

---

7. See Martin, *Corinthian Body*, 248: "Throughout 1 Corinthians Paul attempts to undermine the hierarchical ideology of the body prevalent in Greco-Roman culture. He attempts to make the strong weak and the weak strong. He calls on Christians of higher status to please those of lower status."

8. See Martin, *Corinthian Body*, ix.

9. See Martin, *Corinthian Body*, 208.

10. Certainly, it could be argued that sex with a prostitute is different from the case of incest. But on Martin's reading, the two questions suffer from the same problem—that of sex with outsiders and the associated contagions. On his reading, the question of marriage to outsiders creates the same problem for the immoral brother as it does for sex with prostitutes. Cf. Martin, *The Corinthian Body*, 178: "Thus, whereas in 6:16–17 Paul's rhetoric implied that sexual intercourse between the Christian man and the prostitute enacted sexual intercourse between Christ and the prostitute—in which case,

Christ's body works the other way in the case of mixed marriages."[11] In these cases, Martin thinks that Paul reneges on his own logic. Of course, it is not impossible *per se* that Paul would be inconsistent; certainly many scholars think that he often is. But because of the kind of argument Martin is making, such charges are especially precarious. When Martin applies a schema that is not specified in the text as a programmatic key uniting the letter's various arguments and then argues that Paul is failing to abide by the logic *Martin* claims underlies the letter, he runs the risk of question begging.[12]

If this analysis is correct, Martin's theory on the excommunication may not have quite as much explanatory power as he thinks it does. His attempt to attribute Paul's wrath over the immoral brother to the fact that he is involved in sex *outside* the church[13] falls a little flat when one considers Paul's advice to the spouses of nonbelievers. On this point, as was seen above, Martin punts and accuses Paul of incoherence. But given the explicit theological rationale with which Paul addresses the situation of the spouses of unbelievers, and given the difficulty Martin's thesis faces on other grounds, it may be worth considering whether another thesis can accommodate details Martin's theory struggles with, even as we affirm

---

Christ is sexually penetrating the evil cosmos—in 6:18 the roles are reversed: the man is fucked by sin, so Christ is fucked by the cosmos. In the face of such cosmic consequences of coitus, Paul insists on limiting the freedom of the Christian man. *Again, as in 1 Corinthians 5, what is at stake is the pneuma of God*" (emphasis added).

11. Martin, *The Corinthian Body*, 251.

12. This is not my criticism alone. Margaret Mitchell, in her review of Martin, agrees that he is "too categorical in the application of discrete ideologies to the Corinthians." She also critiques his "reduction of the multifaceted Corinthians conflict to class strife." His sources in ancient medical texts, for example, show that hierarchical conceptions of the body were not everywhere and always at odds with concerns about corporal pollution. She concludes with the puzzle over how the fact that Paul seems himself implicated in both body logics, a fact which Martin recognizes, does not raise the question for Martin over whether the Corinthians themselves, "upper and lower class, likewise had less pure and distinct ideologies and commitments than he reconstructs." See Mitchell, Review, 290–92.

13. Martin, *The Corinthian Body*, 178: "The way Paul deals with *porneia* is soaked in the logic of pollution and invasion. This is sexual immorality that involves a member of the church and an outsider." Martin then imagines a scenario in which there is immorality within the church and argues, on the basis of the logic that "soaks" the passage, that Paul would not have considered that kind of immorality as a pollution: "the real objection to inappropriate sex within the church is put in economic terms: don't defraud your brother!" (Martin, *The Corinthian Body*, 179).

with the majority of 1 Corinthians scholars the basic soundness of at least parts of Martin's project.[14]

III. I Am Because You Are: Discerning an Ecumenical Ethic

(a) The Apostolic Decree as Difference Maker

In 1965, John C. Hurd convincingly argued that Paul's "previous letter" (1 Cor 5:9) was a letter alerting the Corinthians about the content of the Apostolic Decree (Acts 15:22–29; Gal 2:9).[15] Hurd's various proposals concerning the origin of I Corinthians have come under such attack in the four decades since its publication that it may seem unwise to rely upon it in any substantial way.[16] But, for reasons that will become clear,

---

14. This list includes Thiselton and most of the book's reviewers. In the interest of space, this essay has had to deal only with the places where Martin addresses the question of the immoral brother and sexual immorality. That has prevented, regrettably, a more balanced analysis of the many places where he is able to achieve brilliant readings of troubling texts. Below, I will attempt an explanation of this phenomenon in terms of Martin's failure to make many of Paul's final moves with him. That is, while I agree that Corinth presents Paul with conflicting images of the body, Paul's solution is not a straightforward upending of the apple cart. On this score, I must agree with Engberg-Pedersen, who sees in Martin's work the pale specter of Marxism, which overrides Paul's actual arguments.

15. Hurd, *Origin*, 259–62.

16. Despite a basic sympathy with Hurd, it should be observed that our suggestions here are far more modest. While we do suspect the Apostolic Decree to be part of the background of 1 Corinthians, we have far less to say about what (in detail) the "previous letter" must have said. We think it is possible to demonstrate this thesis as the best way of making sense of what is actually in Paul's text. On Hurd, see Greenfield, Review, 63; Pervo, Review; Omanson, Review. In each of these reviews, mention is made of a broad rejection (along with that of the author) of the majority of Hurd's proposals. See also Thiselton, *First Epistle to the Corinthians*, 35: "Hurd's attempt to reconstruct the 'previous letter' (to which 5:9 clearly alludes) remains in the nature of the case more speculative. His hypothesis rests largely on identifying a tone of 'counterarguments' to objections. . . . The most serious difficulty faced by the attempt to reconstruct the previous letter emerges from the last twenty years of research into classical and Pauline rhetoric. Whatever view one takes of Paul and diatribe style, there can be little doubt that Paul's awareness of the widespread use of deliberative rhetoric and its use within epistolary frameworks offers an alternative explanation to Hurd's explanations of the mood or tone of objections and counterarguments. Some of his claims may be valid, but they cannot be demonstrated." In our view, this represents a rare mistake from the ordinarily brilliant Thiselton. For one thing, it fails to note that where diatribe and rhetorical arguments are favored, they are favored on no less shaky a ground than such

I do not think a better hypothesis has been reached that is able to make sense of all of the data. I will thus conclude with him that whatever the other specific content of the "previous letter," it also contained the substance of the Apostolic Decree reported in Acts 15.

First, the relevant data should be assembled. We can follow (initially anyway) Douglas Campbell's dating of Paul's second visit to Jerusalem to late 50/early 51 CE.[17] Secondly, we can join a growing consensus of scholars in dating 1 Corinthians to late 51.[18] Third, there is Paul's own reporting of those events in Gal 2. Additionally, there are Paul's arguments concerning idol-food. Finally, there are Paul's "collection" texts (Rom 15:25–29; 1 Cor 16:1–9; 2 Cor 9).

---

historical proposals as Hurd's. Indeed, where such proposals gain ground, they do so based on (a) the fact that scholars know rhetorical devices to have been common in epistolary literature, and (b) the sense such proposals, once adopted, seem to make of Paul's own arguments (see also Stowers, *Diatribe*, for more on methodological criteria in the evaluation of rhetorical devices). It stands to reason, therefore, that a historical proposal enabling the letter to come together more cohesively does not deserve rejection on the basis of the mere fact of alternative proposals, unless those proposals can be shown to make better sense of the letter. For reasons to be outlined more extensively below, it is here maintained that they do not.

17. Campbell, "Anchor." Based on an enormous survey of Josephus, Vitellius, and other ancient historians, Campbell assembles a strong case that the Aretas referred to in 2 Corinthians must be Aretas IV, who controlled Nabatea for a period of a little less than a year, from sometime in 36 to early 37 CE. This allows a hard date for Paul's escape from Damascus, which then (thanks to Paul's own narration of his activities in Galatians) opens the way for several other strong dates as well. Rainer Riesner disputes the dating, but his Acts-based chronology raises more problems than it solves, such as the absence of any mention of the confrontation between Peter and Paul, as well as the multiplication of Jerusalem visits. Campbell's date is useful because among epistles-based chronologies, like those of Knox and O'Connor (the only ones in which the Apostolic Decree might post-date the founding of the Corinthian assembly), Campbell's chronology introduces the smallest temporal interval between the decree and 1 Corinthians. His chronology presents a limiting case, then, for the hypothesis that the decree might be part of the letter's background. See Riesner, "Chronology." See also Knox, *Chapters*; Murphy-O'Connor, *Paul*; Campbell, *Framing*, 412–14, and the discussion of those dating decisions in 182–89.

18. Thiselton, *First Epistle to the Corinthians*, 29; Murphy-O'Connor, *Paul*, 21; Campbell, *Framing*, 51; Lüdemann, *Apostle to the Gentiles*, 160–62; Jewett, *Dating*, 38–40.

(1) The Collection

Perhaps the best place to begin is with the collection texts, since Paul's collection is deemed by common scholarly consent to arise from the Jerusalem Council.[19] Paul begins his discussion of the matter in 1 Corinthians with this summons: "Now about the collection for the saints, you all should do as I instructed the churches in Galatia" (16:1). This is Paul's only mention of the collection in this letter before he proceeds immediately to give instructions concerning how it should be undertaken. There is in Paul quite a bit of directing and speaking authoritatively; but the size and scope of the project he here enjoins upon the Corinthians is such as would normally call for some further explication if this were the first they had heard of it. Rather, it seems obvious that Paul is giving instructions concerning something about which the Corinthians already know. If the collection has its origin in Paul's Jerusalem visit in late 50 CE ("only that we should remember the poor" [Gal 2:1]), and if in mid-51 Paul can write to the Corinthians about the collection as if they already knew about it, it makes a great deal of sense that the previous letter would be how Paul gets the word to them of what the council had decided. Indeed, it would be strange if such a compromise were struck, one that would compel action on the part of Paul's churches, and Paul didn't write to alert the churches of it.

(2) Idol-food

The question of idol-food, which according to Acts was also part of the Apostolic Decree (15:29), also occupies a significant place in the post-50 letters of Paul. Dale Martin understands Paul's concern with idol-food as a confrontation of the strong on behalf of the weak.[20] He argues (correctly, in my view) that prostitution and eating food sacrificed to idols present

---

19. Thiselton notes disagreement among scholars (Fee, Nickle, Holl, and Bengt Holmberg) as to whether the collection constitutes *mere* obedience rather than something more whole-hearted, but observes no significant disagreement on the origin of Paul's initiative. See Thiselton, *First Epistle to the Corinthians*, 1315, 1318–26.

20. Martin, *Corinthian Body*, 179: "the issue divided the Corinthian church along social status lines and that Paul, while agreeing with the Strong that such eating should not be categorically forbidden, urges them to give up their prerogative, based on superior knowledge, to eat idol-meat so that they may avoid influencing the weak—that is, those of lower status—to do so against the strictures of their conscience."

The Immoral Brother and the Apostolic Decree 55

the same danger.[21] But the text is a larger problem for Martin's broader construal of strong and weak. Paul blends of the language of eating and drinking with the language of sex in 6:12–13 and 10:8 in a way that is instructive for evaluating his schema. Anticipating an objection from the strong against his prohibition of sexual immorality ("All things are lawful for me [*panta moi exestin*]"—6:12), Paul insists that although everything may be lawful, not everything builds up (*sympherō*—lit. bring together).[22] For Martin, the strong are the ones who argue in favor of idol-food, but Paul anticipates that the logic used to justify eating of idol-food[23] (i.e., that all things are lawful) will be marshaled against his directives on uniting the members of Christ with a prostitute (6:13): "Food for the stomach and the stomach for food, but God will destroy them both."[24] But as we have already seen, Martin understands the strong at Corinth to hold an ethic of *askesis*, not licentiousness. On his construal, we should expect those who argue in favor of eating idol-food to also argue in favor of abstinence—as may be the case in 1 Cor 7:1b—rather than in favor of libertinism. Here, then, Martin has difficulty mapping "strong" and "weak" coherently in the Corinthian assembly. As such, Martin's theory about a consistent dynamic of class conflict should be understood in slightly more complicated terms. And since the motivation behind Paul's injunction against idol-food is, for Martin, based on a clear-cut class division, his theory on idol-food may need revision as well.

In Paul's pre-50 letters, the question of food sacrificed to idols does not come up.[25] When it does finally appear in the corpus (1 Cor 8–10), its context is a warning against idolatry (10:14) in language similar to that of the Apostolic Decree. Difficulties in discerning this connection arise from the fact that Paul builds slowly to the chapter 10 directive from what seems to be a different premise in 8:4: "We know that 'an idol has no real existence' and that 'there is no God but one.'"[26] Scholars who think that in

21. Martin, *The Corinthian Body*, 175.
22. This definition will become important below.
23. Martin, *Corinthian Body*, 170.
24. Thiselton notes the majority of translators who see this as a slogan. Thiselton, *First Epistle to the Corinthians*, 462: he notes agreement with Collins and Murphy-O'Connor. Note the slogan's placement in an argument about sexual immorality.
25. That is, again, taking the Thessalonian correspondence to pre-date the Council. Cf. Campbell, *Framing*, 412–14.
26. Martin argues that "Paul's argument in chapters 8–10 is rather confusing. At times he appears to agree with the Strong that idols are 'nothing'—that is, nonexistent

chapter 10 Paul contradicts himself miss his rhetorical question in 10:19 that equates to the sentence above: "What do I say, then? that an idol is anything?" [of course not]. Martin argues not that Paul contradicts himself but that he simply shows the difference between those who possess *gnosis* and those who do not, between those who are strong and those who are weak. That is, for *some* of the Corinthians, an idol is nothing: for others, not. But it seems rather that Paul is warning those who think of themselves as having knowledge that they may not. His echo of their statement, "We know that we all have knowledge" (8:1), is followed by the negation "Not all possess knowledge" in v. 7. And although certainly some who heard v. 7 would still think of themselves as possessing knowledge, as those who "stand" (10:12), Paul says even so that he himself, even if in fact he does stand, will never eat again so that no one *else* would be made to fall (8:13). In fact, he makes himself weak, in order to share in the gospel's blessings with those who are weak (9:22). Finally, he asserts in 10:12 that those who *seem* to stand should be careful lest they fall (*mē pesē*). The subjunctive of the *mē* clause connects with the "seeming" of the previous verse to cast real doubt on the "standing" of those who supposedly do stand. The problem is not, as Martin suggests, that the strong can eat without problems while the weak cannot, but it is rather that those who think they are strong, if they are not living as Paul does (cf. chapters 9 and 13), show themselves to be weak even if they do not know it: "I do not want you to be ignorant" (10:1).[27] Paul is not vacillating; he is dealing with the consequences of life lived according to so-called "knowledge" when that knowledge is not love-knowledge. Those who eat meat sacrificed to idols, when they destroy those for whom Christ died, fracture the body and lay it open to assault by the demons that dominate the nations in their idolatry.

---

or absolutely powerless (8:4). . . . In chapter 10, however, Paul seems to be saying something different, admitting that idol-meat has been sacrificed not to figments of someone's imagination but to demons—his actual word is *daimonion*, the diminutive, which a Greek speaker would understand as a god or some divine being quite near to a god (10:19)." Martin introduces this Pauline tension by arguing that "the only difference between a strong consciousness and a weak consciousness, or between a strong and a weak Christian, is the presence of *gnosis*. Gnosis is the prophylaxis against the pollution that would otherwise result from ingestion of idol-meat" (Martin, *Corinthian Body*, 182).

27. Thus, like Ziesler, I propose in fact that "weak" and "strong" are categories that Paul assumes from the language of the Corinthians themselves but that he assumes it programmatically, effecting a Christological subversion of those categories' integrity. See Ziesler, *Romans*, 326–27.

But who are these weak at Corinth? Why is there any struggle over the question at all? And why does Paul posit such a radical course of action to care for them? Mark Nanos has recently advanced the provocative suggestion that the "weak" at Corinth are unrepentant polytheists, non-believers in Jesus, who might be *confirmed* in their idolatrous practice by the sight of Christians eating meat sacrificed to idols.[28] In this reading, he pursues from the other side of the Jew/gentile divide his thesis that where Paul refers to the "weak" in faith, he refers only to those who are outside the congregation.[29] They are "weak" in faith, Nanos thinks, because they are non-believers. In both the Corinthian and Roman context of the argument, Nanos promotes what he believes are the only theses that can escape the trap into which interpreters fall when their interpretations of "the weak" violate Paul's own command to respect them.[30]

But Nanos' argument, for all the virtue of his attempted ecumenical *rapprochement* with Judaism,[31] does not stand up textually either to Romans or to 1 Corinthians. His major problem is Paul's description of the "weak" as *adelphoi*, as brothers (Rom 14:15; 1 Cor 8:11). Nanos knows he has this problem and attempts to exploit the fluidity of the notion of fictive kinship in Greek and Roman cultures: "At the same time, many of these sources [the Tanakh and other Second Temple literature] use familial language to reach across group boundaries in ways not unlike it is being proposed that Paul should be read in this case."[32] Nanos' examination of the external evidence is compelling but ignores the fact that for Paul, in every other context except (perhaps) these, *adelphos* is a technical term for people in the church.[33] Indeed, in 1 Cor 5:11, Paul speaks of a specific judgment that applies to "any one who bears the name of brother," implying exactly what I am arguing here; it is a name for "insiders" ("those

---

28. Nanos, "Polytheist Identity of the 'Weak,'" 191.
29. For an analogous argument from the Jewish side, see Nanos, *Mystery of Romans*.
30. Nanos, *Mystery of Romans*, 87–95. See also Reasoner, *Strong and Weak*, 19–20.
31. Nanos, *Mystery of Romans*, 159.
32. Nanos, "Polytheist Identity of 'the 'Weak,'" 204.
33. For Romans, see 1:13; 7:1; 8:12; 10:1; 11:25; 12:1; 15:14, 30 (note "*our* Lord Jesus Christ"); 16:14 (in parallelism with "all the saints" in the next verse), 17. For 1 Corinthians, see 1:10, 11; 26 (asking the "brothers" to remember their *call*); 2:1; 3:1 (with a specific mention of "brothers" who were weak in faith); 4:6; 7:23; 7:29; 10:1; 11:33; 12:1; 14:6, 20; 15:1, 6, 30, 50; 16:11, 12, 15, 20.

inside"—5:12). Meanwhile, Paul has a name in 1 Cor for "outsiders," which he applies consistently: they are *apistoi*, or unbelievers.[34]

Indeed, contra Nanos, the "weak" seem to be brothers who have issues of conscience over the consumption of idol-meat. But just here, other problems arise. Mark Reasoner notes the consensus reading of a parallel discussion in Rom 14 that those who are "weak" are Jewish Christians. Whatever the merits of that consensus,[35] the Jewish *character* of their concerns is rightly observed.[36] And such considerations might apply equally as well to 1 Corinthians, as is evidenced, among other things, by Paul's exhortation that the Corinthians should attempt not to offend Jews (1 Cor 10:31). The issue seems, as so many have noted, to be an issue relating to Jewish *halakhic* discipline.[37] This creates something of an issue, since nowhere else in the letter, it should be noted, does Paul express concerns that reveal a significant population of Jewish Christians who might be offended over the matter of idol-meat. Indeed, the brothers Paul worries may be offended are gentiles (1 Cor 8:7). The presence of gentiles who have adopted specifically Jewish concerns is difficult to explain.

There are other problems as well. Nanos is right to note that something in the recent past has occurred to challenge a long-standing consensus: *heōs arti* (8:7).[38] With this observation, Nanos enters into a longstanding discussion concerning what happened after Paul left Corinth. Bruce Winter helpfully summarizes the problem in his observation that 1 Corinthians all but suggests incompetence on Paul's part. Why, he wonders, "had Paul not dealt with some, if not all, of the problems he addressed in 1 Corinthians while he was in Corinth? . . . It is something

---

34. 1 Cor 6:6; 7:12, 13; 10:27; 14:22–25 (four times).

35. Personally, I suspect that this discussion is far better accounted for in terms of *Nebenadressat*, whereby Paul exhorts the Romans to mutual welcome but also reinforces the same point among the Corinthians who are present with him as he composes the letter. See Campbell, *Framing*, 28–29, 54; Hartwig and Thiessen, "*Nebenadressat*."

36. Reasoner notes Origen, Chrysostom, and John Damascene in antiquity, as well as Melanchthon, Godet, Michel, Jewett, Käsemann, Cranfield, Wilckens, and Watson. See Reasoner, *Strong and Weak*, 7–8.

37. See Dunn, *1 Corinthians*, 58: "Certainly on the second question it is hard to avoid the conclusion that the motivations of the 'weak' were primarily Jewish in character. In the ancient world the abhorrence of idolatry was quintessentially and distinctively Jewish, and it is that abhorrence which dominates the discussion, both the fear of the 'weak' (8:1, 4, 7, 10) and also Paul's response (10:7, 14, 19–22); hence also the concluding concern in 10:32."

38. Nanos, "Polytheist Identity of the 'Weak,'" 190.

of an enigma that he responded to many critical issues only when they were raised by letter or report from Corinth."[39] Winter's own answer to the question engages an extraordinary wealth of archaeological information to conclude that social changes in Corinth after Paul leaves are the origin of the lack of clarity the Corinthians seem to have with regard to Paul's teachings. Changing times, on his view, call for a reinterpretation of Paul's intentions. His thesis suffers, however, from two main difficulties: (1) the kinds of changes he suggests, e.g., grain shortages and the relocation of the Isthmian games, are only strange to distant audiences. They represent, in fact, the kind of problems common to ancient cities (grain) under fickle and changing rule (relocating the games). It is hard to imagine a person having grown up in the ancient world teaching ethical behavior that could be so easily dislocated by such changes. Also, (2) only on the most strained readings can Winter find textual evidence of the effects of such changes on Corinth.[40]

To summarize, the problem that must be solved is the presence, among gentile Christians in Corinth who had eaten idol-meat for as long as anyone could remember, of a Jewish halakhic concern. Moreover, that concern must have arisen not while Paul was in Corinth but since: between Paul's visit and the writing of 1 Corinthians, the same period of time during which the "previous letter," containing instructions about the collection and sexual immorality, was composed and sent. Far and away the best explanation for this problem is the fact that Paul's previous letter, in which he alerted them to the terms of the Apostolic Decree, advised a stance toward idol meat that Paul had not adopted himself while he was at Corinth, namely, a stance of abstinence. As will be discussed in more detail below, some, if not many, of the Corinthians apparently resisted Paul's exhortation to abstain. But some of the Corinthians were apparently conscience-stricken over Paul's previous letter and began to abstain from idol-meat and to see the continued practice in it as idolatry. Their obedience to the decree was the object of derision by some in the

---

39. See Winter, *After Paul Left Corinth*, 1.

40. In principle, his methodology works as mine does: he tries these various phenomena on for size and then attempts to discover whether they aid the search for the meaning of Paul's text. This is how all historical work must proceed; proof is a fool's errand for the historian. I agree with Winter that the question of what happened after Paul left Corinth is crucial for making 1 Corinthians coherent, but suspect that the thesis I have proposed has the strength that Paul's encounter with Jerusalem is mentioned at least indirectly in 1 Cor (15:3) and the "collection" texts (Rom 15:25; 1 Cor 16; 2 Cor 9) and directly in other Pauline literature (Gal 2).

congregation, who (correctly) remembered that Paul himself had not preached against idol-meat when he was in Corinth. This dispute was the occasion of their asking Paul about it in the first place.

This hypothesis enjoys the advantage of being able to account for all of the problems that interpreters have struggled to accommodate: namely, the Jewish character of the conviction, apparently carried by gentiles, acquired in the recent past. And in the exhortation to accommodate the weaker brother, Paul implies a compliance with the terms of the Decree from Jerusalem, the brothers behind the "weaker brothers" in Corinth. Nor should Paul's evaluation of the Jerusalem council in those terms be taken as condescending or inflammatory towards Jerusalem, since Paul's assumption of the binaries the Corinthians had used to name themselves were combined with his naming of both himself as weak and of Christ as "the weakness of God," which overcomes the strength of the world. Nanos forgets this when he defends his position that the weak must be outsiders by claiming that on any alternative logic Paul must be ascribing "weakness" to the Church Fathers.[41]

It seems, then, that Paul's entire discourse on idol-meat is a coherent presentation that juxtaposes the "nothingness" of idols in and of themselves (something which Paul probably taught in his original preaching at Corinth; cf. 8:4–6) with the consequences of living outside of charity with the whole body (in every place; 1:2) and thus rendering the body vulnerable to the powers.[42] This summary of the argument allows Paul's climax in 10:14 to achieve its proper volume ("*therefore*, my beloved, shun the worship of idols"). Paul directs the Corinthians to "flee" (*pheugete*) idolatry. It is noteworthy that only one other noun in 1 Corinthians is the object of the verb *pheugō* in 1 Corinthians: namely, sexual immorality (6:18), the other ethical imperative of the Apostolic Decree. It seems quite reasonable then, in light of the mention of the collection and the emphasis on idol-food (the first worry about it that one finds in his letters) and the likely origin of the weaker brothers in the first place at least to suggest that behind Paul's instructions to the Corinthians there is a concern for conformity with the Decree. And if that is true, it might be worth examining why the one instance in the letter in which Paul seems

---

41. Nanos "Polytheist Identity of the 'Weak,'" 189.

42. On this point, a clear resonance with parts of Martin's thesis should be apparent, although I have been at pains to distinguish the broader coherence of his argument from his particular schema for mapping out strong and weak conceptions of the body.

to reject any possibility of tolerable diversity also concerns an issue dealt with in the decree.

(3) Fleeing Immorality

As has been noted already, Paul only warns the Corinthians to flee from two kinds of behavior, namely, those that are banned in the Decree. And although he is willing to confront sin for the most part inside the church, such an open state of immorality in chapter 5 (of a kind not even found among the pagans!) commands instant expulsion. What can make sense of this? If we remember that Paul had almost certainly written to the Corinthians about the collection already, and if we also recall that he himself reminds them that he had written them about sexual immorality (5:9), it seems plausible at least to suggest that Paul had written them previously concerning the accord at Jerusalem. We also know from Paul that the meeting in Jerusalem was over something about which Paul cared quite deeply: whether pagans had to convert to Judaism (and be circumcised) before embracing Christ (Gal 2:2–5). His assertion that the other apostles added nothing to him in spite of fierce opposition by those who came "to spy out the freedom" of the Gentle churches (Gal 2:4) makes clear just how dangerous the situation of ongoing immorality was. The book of Acts likewise preserves memory of charges made against Paul that he had encouraged Jews to abandon the Torah (21:21) and had spoken everywhere against it (21:28). It is my suggestion, then, that Paul excommunicates the immoral brother in compliance with the Apostolic Decree. Were those in Jerusalem to hear of such behavior in Paul's churches, what would be their reaction? His alarm that the immorality at Corinth was of such a kind as even to offend the pagans seems to echo sentiments that might be expressed in Jerusalem by the voices that had lobbied at first for gentile conversion to Judaism before becoming Christians.[43] And what such a case of radical immorality might cost Paul (namely, the revocation of the freedom granted to the Gentle churches, the heart of the Pauline proclamation) is just such a thing as might arouse in him an immediate and decisive judgment.

---

43. It may be helpful to note that nowhere else does Paul write about sin as "greater" in the case of gentiles as would need to be the case for this exasperation to make sense. In fact, in the one place where such a comparison might seem to be at work (Rom 1–2), it seems rather that the Jews are the ones who come off badly in the comparison.

This thesis is not without problems, however. For one thing, the excommunication in 5:11 seems to extend beyond the immoral brother: "But rather I wrote to you not to associate with any one who bears the name of brother if he is guilty of immorality or greed [cf. 11:21a] or an idolater [cf. chs. 8–10] or an idolater [cf. 3:3] or a drunkard [cf. 11:21b] or a swindler [cf. 6:8], not even to eat with a such one." But as the references inserted parenthetically above also indicate, there were instances of every other one of the excommunicable sins going on at Corinth. This is not to suggest that Paul would not eventually have excommunicated more people (who can know?) but merely to point out that there were live instances of each of the other sins mentioned in Corinth. But no one else is excommunicated for those failures. Yet Paul evicts the immoral brother citing Deuteronomic authority (again in a way that is different from the other sins mentioned).

Another problem is that if these observations suggest that Jerusalem's judgments motivate Paul's dealing with sexual immorality in a more stringent way than his confrontation of other sins, they also press the question of his comparative lack of urgency on idol-meat. If it is the Jerusalem Council that speaks behind Paul's excommunication of the immoral brother, why does Paul not banish those who have eaten meat sacrificed to idols? With John Hurd, I would agree that what has happened is that on the question of idol-meat the Jerusalem Council has reversed Paul's earlier teaching.[44] This conclusion is reached on several bases. First, there are four "slogans" that Paul anticipates in the course of his discussion about idol-meat. Two of them ("there is no God but one," and "an idol is nothing at all in the world") would almost certainly have been in Paul's original teaching, as the relationship of 8:4–5 to 8:6 makes clear.

How else, after all, would the Corinthians have learned that the Shema would have purchase with Paul, such that they could use it polemically in defense of a position they held? The other two slogans ("all things are lawful" and "we all possess knowledge" [cf. 1 Cor 2:16]) are both peculiarly Pauline concepts.[45] And that the two monotheist slogans are quoted back *to* Paul in the same way as the other two suggest that the

---

44. Hurd, *Origin*, 278–80. Again, I am not relying on Hurd's arguments; rather, I have found in his work similar conclusions to my own, reached on different grounds although overlapping on occasion.

45. Cf. Titus 1:15 ("to the pure all things are pure"), which is either Pauline or else seemed Pauline enough that someone would use it to pass a letter off as Pauline. Cf., also, Rom 14:14 ("nothing is unclean in itself").

source of those sayings' authority is similar if not the same. Second, as Hurd observed, the rhetorical placement of the two latter slogans seems to suggest a Pauline origin: "the manner in which Paul argued around but not against these principles in I Cor. 8.1–11.1 implies that their ultimate source was Paul himself."[46] Third, one finds later in Paul's writings affirmations *both* of the conviction that would have led Paul to proclaim "all things were lawful" in the first place *and* of the crucial nature of accommodation for the weak brother. On the one hand, Paul writes of his persuasion "in (by?) the Lord Jesus that nothing is common in itself" (Rom 14:14). On the other, he follows Romans 14:14 with the observation that if someone is grieved by what a Christian eats, the Christian is not walking in love (14:15). Paul's first and second convictions together represent a foreshortened version both of what some think was his original preaching at Corinth and the subsequent change in the message following the Jerusalem Council. And Paul's prior preaching that eating idol-meat is not wrong in itself motivates a more patient application of the mind of the Apostolic Council.

The third problem, of course, is the near silence of 1 Corinthians on the Decree. But the letter demonstrates why that might be the case. First, the Corinthian correspondence makes clear that among the problems Paul faced at Corinth, compromised apostolic authority is most assuredly one of them (1 Cor 4:15; 15:10; 2 Cor 3:1–3, 10–13). That Paul makes little of his association with (or indebtedness to) Jerusalem when his own apostleship is in doubt is already clear from the letter to Galatians, in which the Jerusalem Council is explicitly mentioned along with Paul's explicit denial of being taught the gospel by anyone else (1:12–13).

Secondly, although Paul was willing to travel to Jerusalem to ensure that he was in good standing with the apostles there, there is no reason to think that the Corinthians would be swayed by a referral to the mind of Jerusalem. On the reading offered here, in fact, some of the slogans that are proffered back to Paul in light of his previous letter (which, again, because it certainly must have alerted them of the council and most likely concerning idol-food is very likely a notice of the Decree and its terms) are offered in resistance to the decree, at least by some at Corinth. If the Corinthians were not swayed by the original notice of the accord at Jerusalem (or if only some of them were), it makes perfect sense that Paul would not reference it here. This is even more likely if Apollos is part of

---

46. Hurd, *Origin*, 278.

the authority crisis, as seems to be the case (1:12; ch. 3), since Paul's own legitimacy needs repair in the eyes of the Corinthians. At the very least, then, there are reasons why Paul *might* not have mentioned the Decree in the letter even if his intent were to bring the Corinthians in line with it while emphasizing his own rightful place as their apostle.[47] This third problem is clearly the most difficult to overcome, but the fact that there is even a remotely plausible way to deal with it seems to me to advantage my thesis over against others for the ease with which sense it makes, once adopted, of so much of the letter.

While the thesis that the Apostolic Decree underlies the excommunication of the immoral brother is not without the problems noted above, then, none of these problems is terminal. Indeed, this thesis seems to have the best explanatory power for what actually occurs in the letter. We have seen already that Paul's immediate excommunication of the immoral brother is an odd, even singular, action for him to take. Why, when all of the other sins he rebukes in 5:11 are also found in Corinth, does he demand the instant removal of only the one brother? Of the possible answers suggested for so extreme a move by Paul, this hypothesis can actually account for that extremity without making a theological mess of the letter. When the legitimacy of his gospel is in danger, the drastic nature of his action makes sense. We certainly (perhaps only?) see similarly drastic denunciation elsewhere, in Galatians and 2 Corinthians, when that legitimacy is similarly at stake (cf. 2 Cor 11:14; Gal 5:12). It seems reasonable to conclude, then, that Paul's chief concern in excommunicating the immoral brother is a deep concern for compliance with the accord struck at Jerusalem. Why, though, is Paul so zealous to maintain legitimacy in the eyes of Jerusalem and to show the *bona fides* of his churches in the gentile world, that he would literally turn a brother over to Satan rather than alienate his churches from Jerusalem?

(b) Weak and (Therefore) Strong: An Epistemology of Love

As Lou Martyn has noted, Paul's letters are riddled with epistemology.[48] "No one comprehends what is truly God's except the Spirit of God. Now we have received . . . the Spirit that is from God" (1 Cor 2:11b-12). For

---

47. Cf. 1 Cor 5:3, where Paul asserts that *he* casts judgment upon the immoral brother in the Lord.

48. Martyn, "Epistemology at the Turn of the Ages," in *Theological Issues*.

Paul, as 1 Corinthians demonstrates beautifully,[49] humanity's epistemological crisis arises from the bald fact that the "wisdom of this age" was not sufficient to keep its rulers from crucifying "the Lord of glory" (2:6–8), and God's raising him from the dead, in effect, shows creaturely judgment to be not merely misdirected but completely upside down.

This crisis arises again and again in Corinth, as Paul rebukes the faultiness of their judgment and invites them to love one another better and hence know rightly. The mind of Christ is a corporate possession ("we have") held in trust by the Christian charism of love; it is in love for one another that Christians have the mind of Christ (cf. Phil 2:5–11). It follows, then, that division among Christians is an epistemological liability. I take it that this theological truth is behind Paul's insistence that those who think themselves strong should reckon themselves weak lest they find themselves to be so (cf. 1 Cor 8:2). It has already been pointed out that schemas attempting exhaustively to name the weak or the strong at Corinth tend to run into coherence difficulties at some point or another. Instead, it seems that those terms (and their cognate pairs of wise/foolish and spiritual/fleshly) are instances of Pauline irony, whereby he dislocates the judgment of the self-acclaimed "strong" and draws them towards the whole body in the revelation that "the eye cannot say to the hand, 'I don't need you'" (1 Cor 12:21). The realization that Christians need even those who seem to be weakest if they are to know the Lord rightly compels openness and intimacy in an *ethos* of love, which draws weak and strong together in a coinherence of ethics and epistemology, where perfect knowledge is also perfect love (1 Cor 13:12).[50] The Corinthian

---

49. A letter in which the question of "knowledge" is decisively foregrounded, as Paul explicitly calls the Corinthians' knowledge into question no less than thirty-three times.

50. Compare the work of neuroscientist Alexander Clark (*Supersizing the Mind*, 226–30). Clark's research deals with the phenomenon of extended cognition and its relationship to concurrent beliefs. There are many beliefs, Clark observes, that humans have even when unaware of having them in any given moment. Those beliefs typically reside in the memory, concurrent when accessed and latent at other times. He conducts a thought experiment in which the memory is replaced, as it were, by a notebook for an Alzheimer's patient named Otto. Otto gets information, writes it down, and later on looks at the notebook to recall it. In the event that the notebook contains false information, as it does in the case of "Twin Otto," the concurrent belief that is produced in referencing the notebook is inaccurate. Clark's experiment has merit as a theoretical vocabulary for Paul's insistence that the mind of Christ is a corporate possession. For Christians, the church represents a continuous body of memory and testimony. And the Jerusalem church represents the origin of much of that memory. First Corinthians 15 makes clear that Paul sees himself as involved in a *paradosis*, or tradition, of

problem is in fact a problem of differing body images. But the two bodies at play are the self-proclaimed strong (from whatever side of divisions at Corinth), unaware that they are truly weak, and those who by cruciform love for one another acknowledge their weakness and are raised from death in the power of the Spirit (Rom 8:11). The Spirit of Christ and the Body of Christ must coinhere. Thus, a divided Body cannot possibly be in step with the Spirit, whose fruit is love, peace, patience, and kindness. By its paradoxical embrace of weakness, the Church embraces the Spirit who raises the dead and is strengthened against incursions by those of a different spirit (2 Cor 11:4). Thus, the greatest sins for Paul are those that fracture the unity of the Body of Christ, through which Christ's Spirit draws the world to reconciliation with God.

Conclusion

It is this theology that explains Paul's willingness to check even his own convictions about idol-food at the boundary of those in Jerusalem who were alarmed by parts of his practice. Paul knows that he has the Spirit of God (1 Cor 7:40). But he also knows that nobody knows the mind of the Lord alone. And even if all things are lawful, not all things "bring together" (*symphero*). And although Paul is quite sure that his gospel will stand, he also knows that those who think they stand must take heed, lest they fall. For it is in love for the one I take to be the weaker brother that I make myself available to what God reveals in the guise of weakness. Paul's great concern is that Christians should be brought together, since only so can their discernment of the mind of Christ be successful. Thus, although in certain polemical contexts, he will be quick to downplay his association with Jerusalem, it is still true that the prospect of Jewish Christians rejecting his law-free gospel sent him to Jerusalem to present the gospel he preached among the gentiles: "I wanted to *be sure* I was not running and had not been running my race in vain" (Gal 2:3, emphasis

---

memory about Jesus. Although it is clear that in other contexts, Paul makes little of his connection to Jerusalem, it cannot be insignificant for the argument proposed here that the letter where he insists most strongly upon that connection ("I gave to you ... what I also received" [15:3]) is the letter in which he most clearly assaults the world's wisdom and lack of charity. The Corinthians may be Paul's letter (2 Cor 3:2), but the division of the church falsifies the letter, making the kind of knowledge Paul wants the Corinthians to have (and the world to have about Jesus) impossible. The letter can kill; but life together by the Spirit allows life to come to the whole body together.

added; note the epistemological flavor of his language here). "I am because you are": Paul recognizes the need of Christians in every place for unity with Christians in every other place and of Christians in all places to be united with those who first preached the gospel of Jesus to begin with ("For I passed onto you at first what I also received" [1 Cor 15:3]). Thus, it is an ecumenical theology that explains his excommunication of the brother whose life compromises not only Corinth but the relationship of the gentile to Jewish Christians. As Eph 2:11–18 makes clear, Paul saw the reconciliation between gentile and Jew in Christ as an icon of the reconciliation between God and humanity in Christ. Paul was not content that his congregations should merely agree among themselves, but rather that they should also remain in fellowship, even and especially, with the birthplace of the Church in Jerusalem ("together with all those who in every place call on the name of the Lord Jesus Christ" [1 Cor 1:2]), the source of Jesus memory and the fount of the Church's witness before the world that a new people had been begotten in Jesus.

Coda:

> *In the Rule of St. Benedict, monks entering the monastery are enjoined to a vow of "stability," in which they swear to live in the Benedictine monastery for life. The various conflicts that Benedict expects ahead of time to arise in his monasteries are negotiated through an antecedent commitment that "even though injuries are inflicted, [the monk will] accept them with patience and even temper, and not grow wear or give up, but hold out, as the Scripture saith: 'He that shall persevere unto the end shall be saved.'"[51] The stability opens up a theater in which individuals can attempt to know the mind of the Lord while at the same time doubts can be negotiated and the community can sanctify time as it awaits the judgment of God. The Benedictine vision for community thus envisions a complex relationship of one and many that reveals Benedict's careful reading of Paul.[52] Although Paul never mentions anything like a monastic vow, his letters reveal a tight theological bond between stability and the community's ability to know the mind of Christ.*
>
> *This discussion of Paul's ecclesiology presents a slightly different Paul than many scholars are used to seeing. And it must be conceded that Paul himself is partly to blame for this. His*

---

51. *The Rule of St. Benedict* VII.

52. Paul's letters, as Benedict would have understood them, are cited no less than thirty-six times in the Rule.

minimization at certain key points of the relationship between himself and the "pillars" at Jerusalem deserves further study than can be pursued here. But the pastoral circumstances that arise in the post-50 Pauline churches seem in most cases to deal especially with the arrival of those who claim a special relationship with Jerusalem. His reactions to such interlopers, in which he insists upon his own relation with the Lord, reveal attitudes that might be expected in the constant struggle to demonstrate his apostleship. But accounts of Pauline thought that overemphasize these components of his rhetoric seem to overlook the fact that Paul does on occasion boast of his bona fides with the Jerusalem Church (1 Cor 15 and Gal 2, in which Paul makes his boast specifically on the grounds of the agreement reached on his second visit there). Regarding this account, it is worth noting that Paul's comments that "they added nothing to me" (Gal 2:6) ought to be understood alongside the fact that idol-meat does not seem to have been a problem at Galatia—at any rate not so much as to need address. Thus, nothing that Paul had preached in Galatia would have undergone revision by the terms of the Decree. Additionally, what the Jerusalem Apostles did command found a welcome ear in Paul (so much that he risked his life to comply with the command "to remember the poor"), if not in his subsequent presentation.

To Paul's practice of submission to the mind of the Jerusalem Council might be added Paul's insistence upon, and observance of, geographical boundaries for his mission work,[53] his hermeneutics, his participatory soteriology, his apostolic ambassadorship, and his insistence upon communal phronēsis, in order to discover a truly Pauline ecclesiology. This would be an interesting locus for more study, as it raises the potential for a much less tortuous line than has usually been drawn between the Damascus Road and the powerful episcopacies of the second-century church.

---

53. Gal 2:9–10. See also Harris, *2 Corinthians*.

3

Pauline Evidence for Markan Posteriority

BRENDAN CASE

BEFORE THERE WERE GOSPELS, there was Paul, and the far-flung community of churches within which he found himself a leader. The Gospels took shape within this community, and were fashioned from traditions, whether oral or written, which were borne by it, as is evident from our earliest witnesses to the Gospels' formation, namely the Prologue to Luke and the fragments of Papias.[1] Now, to the extent that any of these proto-Synoptic traditions are visible to us, they provide useful aids for the study of the Synoptic Problem, concerning the literary relationships among

---

1. Luke, alone of the Evangelists, explicitly flags his dependence on earlier traditions, particularly those which he derived from eyewitnesses of Jesus' ministry: "Inasmuch as many have undertaken to compile a narrative of the things which have been accomplished among us, just as they were delivered to us by those who from the beginning were eyewitnesses and ministers of the word" (Luke 1:1-2). And Papias writes that Mark incorporates the reminiscences of Peter, while "Matthew set in order the oracles (*synetaxato ta logia*) in the Hebrew language (Papias, *Fragments* 3.15-16, in Holmes, *The Apostolic Fathers*, 740-41). The precise balance in these materials among sayings and extended narratives, or oral and written sources (or even—though certainly not only—full Gospels), when Matthew, Mark, and Luke drew on them, is irrelevant for our present purposes.

Matthew, Mark, and Luke.[2] In particular, if Mark were first to write among the Synoptists (Markan Priority, as Styler informs us, representing "the one absolutely assured result" of Synoptic studies),[3] then we might expect early references or allusions to "Markan traditions" to bear a distinctively Markan profile,[4] since the Matthean and Lukan versions of those pericopes would generally represent later redactions of Mark.[5] After all, while Matthew or Luke might be allowed to have recovered some traditions which were largely independent of their parallels in Mark, it would be strange if Mark were the earliest Gospel and yet his versions of a pericope were rarely or even *never* discernible among the crowd of allusions in the earliest church to their Matthean and Lukan cousins.

This essay tests that hypothesis about the probable shape of the nascent Synoptic tradition against one of its earliest witnesses, the Pauline epistles. (Of course, that Paul took more than a passing interest in the words and actions of Christ prior to the crucifixion is itself controversial;

---

2. Cf., e.g., Tuckett, *From the Sayings to the Gospels*, 309-10.

3. Styler, "The Priority of Mark," 64.

4. All but three Markan pericopes (the Seed Growing Secretly [Mark 4:26-29], the Healing of the Deaf-Mute [Mark 7:31-37], and the Healing of the Blind Man of Bethsaida [Mark 8:22-26]) have parallels in Matthew or Luke, which makes "Markan tradition" a convenient label for the material we will consider, namely pericopes which appear in Mark and at least one other Synoptic Gospel. Nonetheless, the label implies nothing about the relative order among the Synoptics. (For this usage, cf. Butler, *The Originality of St. Matthew*.) The Markan traditions treated here are as follows: the Traditions of the Elders (Matt 15:1-20; Mark 7:1-23), Peter's Confession (Matt 16:13-20 and par.), the Transfiguration (Matt 17:1-8 and par.), the Controversy over Divorce (Matt 19:1-11; Mark 10:1-10), the Rich Young Man (Matt 19:16-22 and par.), the Synoptic Apocalypse (Matt 24 and par.), and the Institution Narrative (Matt 26:17-29 and par.).

5. At least, this is the case for Markan traditions whose versions are sufficiently alike in substance and style as to require direct literary dependence by the later versions on their predecessors, however supplemented by additional testimony (or literary invention). James Dunn, however, has pointed out that even if a later Evangelist knew his predecessor's version of a story, he might well have preferred to incorporate a different version which was more familiar to him into his Gospel—multiple versions might thus be equally "primitive," with little literary dependence between them. (Possible examples include Matt 15:21-28/Mark 7:24-30; Mark 9:14-27 and par.; Mark 9:33-37 and par.; cf. Dunn, *Jesus, Paul, and the Gospels*, 28-31). John Wenham mounts a similar argument in *Redating Matthew, Mark, and Luke*, 54-87, as does B. Ward Powers for the relation of Luke to Matthew in *The Progressive Publication of Matthew*, 353-88.) The Markan traditions discussed in this essay (cf. n4 above), however, are close enough in content and wording that their primary relation must (in my judgment) be literary.

the evidence for that interest is set out at length in what follows.)[6] We will consider nine Pauline allusions or references, spread across six letters, to a variety of Markan traditions.[7] Perhaps surprisingly, the results of this survey pose a distinct challenge for Markan Priority: seven of the nine echoes are unambiguously Matthean or Lukan, and the remaining two are at best ambiguously Markan. I conclude by suggesting that this data provides substantial external support for Mark's posteriority to Matthew and Luke (the Griesbach hypothesis, or GH), and particularly for B. Ward Powers's proposal that Paul was acquainted with a number of proto-Matthean and proto-Lukan traditions (and perhaps even texts) which circulated in the earliest church prior to their incorporation into the canonical Gospels.[8]

I. Markan Traditions in Paul

(a) Matthew's "Little Apocalypse" in 1–2 Thessalonians

We can begin by considering the extensive use which Paul apparently makes of an extended Synoptic discourse in 1–2 Thessalonians,[9] where his reflections on the last things are strikingly similar to the "Synoptic Apocalypse" (cf. Matt 24/Mark 13/Luke 21) and particularly to the

---

6. This essay seeks to chart a course between the maximalism of W. D. Davies, who insisted, "It was the words of Jesus Himself that formed Paul's primary source in his work as ethical *didaskalos* (Davies, *Paul and Rabbinic Judaism*, 136) and the minimalism of Rudolf Bultmann, who claimed, "The teaching of the historical Jesus played no role or practically none in Paul" (Bultmann, *Theology of the New Testament*, 1:35). (Donald Dungan evokes these two extremes at the outset of his *The Sayings of Jesus in the Churches of Paul*, xvii.) At the very least, we need to take seriously C. H. Dodd's quip that shortly after his call, Paul "stayed with Peter a fortnight, and we may presume they did not spend all that time talking about the weather" (Dodd, *The Apostolic Preaching and Its Developments*, 16; cf. Gal 1:18–19).

7. For the sake both of brevity and clarity, we will limit our consideration to cases in which (1) there are sufficiently close lexical and thematic overlaps between a Pauline epistle and a Synoptic tradition to suggest a literary relationship, and (2) there are either explicit or implicit indications that Paul is drawing on a prior dominical tradition, rather than (or at least, in addition to) the Evangelist drawing on Paul.

8. Powers, *The Progressive Publication of Matthew*, 230.

9. There isn't space here to adjudicate the long debate over the authenticity of 2 Thessalonians. For a recent argument for reading it as a forgery, see Ehrman, *Forgery and Counterforgery*, 137–47; for a convincing response to Ehrman, see Campbell, *Framing Paul*, 204–16.

version preserved in Matt 24.[10] Just in plotline, the composite eschatology presented by 2 Thess 2 (on the events to presage Christ's return) and 1 Thessalonians (on the events ingredient in that return itself) has a distinctly Matthean accent: the desecration of the Temple will precede Jesus' return in glory to judge the world and to gather his saints with a trumpet-cry (cf. Matt 24:15–31; 1 Thess 4:16–17; 2 Thess 2:3–4). That precise story is Pauline and Matthean, and appears nowhere else in the NT—and note that the trumpet has stuck around into 1 Cor 15:52.[11]

Paul's comments on the last things in these letters don't merely conform to the broad outline of Matthew's "Synoptic Apocalypse," but do so by way of repeated verbal echoes.[12] Not only the angel and the trumpet (cf. also Isa 27:13), but also talk of those who killed the prophets filling up their sins,[13] of the thief in the night,[14] of wakefulness enjoined and contrasted with drunkenness,[15] of false signs and wonders,[16] and other details besides—these conspire to create a dense network of resonances between Paul's eschatology and the sequence of events set out by Christ in Matt 24–25, and, to a lesser extent, in Luke 12 and 21.

Given these lexical links, it is significant that in both letters, Paul reminds his readers that these are teachings which he received so as to hand on to them. Consider that in 1 Thess 4:15, Paul prefaces his teaching about the role of the dead in the "appearance (*parousia*)" of Christ by saying, "We say that to you by a word of the Lord (*en logō kyriou*)." To what is he appealing here? While Paul's account of these penultimate events is strikingly resonant with Jesus' description of the "appearance of the Son of Man" in Matt 24:30–31,[17] some commentators prefer to see him as referring to a dominical word delivered spiritually to a contemporary prophet,

---

10. Cf. Riley and Orchard, *The Order of the Synoptics*, 119.

11. Cf. Wenham, *Paul and Jesus*, 98.

12. "Part of the fascination of the phenomenon of the parallels between 1 Thessalonians and the synoptic tradition is that many of the parallels occur together both in Paul and in the gospels, above all in the eschatological discourses" (Tuckett, *From the Sayings to the Gospels*, 319).

13. Cf. 1 Thess 2:14–16 / Matt 23:31–32, 37 [Luke 11:49–50].

14. 1 Thess 5:2 / Matt 24:42–43 [Luke 12:39–40].

15. 1 Thess 5:6–7 / Matt 24:42, 47–49 [Luke 12:37, 45].

16. 2 Thess 2:9 / Matt 24:24 [Mark 13:22].

17. Cf. the "(arch)angel(s)," "trumpet" and "clouds" in both 1 Thess 4:16–17 and Matt 24:31. Paul's concern "about the appearance (*parousias*) of our Lord and our being gathered (*episynagōgēs*) to him" (2 Thess 2:1) similarly echoes Matt 24:27 and 31.

pointing in particular to Matt 24's apparent irrelevance to the problems addressed in 1 Thess 4:15–17.

So, Christine Jacobi notes that this is an appeal to a dominical word "which remains without Synoptic parallels and in which, additionally, it is somewhat unclear whether it relates at all to a concrete text."[18] After all, as Tuckett observes,

> It would seem most plausible to assume that Paul's decision to cite his tradition here indicates that the latter relates directly and positively to the situation addressed. Otherwise there would be little point in citing it. With this in mind it seems very improbable that a saying like Matthew 24.30–31 could be the tradition cited by Paul here. For Matt 24.30–31 says nothing about the resurrection of the living and the dead and the relative order of the two. Yet it is this which is the key point of Paul's argument.[19]

Indeed, while favoring the "prophetic inspiration" reading of this dominical word, Tuckett even wonders whether John 11:25–26 might provide a clearer background than Matt 24 for Paul's response to Thessalonian concerns about the fate of deceased Christians, since it can be read as addressing, however obliquely, both the fate of those who have died in Christ, and then the fate of those who are yet living.[20]

The extent and volume of the echoes of the Matthean Apocalypse both in 1 Thess 4:13—5:11 and its sister-text in 2 Thess 2 (see below) make it unlikely, in my judgment, that the dominical word to which Paul refers is Johannine, particularly given the similarities in both wording and content between Matt 24:30–31 and 1 Thess 4:15–17. Nonetheless, it is true that nothing on the surface of those two verses seems to bear directly on the resurrection of the dead, and particularly its relative order in the events surrounding Christ's return.

Proponents of Matt 24:30–31 as the appropriate intertext have proposed several interpretations of Paul's reading. Seyoon Kim, for instance, suggests that it was this passage, relayed to the Thessalonians by Paul, which initiated their crisis of confidence in the fate of the deceased, and that "*Paul refers to the 'word of the Lord' that has given rise to their grief, and expounds its full implications, emphasizing that one of them is the*

---

18. Jacobi, *Jesusüberlieferung bei Paulus?*, 45.

19. Tuckett, *From the Sayings to the Gospels*, 337.

20. "Jesus said to her, "I am the resurrection and the life; he who believes in me, though he die, yet shall he live, and whoever lives and believes in me shall never die" (John 11:25–26; cf. Tuckett, *From the Sayings to the Gospels*, 337).

resurrection of the dead prior to ingathering."[21] Paul, that is, simply underscores that the resurrection is *presupposed* in the Lord's words regarding his return. The liability of this approach, of course, is that it requires positing a substantial theological inference by Paul without any explicit basis in the authority he has cited.

Lars Hartman, by contrast, suggests an exegetical explanation for this inference from the *parousia* to the resurrection, in the possibility that Paul "knew about the 'midrash' structure of his *logos* [i.e., Matt 24:30–31] and how it was based on Daniel," and linked Jesus' references to "the Son of Man" from Dan 7 with the description of the resurrection in Dan 12.[22] "The statement that precisely 'those who have fallen asleep' will be included in this multitude is probably taken from Dan 12,2 f.," he proposes, since in "both texts death is spoken of as a sleep from which one awakes."[23]

Where Hartman seeks for a "vertical" explanation of Paul's inference, in the OT background of Jesus' saying, David Wenham instead proposes a "horizontal" explanation for that reasoning, in the Parable of the Ten Virgins (Matt 25:1–13), which in canonical Matthew comes close on the heels of the "Coming of the Son of Man." As Wenham notes, Paul seems to allude to the Parable of the Virgins alongside the Son of Man discourse in 1 Thess 4:17. In particular, Paul's, "We who are alive, who are left, shall be caught up together with them in the clouds to meet the Lord (*eis apantēsin tou kyriou*) in the air," might echo the announcement in the Parable: "Behold the Bridegroom: come out to meet him (*eis apantēsin autou*)" (Matt 25:6).[24]

More interesting still than that lexical overlap is the Parable's overall plotline, in which the virgins "lied down" (Matt 25:5) and then "were

---

21. Kim, "The Jesus Tradition," 241.

22. I.e., "Many of those who are sleeping in the dust of the earth will be raised up, some to eternal life and some to a curse and to eternal shame" (Dan 12:2).

23. Hartman, *Prophecy Interpreted*, 189; cf. 1 Thess 4:13. Similarly, while Abraham Malherbe is inclined to see Paul as delivering traditions that he received directly from the ascended Christ, he also acknowledges the possibility that "Paul uses a tradition closely related to Matt 24 and its parallels but supplements and interprets it in light of Jewish apocalyptic speculation based on Dan 7:13 and 12:2–3" (Malherbe, *The Letters to the Thessalonians*, 268).

24. As David Wenham notes, this is "a somewhat unusual phrase, at least in the New Testament" (Wenham, *Paul and Jesus*, 100). Is this the "command" which Paul associates with the Lord's return in 1 Thess 4:16?

raised (*ēgerthēsan*)" (Matt 25:7) before going to meet the bridegroom.²⁵ As Wenham points out, Paul's trope of death as "sleep" (1 Thess 4:13) seems to have been deeply-rooted in the earliest church, arguably going back to Jesus himself (cf. Mark 5:39; John 11:11), and beyond him, to Dan 12:2.²⁶ If Paul knew it, the Parable of the Virgins, interpreted as describing the death and resurrection of Christians prior to Christ's return, would have suggested a natural clarificatory supplement to Jesus' warning about the Coming of the Son of Man, explaining the importance of resurrection for "those who sleep" prior to believers' "going out to meet" the Lord.

After addressing the Thessalonians' concerns about the fate of those who had died, Paul turns next to a related problem, concerning the timing of the "day of the Lord" (1 Thess 5:1-11). Once again, he seems to allude to a parable from Matthew 24 as an authority already delivered to the Thessalonians: "For you yourselves know well (*akribōs*) that the day of the Lord will come (*hēmera kyriou* . . . *erchetai*) like a thief (*kleptēs*) in the night" (1 Thess 5:2), echoing Christ's warning that "you do not know on what day your Lord is coming . . . if the householder had known on what day (*poia hēmera*) the thief was coming (*kleptēs erchetai*), he would have watched" (Matt 24:42-43; cf. Luke 12:39-40).²⁷ Jacobi rightly notes that Joel 2 is likely in the background of both Jesus' parable and Paul's simile,²⁸ but the latter two have common features which Joel cannot explain. These include the thief's arriving by night, and the moral drawn from this that the hearers must keep sober and wakeful so as not to be taken by surprise.²⁹

25. Cf. Wenham, *Paul and Jesus*, 99.

26. Given that, Hartman's "vertical" explanation is in fact complementary to Wenham's "horizontal" one—awareness of either Dan 12 or the Parable of the Virgins would have reinforced the relevance of the other for interpreting Matt 24:30-31.

27. Cf. Kim, "The Jesus Tradition," 238. Jacobi is right to observe that whereas the "thief" in the latter is identified with "the Son of Man" (Matt 24:44), for Paul, it is a simile for the "day of the Lord" itself (Jacobi, *Jesusüberlieferung bei Paulus?*, 139). But her inference from this that Paul cannot be dependent on Jesus' parable depends on a needlessly restrictive sense of how literary influence works—Paul's usage is continuous with the parable's, and could surely reflect nothing more than the ordinary divergences we might expect from someone (for instance) drawing on a remembered tradition (cf. the discussion of memory and orality in Bauckham, *Jesus and the Eyewitnesses*, 240-63).

28. Joel announces that on the "day of the Lord" (Joel 2:1), Israel's enemies "leap upon the city, they run upon the walls; they climb up into the houses, they enter through the windows like a thief" (2:9). Cf. Jacobi, *Jesusüberlieferung bei Paulus?*, 143.

29. "So then let us not sleep, as others do, but let us keep awake (*grēgorōmen*) and be sober. For those who sleep sleep at night, and those who get drunk (*hoi*

Given Paul's repeated appeals to the Matthean Apocalypse in developing his teaching on the Lord's Parousia in 1 Thessalonians, it is no surprise that when he takes up the same topic in 2 Thessalonians, now considering principally the events which will precede and announce that return, Paul's words once again echo Matt 24.[30] Nor is it surprising to find Paul again reminding the Thessalonians that he had taught them these things during his earlier visit (2 Thess 2:5), and even referring to them as the "traditions (*paradoseis*)" which he had handed on (2 Thess 2:15).

Second Thessalonians 2 centers on Paul's warning that the Day of the Lord will be preceded by the coming of "the man of lawlessness, the son of destruction," who will "seat himself in the Temple, showing himself to be God" (2 Thess 2:3b-4). Given the echoes of Matt 24 present throughout this passage, might this be an allusion to Jesus' prediction of "the abomination of desolation . . . standing in the holy place" (Matt 24:15; cf. Mark 13:14)? The difference between Paul's and Jesus' descriptions is that, as Wenham and Douglas Campbell have noted, in 2 Thess 2 the desecrating event has come into focus as the crisis precipitated in 40 CE by Caligula's plot to install an image of himself in the Jerusalem Temple—the lawless one will attempt to prove himself divine by seating (a statue of) himself in the Jewish Temple.[31]

Gerd Theissen has proposed that the Markan "Little Apocalypse" is similarly shaped by this crisis: he suggests in particular that Mark's ungrammatical participle "*hestēkota*" (whose masculine gender doesn't agree with its neuter antecedent, "the abomination (*to bdelugma*)"—cf.

---

methuskomenoi) are drunk at night" (1 Thess 5:6-7) / "So then keep watch (*grēgoreite*), for you do not know on what day your Lord is coming. . . . But if that wicked servant says to himself, 'My master is delayed,' and begins to beat his fellow servants, and eats and drinks with the drunken (*methuontōn*)" (Matt 24:42, 47-49; cf. Luke 12:37, 45). A further Synoptic echo appears later in the passage, this time of Luke: "When people say, 'There is peace and security,' then sudden (*aiphnidios*) destruction will come upon them (*ephistatai*)" (1 Thess 5:3) / "that day [will] come (*epistē*) upon you suddenly (*aiphnidios*) like a snare" (Luke 21:34-36).

30. "The parallels are very striking, and indeed, there is a case for seeing 2 Thessalonians 2 almost as a brief précis of the teaching of Jesus in Matthew 24 and Mark 13" (Wenham, *Paul and Jesus*, 117). The following echoes are particularly noisy: 2 Thess 2:1/Matt 24:27, 31; 2 Thess 2:2/Matt 24:6 (cf. Mark 13:7); 2 Thess 2:3/Matt 24:4 (Mark 13:5); 2 Thess 2:7, 10/Matt 24:12; 2 Thess 2:8/Matt 24:27; 2 Thess 2:9/Matt 24:24 (Mark 13:22).

31. Campbell, *Framing Paul*, 220-25; Wenham, *Jesus and Paul*, 116. Cf. Josephus, *J.W.* 2.184-203; Josephus, *Ant.* 18.256-309; 19.15-114; Philo, *Embassy to Gaius* 29.188, 31.207-8, all discussed in Campbell, *Framing Paul*, 221.

the more appropriate "*hestos*" in Matt 24:15) reflects an implicit awareness that the desecrating object is a "he," viz. a statue of Caligula.[32] He takes this to suggest that Mark's account is more primitive than Matthew's, but if this slip implies anything, it is the reverse, since the scenario envisaged in Matthew (and indeed in Mark, except for the awkward participle) makes good sense simply in light of Old Testament parallels and recent Jewish experience.[33] As N. T. Wright has argued, nothing in the "Synoptic Apocalypse" reflects views that could not have been espoused by an intelligent observer of Palestinian politics in the early 30s AD: "It is far more plausible to regard the details of the passage as extrapolations from ancient biblical prophecy than to read them as lame and inaccurate attempts to turn history, after the fact, into pseudo-prophecy."[34]

Given the striking parallels of 1 Thess 4–5 and 2 Thess 2 with Matt 24, and particularly given Paul's clear statements in both 1–2 Thessalonians about his dependence on prior (and, in 1 Thessalonians, dominical) tradition, it seems that even if the Thessalonian correspondence has influenced Matthew, we would still have to posit an eschatological tradition, related in some way to the "Synoptic Apocalypse," which Paul had received and handed on to his first congregations. Surprisingly, given the expectations raised by the hypothesis of Markan Priority, the version of this tradition with which Paul seems to have been acquainted is most closely related, not to Mark, but rather to Matthew.[35]

---

32. Theissen, *The Gospels in Context*, 121-65.

33. The disciples, like Mattathias and his sons, must flee to the hills (Matt 24:16/1 Macc 2:28; cf. Mark 13:14), and the sun will turn to blood, just as Isaiah and Joel predicted (Matt 24:29/Isa 13:10; Joel 3:15; cf. Mark 13:24), but the days will be shortened because of the elect (Matt 24:22/Isa 65:8; cf. Mark 13:20). Mark and Matthew also envisage the desecration of the Temple (Matt 24:15; cf. Mark 13:14), in terms drawn from Daniel (cf. 11:31) and 1 Maccabees (1:54). But the Pompey's entrance into the Holy of Holies in 63 BC (Josephus, *Ant.* 14.70-71), or Pilate's attempt, during Jesus' lifetime, to install Roman battle standards in the Temple (Josephus, *Ant.* 18.55-59) would have provided sufficiently ominous precedents even without a knowledge of the events of 70 CE. Even Luke's Jesus' description of Jerusalem's "desolation" in terms of a Roman siege (Luke 21:20) hardly need be a *vaticinium ex eventu*; this was always the most probable outcome for a Jewish rebellion against Rome, as for the earlier rebellion against Babylon (cf. 2 Kgs 25:1).

34. Wright, *Jesus and the Victory of God*, 345.

35. Hartman observes that "Matthew's version of the eschatological discourse has yielded the closest parallel to 2 Ths 2.... We may add that in 1 Ths it was Matthew's Gospel that was the sole basis for certain parallels.... This agrees with other observations that Paul seems to use a Gospel tradition that is related to Matthew" (Hartman, *Prophecy Interpreted*, 203).

(b) Two or Three Synoptic Traditions in 1 Corinthians

We'll turn next to two points at which Paul clearly undoubtedly appeals to Markan Traditions in 1 Corinthians, and briefly consider a third point at which such an appeal is possible, but difficult to demonstrate: the former two are Paul's command from the Lord concerning divorce (7:10–11) and his rehearsal of the Institution narrative (11:23–26); the latter is his citation of a dominical command regarding support for Apostles (9:14).[36]

One of the clearest Pauline appeals to a dominical word comes in his discussion of divorce in 1 Cor 7:10–11. Paul frames his teaching regarding divorce as a command from "the Lord" (cf. 1 Cor 8:6): "To the married I give charge, not I but the Lord, that the wife should not separate from her husband (but if she does, let her remain single or else be reconciled to her husband)—and that the husband should not divorce his wife." The dominical command in view here is almost certainly Jesus' prohibition of divorce, a teaching which appears in both Mark 10:2–12 and Matt 19:3–12, and also, briefly, in the "Double Tradition" (Matt 5:31–32; Luke 16:18).[37]

Is there any indication, though, whether the tradition Paul knows regarding this command is closer to Matthew's, Mark's, or even Luke's? (The latter lacks the controversy dialogue in which Mark and Matthew set this teaching, having only the bare saying, corresponding to Matt 5:31–32.) The dominant view is that the command known to Paul is closest to Mark's,[38] but in fact, the evidence here is mixed, and perhaps favors a Matthean echo. On the one hand, Paul, like Mark's Jesus, addresses the duties of both husbands and wives (cf. Mark 10:11–12; 1 Cor 7:10–11).[39] Collins's comment on this detail is significant, however: "Only Mark, *in what is clearly a Markan addition to the tradition*, speaks of a wife divorcing her husband," which was allowed under Roman, but not Jewish, law.[40]

---

36. For reasons of space and because the echo is relatively weaker, we will set aside a fourth possible allusion in 1 Corinthians to a Matthean tradition, namely Paul's comment that "Jews ask for signs . . . but we preach Christ crucified" (1 Cor 1:22), which might echo Matt 12:38–40 (cf. also Luke 11:28 and, more distantly, Mark 8:12).

37. For Paul's dependence here on a dominical word, cf. Collins, *First Corinthians*, 264; Fee, *The First Epistle to the Corinthians*, 323; Hays, *First Corinthians*, 119–20.

38. Cf. Hays, *The Moral Vision of the New Testament*, 358; Fee, *The First Epistle to the Corinthians*, 324.

39. Cf. Fee, *The First Epistle to the Corinthians*, 324; Thiselton, *The First Epistle to the Corinthians*, 520–21.

40. Collins, *First Corinthians*, 264, my emphasis.

Is Paul following Mark here, or reflecting a later amplification of the more primitive Matthean tradition, which was also incorporated into Mark?[41]

A second apparently "Markan" element in 1 Cor 7 is that Paul shows no awareness of the Matthean Jesus's seeming allowance of divorce in cases involving *"porneia"*: "Whoever should divorce his wife (lit. send away his woman (*apolusē tēn gunaika*)), except for sexual immorality (*porneia*), and should marry another, makes that other an adulteress" (Matt 19:9).[42] Rather, like Mark and Luke, Paul's teaching both in 1 Cor 7 and in Rom 7:2-3 seems to be that marriage—at least among Christians—is indissoluble.[43] (He might, however, make an exception for cases in which an unbelieving spouse leaves a Christian—"But if the unbeliever separates himself, let him be separated; the brother is not bound" [1 Cor 7:15]—although the phrase "he is not bound" is a rather slender thread with which to anchor a permission to remarriage.)[44] Nonetheless, even if Matthew's Jesus did, like the House of Shammai (cf. n41 ve), permit divorce and remarriage after sexual misconduct by one's spouse,[45] Paul

41. Another indication that Matthew's version is more primitive than Mark's comes in the setting of the dialogue. In Matthew, the presenting question is whether divorce is permissible "for any reason (*kata pasan aitian*)" (Matt 19:3), which, according to the Misnah, was the position of "Beit Hillel" in Jesus' day. Beit Hillel was principally opposed by "Beit Shammai," which maintained, "A man may not divorce his wife unless he finds out about her having engaged in a matter of forbidden sexual intercourse (*dabar 'rvah*)" (Tract. Gittin 90a, in the *Talmud Bavli*). This formulation is quite close to Jesus' own apparent exception for divorces "in case of sexual immorality" (Matt 19:9). Mark's controversy, by contrast, is over whether divorce is permissible *at all* ("Is it permissible for a man to divorce his wife?" [Mark 10:2]), a question which more closely reflects the concerns of the later Pauline churches than it does those of Jesus' Palestinian contemporaries.

42. Unsurprisingly, some scribes later clarified Matthew's gnomic statement here by partially conflating it with Jesus' clearer teaching from Matt 5:32.

43. Dungan suggests that, while Paul knows Matthew's more original account (cf. Dungan, *The Sayings of Jesus in the Pauline Churches*, 102-24), "in using this account . . . Paul tended to fasten upon the final saying, which rejected all remarriage and required divorce under certain circumstances. In using the saying, however, the original formulation became distorted slightly so that it came to be just a prohibition of divorce and remarriage or, in the case of Paul, no more than a prohibition of divorce" (Dungan, *The Sayings of Jesus in the Pauline Churches*, 131).

44. "Thus 'no divorce' is not turned into law, and the woman who does so is not put out of the community. What is disallowed is precisely what one finds in the teaching of Jesus: no adultery. Hence if she does separate, she must continue to follow the dictum, 'Stay as you are,' meaning now, 'Remain unmarried'" (Fee, *The First Epistle to the Corinthians*, 327).

45. There are complications here as well. For instance, earlier in the passage,

would hardly have been the last to interpret the Matthean version of the story as also requiring an absolute ban on divorce.[46]

Finally, consider a detail which arguably favors a Matthean rather than a Markan setting for Paul's divorce-command, namely that Matthew ends this pericope much in the way that Paul begins 1 Cor 7, with the observation that it is in fact better not to marry, that the single life—a life of voluntary eunuch-hood for the kingdom of heaven—is the higher state, though not all are called to take it up (Matt 19:10–12; 1 Cor 7:1–7). Indeed, however Paul's understanding of divorce relates to Matthew's, 1 Cor 7:1–16 might well presuppose the surrounding context of Matt 19, or something much like it.

Paul's second citation of a dominical command in 1 Cor comes in 9:14, where he writes, "Thus also the Lord commanded (*ho kyrios dietaxen*) those who preach the gospel to live by means of the gospel." There is general agreement that Paul is alluding both to the command found in slightly different forms in Matt 10:10 and Luke 10:7,[47] and perhaps even to the broader "missionary discourse" of which it is a part.[48] As to whether Paul knows the Lukan or Matthean form (or setting) of the command, the evidence is mixed: some aspects of 1 Cor 9 could echo either

---

Matthew's Jesus seems to categorically forbid divorce ("So then, what God has joined, let man not separate," Matt 19:6), and the exception offered later concerns "sexual immorality (*porneia*)" rather than "adultery (*moicheia*)" (Matt 19:9), which might suggest that what is in view is extra-marital sex prior to the consummation of the marriage (cf. Deut 22:13–24), or perhaps marriages which Leviticus would class as "incestuous," and so invalid (cf. Lev 18:7–18). For these possibilities, cf. Hays, *The Moral Vision of the New Testament*, 195; France, *The Gospel of Matthew*, 208–9.

46. E.g., "Now that the Scripture counsels marriage, and allows no release from the union, is expressly contained in the law, 'You shall not put away your wife, except for the cause of fornication'; and it regards as fornication, the marriage of those separated while the other is alive" (Clement of Alexandria, *Stromateis* 2.23). Clement interprets the "fornication" at issue as a putative "second marriage" while one's spouse is still living—the "wife" who is to be put away on account of fornication is a wife in name only, and the call to separate is in fact a call to respect the vows undertaken in the first, genuine marriage.

47. E.g., Dungan, *The Sayings of Jesus in the Churches of Paul*, 3–75; Fee, *The First Epistle to the Corinthians*, 455–56; Hays, *First Corinthians*, 152; Thiselton, *The First Epistle to the Corinthians*, 692–93.

48. Allison concludes that "Paul knows more than isolated sayings. He seems to know a block of material, a missionary speech," which is closest to Luke 10:1–16 (Allison, "The Pauline Epistles and the Synoptic Gospels," 10). Cf. also David Wenham: "Paul was familiar not just with this one saying, but with the whole mission discourse of Jesus" (Wenham, *Paul and Jesus*, 158).

Matt 10 or Luke 10,[49] while some features seem particularly responsive to Luke,[50] and others to Matthew.[51]

Now, the indeterminacy of the Pauline evidence means that 1 Cor 9:14 is not really relevant to our purposes in this essay, since the command in Matt 10:10 and Luke 10:7 is properly "Double Tradition" material; advocates of the Two-Document Hypothesis (2DH), for instance, typically regard Luke as preserving the more primitive form of the "Q-logion," which Matthew redacted and conflated with Mark 6:6b-13.[52] As

---

49. E.g., "apostle (*apostolos*)" and cognates (Matt 10:2; Luke 10:1, 3; 1 Cor 9:1, 2, 5); "authority (*exousia*)" (Matt 10:1; Luke 10:19; 1 Cor 9:4-6); "work (*ergon*)" and cognates (Matt 10:10; Luke 10:2, 7; 1 Cor 9:1, 6, 13); eating and drinking (Matt 10:10; Luke 10:7-8; 1 Cor 9:4, 7, 13); "harvest (*therismon*)" and cognates (Matt 9:37; Luke 10:2; 1 Cor 9:11).

50. Paul's most interesting connection to Luke in particular is his repeated reference to a "wage (*misthon*)" for apostolic labor (Luke 10:7; 1 Cor 9:17-18; cf. also 1 Cor 3:8, 14). This might well betray his awareness of the Lukan form of the command at Luke 10:7. First Timothy 5:18 is of course relevant to this question as well, as it appears to cite Luke 10:7 alongside Deuteronomy as Scripture: "For the Scripture says, 'Do not muzzle a plowing oxen,' and 'The worker is worthy of his wages.'" However, assessing its relevance would require wading into questions of its date and authorship, which would take us too far afield. A second striking parallel is that between Luke 10: 8 ("Eat what is set before you (*esthiete ta paratithemena humin*)") and 1 Cor 10:27 ("*to paratithemenon humin esthiete*"), although, as Dungan points out, this one of the features of the Lukan discourse which most clearly betrays its secondary character in comparison with Matthew: worries about whether a missionary could in good conscience accept the food offered by a host much more clearly reflect the milieu of Paul's Torah-flexible mission to the gentiles than that of Jesus' own ministry of preaching and healing, which, as Matthew explicitly notes, was (largely) restricted to Jews (Matt 10:5-6; the two exceptions in Matthew are of course the Centurion's Servant (8:5-13) and the Canaanite Woman (15:21-28).

51. As David Dungan notes, the surrounding context of 1 Cor 9:14 indicates that the command of the Lord to which he alludes specifically concerns food. For instance, Paul "says that he has 'the authority to be provided with something to eat and to drink' (9.4). Furthermore, this specific idea of 'food' appears again in the priest-Levite analogy, which is the actual point at which Paul introduces the command of the Lord" (Dungan, *The Sayings of Jesus in the Churches of Paul*, 79). Further, both Matthew's Jesus and Paul figure the evangelist/evangelized relation in terms of a shepherd and his flock (Matt 9:36; 1 Cor 9:7). And while the verbal correspondence is weak, both Matthew and 1 Corinthians refer to preaching the gospel without charge (*dōrean*), Matt 10:8; *adapanon*, 1 Cor 9:18, a NT *hapax*).

52. E.g., "Matthew combines Mark 6:8-11 and Q = Luke 10:4-12 into a new text" (Luz, *Matthew 8-20*, 71). Cf. Q 10:7-8 in Robinson et al., *The Critical Edition of Q*. As David Dungan has shown, however, the internal evidence in fact supports the priority of Matt 10:1-15 to Luke 10:1-16 (Dungan, *The Sayings of Jesus in the Churches of Paul*, 42-63; cf. also n50 above).

such, they have no more trouble than defenders of the GH in accepting that Paul might have known something like Luke 10:1–16. By contrast, if Paul knew something like Matt 10:1–16, that would strongly suggest that it is not, as both the 2DH and the FH require, posterior to Mark 6:6–13; at this point, however, 1 Cor 9 seems not to provide clear support for either position.

By way of concluding this survey of Markan traditions in 1 Corinthians, we can consider Paul's appeal to one such tradition in 1 Corinthians which is distinctively Lukan, namely his version of the Institution narrative (1 Cor 11:23–26).[53] This passage has several similarities to Luke which are not shared by Mark or Matthew: in both, Jesus speaks of "the new covenant (*hē kainē diathēkē*)" as opposed to simply "the covenant" (Matt 26:28; Mark 14:24; Luke 22:20; 1 Cor 11:25), and both have "do this in remembrance of me" (Luke 22:19; 1 Cor 11:25).[54] And moreover, as Michael Goulder observes, Luke's Last Supper includes a "dispute (*philoneikia*)" among the disciples, over "which of them seemed to be (*tis dokei*) the greatest" (Luke 22:24). But this is also echoed in 1 Cor 11:16, where Paul, just prior to cataloguing the Corinthians' own deplorable behavior during the Eucharist, writes, "But if someone seems to be disputatious (*tis dokei philoneikos*)."[55] In this case, Paul seems to presuppose, not simply the Lukan version of this Markan tradition, but indeed the larger narrative setting which those words are given in Luke.

---

53. For a similar Luke-Paul overlap in the "Double Tradition" material evoked by 1 Corinthians, consider Paul's rehearsal of the "tradition" (cf. 1 Cor 15:3) that the resurrected Christ appeared to Peter first among the disciples (Luke 24:34; 1 Cor 15:5; cf. Matt 28:17; John 20:19). Moreover, Paul, also like Luke and unlike Matthew and John, does not mention an initial appearance by Jesus to his female followers (compare 1 Cor 15:5-7 and Luke 24:1–11 to Matt 28:1–10; John 20:1–2, 11–18; cf. also Mark 16:9–11).

54. Cf. Marshall: "Luke's introduction to the cup saying is almost identical to that in Paul" (Marshall, *The Gospel of Luke*, 805). Cf. also Hays, *First Corinthians*, 198; Thiselton, *The First Epistle to the Corinthians*, 878.

55. Cf. Goulder, "Did Luke Know Any of the Pauline Letters?," 106. Goulder presupposes, throughout his essay, that such echoes are evidence of Pauline influence on Luke, but he doesn't take sufficient account of the fact that evidence for a literary relationship between Paul's letters and the Synoptic tradition is particularly pronounced when Paul has overtly signaled his dependence on traditions about Jesus.

(c) Christ's Transfiguration in 2 Cor 3-4

Paul also alludes to Matthew's account of Christ's Transfiguration in 2 Cor 3:18—4:6. Just prior to this passage, Paul has been weaving together Jeremiah's promise of a "new covenant," in which the Law would be written on the heart (Jer 31:31–34; cf. 2 Cor 3:3–6) with the account of Moses' shining face in Exod 34:29–35 (cf. 2 Cor 3:7–15). He goes, however, to evoke the Transfiguration of Christ,[56] though not simply to reprise it, but rather to enfold his churches within it.

Consider: in 2 Cor 3:18, Paul and his churches are transformed as they "behold the glory of the Lord"; but the Lord must be Jesus (cf. 2 Cor 4:5), the one in whose face shines the glory of God (2 Cor 4:4, 6). Second Corinthians 4:4–6, that is, offers an extended restatement of the point made more elliptically in 3:18—Christians are transformed by looking on God's glory; but God's glory is "in the face of Jesus Christ."[57] Paul is assuming the implicit comparison between Christ's and Moses's Transfigurations already present in the Synoptics—it is Christ's glorious face that pours forth the glory by which and to which believers are conformed.

Once again, it's striking how many more verbal resonances Paul has with Matthew than with Mark or even with Luke. Just as Jesus' face "was transformed (*metemorphōthē*)" on Tabor (Matt 17:2; Mark 9:2), so too are we are transformed (*metamorphoumetha*) by "beholding the glory of the Lord in a mirror" (2 Cor 3:18); unbelievers cannot see "the light of the gospel (*ton photismon tou euangeliou*)" (2 Cor 4:4; cf. the "bright cloud [*nephelē phōteinē*] in Matt 17:5); and just as Christ's "face shone (*elampsen to prosōpon autou*)" (Matt 17:2), so too God "shined (*elampsen*) in our hearts the light of the knowledge of the glory of God in the face (*en prosōpō*) of Jesus Christ" (2 Cor 4:6). Strikingly, the only parallel between 2 Cor 3–4 and the Transfiguration not accounted for by

---

56. Which, of course, is surely also engaged with Moses' transfiguration (cf. Matt 17:4; cf. also Matt 17:2/Exod 34:29; Matt 17:6/Exod 34:30 and par.). Curiously, this allusion often goes unrecognized by commentators, such as Thrall, *The Second Epistle to the Corinthians*, 282–320; Furnish, *II Corinthians*, 234–52; Barclay, who writes, "There is no reference [in Paul] to . . . the Transfiguration" (Barclay, "Paul and Jesus," 498). A welcome exception to this neglect is Simon Lee, who notices the connection (Lee, *Jesus' Transfiguration*), as did the editors of the Revised Common Lectionary, in assigning 2 Cor 3:1–9, 18 to the Eve of the Transfiguration, and 2 Cor 4:1–6 to the Feast of the Transfiguration (*The Book of Common Prayer*, 998).

57. Cf. Lee, *Jesus' Transfiguration*, 81–82.

Matt 17 is the term "glory (*doxa*)" (2 Cor 3:7–11, 18, 4:4, 6; cf. Luke 9:32), which is already prominent in Exodus (cf. 34:29–30, 35 LXX).

Given these links, Lee is simply mistaken to take Mark's account to be nearest to Paul's.[58] The difficulties with this view occasionally betray themselves in Lee's argument, as in the following:

> Since there is a Moses-Jesus parallelism in terms of glory on the face, as is attested to in Paul, Matthew, and Luke, this parallelism suggests that an earlier version of the Transfiguration story contained the idea of glory on the face of Jesus as well. Mark or Mark's source seems to remove this feature in order to surpass Mosaic typology.[59]

That is, Lee also seems to need a Matthean tradition *prior to* as well as following Mark!

Furthermore, it seems that Paul not only knows a tradition about the Transfiguration of Christ, but also that he expects this tradition to be sufficiently familiar to the Corinthians that he can simply presuppose it in contrasting the glory of Christ with the fading glory of Moses' ministry. As with Paul's appeal to the "Synoptic Apocalypse" in the Thessalonian correspondence, or to Christ's teachings regarding divorce or the rights of apostles in 1 Corinthians, the role of the Transfiguration in 2 Cor 3–4 suggests that he had already handed on this tradition during his initial preaching in the eighteen months he spent with them (Acts 18:11), so that—just as with his use of Jer 31 and Ezek 36–37 in this passage—allusions were all that was needed to summon the fuller story.

(d) Petrine Primacy as a Problem in Galatians

Let's now turn briefly to Galatians, where Paul arguably alludes to Matthew's version of Peter's confession at Caesarea Philippi (Matt 16:13–20; cf. Mark 8:27–30; Luke 9:18–22). In Matthew's version alone, Jesus praises Peter: "Blessed are you, Simon Bar-Jonah, for flesh and blood did not reveal [this] to you (*sarx kai haima ouk apekalypsen soi*), but my Father who is in the heavens. . . . You are Peter, and upon this rock I will build my church" (Matt 16:17–18). Paul's account of his own call in Gal 1:15–16 echoes this commissioning of Peter: "When God was pleased . . . to reveal (*apokalypsai*) his Son in me, so that I might preach the gospel about him

---

58. Lee, *Jesus' Transfiguration*, 49.
59. Lee, *Jesus' Transfiguration*, 82.

among the nations, I did not immediately consult with flesh and blood (*sarki kai haimati*)" (Gal 1:15-16). Giuseppe Barbaglio and David Wenham agree that this story likely was originally attached to Peter, and that Paul drew on it in Galatians as part of his general strategy of leveling the field between himself and the Jerusalem Apostles (Gal 2:1-15), but perhaps especially Peter, James, and John (cf. Gal 2:9), and more particularly yet, Peter himself (cf. Gal 2:7-8, 11-14).[60]

Moreover, there are good reasons to think that Paul is being influenced by the Matthean tradition, rather than vice versa, since, while a concern with Peter is everywhere evident in the surrounding context of Gal 1:15-16, a corresponding concern with Paul is difficult to discern in the surrounding context of the Matt 16.[61] Is it simply a coincidence that this echo of Christ's calling of Peter to lead the church comes in a passage in which Paul is defending his own calling against the authority of Peter?[62] Wenham rightly notes that, despite the usual presupposition that Matthew's version of Peter's confession must be a redaction of Mark in light of later ecclesiological developments, "Paul may be an early witness to Matthew's account."[63]

(e) Markan Traditions in Romans

Finally, we can consider two possible echoes of Markan Synoptic traditions in Romans. There is a widespread agreement among commentators on this letter that chapters 12-14 in particular reflect Paul's use of (especially non-Markan) Synoptic traditions, from faint echoes to noisy allusions.[64] We will focus here, however, on two particularly clear echoes of Markan Traditions in Rom 14, in which Pauline dependence on traditions about Jesus is reasonably certain, namely his summary of the Law

---

60. Barbaglio, *Antipaolinismo*, 21; Wenham, *Paul and Jesus*, 69.

61. Contra Sim, *The Gospel of Matthew*, 201. Luz rightly rejects reading this passage as anti-Pauline, though he regards the two passages as independent (Luz, *Matthew 8-20*, 359).

62. Consider also that there might be a more distant echo of Matt 16:18 in Eph 2:20—Christ promised to build his church upon the rock named Peter, and Paul declares that the church is built upon the foundation of the prophets and apostles.

63. Wenham, *Paul and Jesus*, 70.

64. Cf. Fitzmeyer, *Romans*, 656, 679, 696; Jewett, *Romans*, 766, 810; Moo, *The Epistle to the Romans*, 781, 784, 815; Neirynck, "Paul and the Sayings of Jesus," 270.

with the love-command and his comments on the permissibility of all foods in Rom 14.

To begin, compare Paul's and Jesus' summaries of the commandments in Rom 13:9 and Matt 19:18–19 (in "the Rich Young Man"),[65] which both conclude with the command to neighbor-love:

> For the "you will not commit adultery, you will not murder, you will not steal, you will not covet," and whatever other commandment are summarized in this word, in the "you will love your neighbor as yourself." (Rom 13:9)

> The "you will not murder, you will not commit adultery, you will not steal, you will not bear false witness, honor your father and mother," and "You will love your neighbor as yourself." (Matt 19:18–19)

Paul agrees here with Mark 10:18 and Luke 18:20 as to the order of the first three commands (against adultery, murder, and stealing), but agrees with Matthew's use of the future tense (Luke and Mark each have aorist subjunctive verbs). Paul and Matthew also agree against Luke and Mark in introducing the commandments with the neuter article "*to*" as though indicating a stock list. Finally, and most striking of all, they agree in their quotation of Leviticus 19:18 as a concluding command, which Paul also introduces with the tell-tale article: "in the (*en tō*) 'You will love your neighbor as yourself,'" as though indicating that this command too ought to be familiar to them as a summary of the Law.[66] Indeed, Paul's formulation reads like an explanatory gloss on Matthew's comparatively shapeless list—the command to neighbor-love, he emphasizes, is not simply a final commandment tacked on at the end, but rather sums up all the preceding commands in itself.

Now, as James Dunn has observed, Paul's appeal to Lev 19:18 as a familiar summary of the Law is likely dependent on Jesus' teaching:

> Explicit references to Lev. 19:18 are lacking in Jewish literature prior to Jesus. And such allusions as there are give it no particular prominence, though subsequently the opinion is

---

65. The "Rich Young Ruler" is of course a composite character—Jesus' interlocutor is a young man in Matthew (19:20), a ruler in Luke (18:18), and neither in Mark 10:17–27.

66. Cf. Dunn's comment: "Literally 'in the "You shall love your neighbour as yourself"', so the reference is clearly to something familiar, as in Rom 13:8–9, written to a church Paul had never previously visited" (Dunn, *Jesus, Paul, and the Gospels*, 98).

later attributed to Rabbi Akiba (early second century) that Lev. 19:18 is 'the greatest general principle in the Torah' (*Sifra on Lev.* 19:18). Almost certainly, then, it was Jesus himself who extracted Lev. 19:18 and gave it this preeminent status within the law. And quite possibly Rabbi Akiba was influenced by Jesus, knowingly or unknowingly, in giving Lev. 19:18 a similar key role in interpreting the Torah.[67]

And that this teaching was not a Pauline contribution to the development of Christianity seems to be clear from the fact that the Epistle of James—whatever its date and provenance, by no means the product of a Pauline school—also quotes it as the "royal law (*nomon basilikon*)" (Jas 2:8). It seems reasonable to conclude, then, that Paul is not only dependent here on Jesus' teaching about neighbor-love (Dunn goes so far as to call this material "the most striking evidence of the influence of Jesus' teaching on Paul"),[68] but is even familiar with it in the particular setting handed down to us in Matt 19:18-19, a fact which might also explain why Paul does not include the command to love God (Deut 6:5) alongside the command to neighbor-love, as Jesus does elsewhere in the Synoptics (e.g., Matt 22:36-40 and par.).

A further instance in Romans in which Paul seems to be dependent on a Synoptic tradition is in his insistence, "I have been persuaded *en kyriō Iēsou*"—perhaps not merely "in the Lord Jesus," but rather "*by the Lord Jesus*"—"that nothing is common in itself (*koinon di' heautou*)," since "all things are pure (*panta kathara*)" (Rom 14:14, 20). Is this another indication by Paul of his dependence on a dominical tradition? That seems all the more likely given that Paul's statement here is particularly resonant with Jesus' declaration in Mark, "Nothing external which enters into a man can make him common (*koinōsai*), for it does not enter into his heart, but into his belly, and it goes out into the sewer (purifying all foods (*katharizōn panta ta brōmata*))" (Mark 7:18-19). As such, it provides the clearest piece of evidence so far considered for Paul's dependence on a Markan version of a Markan tradition.

Even this echo is weakened, however, by the fact that the phrase which brings the Markan version particularly in line with Paul's is an editorial aside—"purifying all foods"—which is missing in Matt 15:11. Moreover, there are good reasons for taking Matthew's account to be

---

67. Dunn, *Jesus, Paul, and the Gospels*, 97.
68. Dunn, *Jesus, Paul, and the Gospels*, 98.

more primitive than Mark's,[69] not least that if Jesus had explicitly abrogated kosher restrictions during his Galilean ministry, the wracking controversy over these observances in the early church,[70] to say nothing of the dismay with which Peter met the ascended Christ's command to eat unclean foods,[71] would be something of a puzzle.[72] But if Mark's version of this story in fact derives from (something like) Matthew's, then there seems to be no way to tell whether the tradition known to Paul already included the editorial aside about Jesus' purifying all foods, or whether Rom 14 represents an interpretive gloss on the more original (sc. Matthean) pericope along the same lines which we later find in Mark.

II. Paul's Use of Synoptic Traditions: Two Implications

In sum, over long sections of 1–2 Thessalonians, 1–2 Corinthians, Galatians, and Romans, we find Paul referring or alluding to traditions about Jesus later recorded in the "Markan Tradition" of the Synoptic Gospels. Where these allusions or references display an intimacy with one Gospel among the three, that Gospel is most often Matthew, followed by Luke, with Mark registering only two ambiguous echoes. (Recall that judgments about Pauline dependence on Markan versions in these two cases were complicated by the fact that in both, Mark's versions are arguably less primitive than Matthew's, and can be shown to be so by virtue of the very details which bring those pericopes into close alignment with Paul.)

This indicates, first, that Davies was much more right than wrong to emphasize the importance of Jesus's actions and teachings, and not merely his death and resurrection, for Paul's letters.[73] Whatever the significance of Paul's claim, "But now, we no longer know Christ according to the

---

69. Cf. Thompson: "Matthew probably preserves the logion's original intention" (Thompson, *Clothed with Christ*, 191). And Dunn proposes that "Mark's version of Jesus' teaching on the subject of food purity seems to reflect the strong affirmation of Paul. In other words, it is in this teaching in particular that we can see the influence of Jesus's priorities being further reflected on by Paul, and the inferences drawn from his teaching being reflected back into the memory of his teaching" (Dunn, *Jesus according to the New Testament*, 21).

70. Not least in Rom 14, but cf. also Gal 2:11–14; Col 2:16.

71. Acts 10:9–16. We find the same "Markan" contrast between "cleansed" and "common" food in this passage: "What God has purified, you must not make common" (Acts 10:15).

72. Cf. Sanders, *Jesus and Judaism*, 266; Dunn, "Jesus and Purity," 463.

73. Davies, *Paul and Rabbinic Judaism*, 136.

flesh" (2 Cor 5:16),⁷⁴ we in fact repeatedly found him presupposing or referring to, not simply isolated dominical sayings or general themes, but to versions of developed Markan traditions (the Synoptic Apocalypse, the Mission Discourse, the Institution Narrative, the Transfiguration, etc.) which are familiar to us from Matthew or Luke. For instance, when Paul reflects on eschatology in 1–2 Thessalonians, he offers a teaching that is not only Matthean in plotline, but one which also has dense verbal correspondences with Matthew's "Synoptic Apocalypse." Paul does not simply refer to the words of Jesus, but deploys Matthean ideas in Matthean language, albeit without direct quotation.

Paul's preference for Matthean and Lukan versions of Markan traditions is difficult to explain on the hypothesis of Markan Priority, according to which Matthew and Luke each draw on and redact Mark. Indeed, far from supporting that picture, the Pauline data we have surveyed would suggest that Mark consists in large part of revised Matthean and Lukan pericopes. Moreover, Paul is not alone in this. It would go beyond the scope of this essay to document the extent of the early witnesses' preference for Matthean traditions in particular,[75] but to take just a few examples, it is striking how many echoes of Matthean versions of Markan traditions appear in the Epistle of James,[76] 2 Peter,[77] and the *Didache*.[78] (Even if these texts are half a century after Paul, we might still wonder why a later Gospel's versions would so consistently crowd out the earliest one's.)

Now, if this situation—in which the Major Synoptics' versions of Markan traditions predominate in the earliest witnesses, and then ever

---

74. The prepositional phrase "according to the flesh" could just as easily modify "we have known" as "Christ." And of course, in the immediately preceding clause, Paul disavows knowledge of *anyone* which is "according to the flesh" (2 Cor 5:16).

75. Cf. Massaux's *Influence de l'évangile de saint Matthieu*.

76. Consider the following parallels: Jas 1:6/Matt 21:21; Jas 1:10/Matt 13:6; Jas 1:27; 2:15–16/Matt 25:42–43; Jas 4:12/Matt 10:28; Jas 5:9/Matt 24:33.

77. The reference in 2 Peter to the Transfiguration, like Paul's allusions in 2 Cor 3–4, is a clear echo of Matthew's version: "For when he received honor and glory from God the Father and the voice was borne to him by the Majestic Glory, 'This is my beloved Son, with whom I am well pleased'" (1:17). This is much closer to Matthew 17:5 ("This is my beloved Son, with whom I am well pleased: listen to him") than to Mark 9:7 or Luke 9:35.

78. The majority of the allusions to the Markan Tradition in the *Didache* (as footnoted by Holmes in *The Apostolic Fathers*) are (or could be) to Matthew: in 1:2, cf. Matt 22:37 (Luke 10:27); in 11:7, cf. Matt 12:31; in 13:1, cf. Matt 10:10 (the worker is worthy of his food); in 16:1, cf. Matt 24:42 (Mark 13:35, 37; Luke 12:35); in 16:8, cf. Matt 24:30.

after—fits awkwardly at best with Markan Priority, it is just what we would expect if, as Clement of Alexandria reported and J. J. Griesbach and his followers argued, "The Gospels containing the genealogies were written first (*progegraphthai*)."[79] Read carefully, Paul's letters provide substantial support for the oldest solution to the Synoptic problem: Markan Posteriority.

---

79. Clement of Alexandria in Eusebius, *Hist. Eccl.* 6.14.5–7. Stephen Carlson has argued that Clement was contrasting the *manner* of the Gospels' publication rather than their order (with the Major Synoptics being published openly, unlike Mark, which was written initially for private circulation) (Carlson, "Clement of Alexandria," 118–25). However, as Francis Watson has pointed out, Clement's use of "*eschaton*" for John indicates a clear chronological interest, which ought to control our interpretation of "*progegraphthai*" (Watson, *Gospel Writing*, 433n85). For additional patristic testimony to Matthean priority to Mark, cf. Irenaeus, *Adv. Haer.* 3.1.1; Eusebius, *Hist. Eccl.* 3.24.7; Jerome, *Ad Damasum*. Cf. also the "anti-Marcionite" prologue to Luke (*Die antimarcionitischen evangelienprologe*, 16 [Greek], 30–34 [Latin]).

The Legacies of Paul

4

Apollos and the Pauline Influence on Hebrews

A Proposal of Origin and Occasion

WILLIAM GLASS

IT WOULD PROBABLY NOT be too much of a stretch to suggest that there have been almost as many proposals about Hebrews' authorship as there have been readers of Hebrews. Answers range from Paul[1] to Barnabas[2] to the Virgin Mary. The plurality of suggestions[3] has convinced many that

1. Hence the inclusion of Hebrews in the Chester Beatty II collection of Pauline letters (P46). Harold Attridge observes that P46 reveals judgments about the authorship of Hebrews that were current in Alexandria since the middle of the second century. See Attridge, *Hebrews*, 1.

2. Johnson, *Hebrews*, 41.

3. Spicq (*Hébreux*) and Montefiore (*Hebrews*), following Luther, propose Apollos, a figure Johnson finds plausible as well. Origen speculated that it could be Clement of Rome or Luke, while others have proposed Priscilla (See Attridge, *Hebrews*, 4; cf. Hoppin, *Priscilla*). Attridge suggests that "the list of other possibilities which have been advanced reads like a roster of the supporting actors on the stage of the New Testament" (Attridge, *Hebrews*, 4–5): Silas, or Epaphras (under the assumption that Hebrews is the lost letter to the Laodiceans). This hypothesis relies on a few verbal similarities between Hebrews and Colossians, similarities that Attridge believes have been exaggerated. Lukan authorship has been seriously proposed as recently as 2010, in David Allen's *Lukan Authorship of Hebrews*. Allen's book is very interesting, but it

there can in the end be no decisive answer and that Origen is correct after all when he says that only God knows who it was.[4] These theories are all the more remarkable, when one remembers just how many patristic and later readers were convinced (and not without reason, I will suggest) that the author was Paul!

Attridge sums up the modern critical resignation by concluding that the "beginning of sober exegesis is a recognition of the limits of historical knowledge and those limits preclude positive identification of the author."[5] And Luke Johnson attempts to make a virtue of necessity, arguing that hypotheses concerning authorship do not in any case significantly affect the reading of the letter.[6] I will suggest in this essay, however, that there are several lingering questions about Hebrews that might be helped towards settlement if the letter's author can be plausibly identified. In what follows, then, I will first gather several pieces of data together to propose an author for the letter. Secondly, I will test that hypothesis on other parts of the letter that do not necessarily suggest an author but seem to make better sense given a particular account of the letter's authorship. I will regard the corroboration in the second stage of a hypothesis reached in the first as strong evidence for accuracy of the hypothesis. Thus, thirdly, I hope to construct as full an account as possible of the epistle's context, in the hopes that the epistolary context

---

is plagued by several crucial weaknesses: first, the argument depends upon a number of features of both Luke-Acts and Hebrews that are supposedly unique to them. The extent of these similarities is initially impressive, except that he compares his findings to no control group (other than the letters of Paul). For example, when one compares Hebrews to 1 Peter, keeping in mind the brevity of the latter, the unique verbal and stylistic echoes between Hebrews are comparatively at least as impressive (if not far more so) than those between Hebrews and Luke-Acts. Allen does little to distinguish the features uniquely to Hebrews and Luke-Acts from what may be found in other works of Christian, or even just literary, Greek. Second, he makes numerous important factual errors in his list of supposed unique commonalities (a representative example: he claims that the phrase *dia* with *pneumatos* occurs only in Heb 9:14 and Acts 1:2; 11:28; and 21:4 [p. 118]. In fact, it occurs also in Rom 5:5, 2 Thess 2:2, and 2 Tim 1:14). Thirdly, Allen's discussion of the Spicq hypothesis amounts to little more than a page and a couple of citations of Hurst and Williamson, as if those amount to decisive refutation of Spicq. But one wonders whether Allen has sufficiently considered either Spicq or his opponents; when the analytical tools of Hurst and Williamson are applied to Allen's own findings, he comes off far worse than Spicq did. It is well to take one's medicine before administering it to others.

4. Eusebius, *Hist Eccl.* 6.25.11–13.

5. Attridge, *Hebrews*, 5.

6. Johnson, *Hebrews*, 44.

will yield a fuller understanding of Hebrews and its place in the early Christian movement.

I. Toward a Hypothesis

Several traits of Hebrews have historically both compelled and bedeviled hypotheses concerning the book's authorship. The presence of what has seemed to many to be conspicuous philosophical language has led to speculations of a Platonic or Philonic background. Although the presence of philosophical language within Hebrews has been strongly contested,[7] there is a broad consensus that the book of Hebrews bespeaks a philosophically literate and rhetorically capable author. On the other hand, many have seen in Hebrews evidence of the influence of Paul, leading some to credit Paul as the book's author while other readers suspect it was someone in a Pauline "school." I will now attempt to analyze the character of these two influences in the letter, to see if they lead to any plausible hypothesis concerning the letter's origin.

(a) Philo of Alexandria

In the first chapter of his book on possible backgrounds for Hebrews, Lincoln Hurst engages a long scholarly tradition of seeing philosophical ideas at work in Hebrews. Championed by Sowers, Ménégoz, and Spicq *inter alia*, this tradition sees in Hebrews a broadly Platonist worldview in some of its key terms ("copy/shadow") and its "vertical" ontology. Additionally, Hurst notes significant discussion around terms like *hypodeigma* ("copy") and *skia* ("shadow"), *antitypos*, *eikōn* ("image"), and *pragma*, the nature of the true tent, and other such themes as supposed evidence of a broad Platonic or philosophical context for the letter. He also observes that at least some of these scholars detect in Hebrews the further influence of Philonic Judaism in the epistle's use of the OT, vocabulary, hermeneutics, and its characterization of faith in chapter 11.[8] But all these phenomena can be explained at least as well by other contexts, not least of which are Jewish Apocalyptic or the Qumran community

---

7. See Hurst, *Hebrews*.

8. Hurst, *Hebrews*, 13–21, responding to Spicq (*Hébreux*) and Sowers (*Hermeneutics of Philo and Hebrews*), following Eugéne Ménégoz, (*Hébreux*).

attested in the Dead Sea Scrolls.[9] Thus, Hurst remains unconvinced that the parallels that have served for others as evidence of indebtedness to Platonism or to Alexandrian Judaism suffice to make claims about the provenance of Hebrews.

Hurst must be given his due; his arguments point out a significant methodological weakness in the arguments of Spicq and others.[10] Terminological parallels are sufficient to raise the possibility of influence, but they are enormously tricky bases for strong conclusions. For one thing, demonstrating parallels requires not only noting presence in two loci but conspicuous absence in literature that seems to pursue similar themes. For another, apparent parallelism is often determined by judgment. In the case of Hebrews, Hurst contends that what seems to be philosophical language functions, when rightly read, to denote not a world of ideas and matter but of a thoroughly Jewish "two ages" salvation history.[11] The presence of apparent parallelism between Hebrews and a Philonic or Platonic background, then, cannot be determinative in the way that Spicq and others seemed to think.

But there are several facets of Hebrews left out of Hurst's discussion that might shape scholarly judgment on the questions of influence. The first of these is what seems to be a direct quotation of Philo in Heb 13:3, where the author encourages his audience[12] to remember to look after those who are tortured as though they were in one body with them (*hōs*

---

9. For the question of Qumranic influence on Hebrews, see Hurst, *Hebrews*, 43–66. See also, for Jewish apocalyptic, p. 42: "the ambiguity of the four crucial texts considered (9:8f., 11, 24, and 10:20), together with certain other indications in the epistle, provides and equally plausible cumulative argument in the direction of certain currents within Jewish apocalyptic."

10. Spicq here serving as the head of that tradition for Hurst: "although others have continued to present arguments for Philonic influence, it is Spicq who represents the climax of approximately sixty years of research, during which there was an extraordinarily unanimous approach to the background of Hebrews" (Hurst, *Hebrews*, 8).

11. Hurst, *Hebrews*, 17–18.

12. It may be thought that here I am prejudging the entire question of authorship by asserting that the author was a male. Rather, I merely follow the fact of a masculine self-reference in Heb 11:32 with the appropriate caution that if there are plausible grounds for such self-reference in the case of a female author, the judgment can be revised. For a vigorous (if ultimately unconvincing) argument that Hebrews is in fact the letter of a female author, see Hoppin, *Priscilla*; Hoppin, "Hebrews Is Priscilla's Letter." Johnson notes these sources but observes, in addition to the problem of 11:32, the rarity for rhetorical training among women in the Roman Empire, and the fact that everything supporting her candidacy would apply equally to other men in the NT, not least her husband Aquila. See Johnson, *Hebrews*, 41.

kai autoi ontes en sōmati). The phrase, especially given the context, echoes a statement of Philo concerning witnesses of a brutal tax collector's punishments. Philo states that some of them felt "as if they had been wronged in the bodies of others (*hōs en tois heterōn sōmasin autoi kakoumenoi*) and hastened to take leave of life either by drug or sword or noose."[13] The use of this metaphor in the same context as in Philo (i.e., one of observation of suffering) is conspicuous, making the suggestion that this is an allusion to Philo difficult to avoid.[14] And while familiarity with Philo would not itself demonstrate the arguments of Spicq and others, the presence of a Philonic inter-text places pressure in a Philonic direction where that interpretation competes with other plausible judgments.

As has often been observed, Philo and Hebrews also seem to use the Old Testament in similar ways.[15] But in my judgment, scholars have not sufficiently processed the importance of the citation in Heb 13:5. In an exhortation of his audience to avoid the love of money, the author asserts that God has sworn, in first-person, "I will never leave you nor forsake you" (*ou mē anō oud' ou mē se engkatalipō*). This verse, found nowhere in the OT as-is, seems to be a combined citation of Deut 31:6a, which has the promise made in third person and on God's behalf (*ou mē anē*—"he will never leave you"—*oud' ou mē se engkatalipē*), and Gen 28:15, in which God says himself "I will never forsake you" (*ou mē se engkatalipō*). It may be instead that the author had to hand a manuscript of LXX that either had Deut 31:6 spoken in the mouth of YHWH or one of Gen 28:15 that added the second clause in first person, but no such manuscript survives. In any case, the citation in Hebrews does *exactly* parallel Philo's *De Confusione Linguarum* 166, in which the quotation is used in the context of comfort for the soul that thinks her sins too great for God's forgiveness. There are good reasons to suspect that the author's text of Deut 31 looks much more like surviving texts. As Paul Ellingworth has observed, Hebrews quotes Deut 31 in 1:6 and 10:30 and alludes to it elsewhere, all in third-person, as in our manuscripts.[16] If the author and Philo each have texts of Deut 31 that look more like surviving versions, then the mode of their citation here suggests a combination of texts, which is all but impossible to account for except in terms of dependence, either direct

---

13. Philo, *Special Laws*, 3.161.

14. See Johnson, *Hebrews*, 341: "The phrase . . . is a bit odd but is paralleled almost exactly by a passage in Philo."

15. See Sowers, *Hermeneutics of Philo and Hebrews*.

16. Ellingworth, *Hebrews*, 700.

or indirect. But whether the citation is in fact a combination of Deut 31 and Gen 28 or not, it must not be overlooked that the citation appears in Hebrews, in Philo, and *nowhere else* in all of ancient Jewish or Christian literature. Moreover, the absence of the citation from Christian literature suggests that the author inherits the citation from a source he shares with Philo. The fact that the phrase does not appear in any contemporary or subsequent Christian literature, given the remarkable presence of shared traditions throughout the NT, seems to corroborate at least that the author pulls this citation from a store he shares with Philo rather than with Christian exegesis of the OT.

The remembrance of the Wilderness period in Hebrews also overlaps conspicuously with similar treatment in Philo. In Heb 12:7, the author exhorts the hearers to count "discipline" "*paideian*" as fatherly treatment from the Lord. The hearers' endurance is the appropriate response to what Matthew Thiessen calls Hebrews' "re-narration of Israel's history—a narration in which the author has placed both himself and his readers in the wilderness period together with all the generations of God's people who have been awaiting entry into God's promised rest."[17] This re-narration is meant to encourage the hearers to see themselves as those who are loved, and hence disciplined, by God. And the author's association of Israel's testing in the wilderness with *paideia* (discipline in the ancient pedagogic sense) has a long history in Alexandrian Judaism. The LXX translates Deut 8:5 with a statement that YHWH has led the people in their wandering "as a man might *discipline* (*paideusai*) his son." Wisdom similarly groups the wilderness period with *paideia* and the instruction of contemporary readers. While it may be argued that all of this merely shows the influence of the LXX on first-century Jewish thought (Thiessen notes that these motifs appear in the work of Jerusalemite Josephus as well as in the Alexandrian sources),[18] Hebrews' particular development of these traditions, again, has only one analogue in ancient Judaism. In *Preliminary Studies* 163–77, Philo understands the wilderness period as an allegory for moral life, linking Deuteronomy 8, Prov 3:11–12, and the figure of Esau.[19] Thiessen notes that Philo resumes discussion of Esau in several texts (*Alleg. Interp.* 3.2, *Prelim. Studies* 61,

---

17. Thiessen, "Hebrews 12.5–13," 368.

18. Thiessen, "Hebrews 12.5–13," 373.

19. Thiessen, "Hebrews 12.5–13," 371. Cf. Heb 12:3–16. The coincidental confluence of this particular suite of themes, again unique only to Philo and Hebrews, is difficult to imagine.

Questions and Answers on Genesis [QG] 4.165), coming closest to the tradition found in Hebrews in *QG* 4.168:

> For it was not for the sake of a trifling cooked pottage that [Esau] gave up his rights as first-born and yielded to the younger [brother] but because he made himself a slave to the pleasures of the belly. Let him be reproved and condemned as one who never was zealous for restraint and continence.[20]

Esau becomes for Philo a paradigm for taking God's discipline badly. And he is deployed in exactly the same way in Hebrews, giving up his "birthright" (*prōtotokia*) for a single meal, unlike the *prōtotokos* Jesus, who received the inheritance of a better name (Heb 1:4).[21]

There are grounds, it seems, to assert that the author to the Hebrews knows at least some of the work of Philo (see the comment on Heb 13:3 above). And this familiarity may explain the deployment in Hebrews of exegetical traditions found only in Philo. On this score, however, some critics have noticed that in the very places where pro-Philo scholarship has noticed seeming parallels, Hebrews seems thematically to be about something else. Hurst's protest concerning the possibility of reading ontological language in terms of *Heilsgeschichte* is but one such example. In Heb 13:5, where the author cites the combined Deut 31:6 and Gen 28:15, Ellingworth notes arguments that here Hebrews is merely quoting a source common to itself and to Philo.[22] In favor of such arguments, Ellingworth suggests, "is the fact that Philo's exposition has little in common with that of Hebrews."[23] Philo's citation of the combined Deuteronomy/Genesis verse comes in a discussion about the endless mercy of God to a soul that thinks itself beyond forgiveness: "my wickedness is too great for me to be forgiven."[24] Hebrews' deployment of the very same verse arises in a discussion about God's ability and willingness to provide for the needs of the hearers. But this conclusion is overcooked. In both cases,

---

20. Thiessen, "Hebrews 12.5-13," 377.

21. Thiessen, "Hebrews 12.5-13," 377. Thiessen suggests that Esau may have served as the paradigmatic example in some wider Jewish tradition of an undisciplined person (p. 376), but he suggests this only on the strength of its frequent appearance in Philo. If it was a tradition, then, that tradition seems at least to be in Philo's vicinity.

22. See Williamson, *Philo and the Epistle to the Hebrews*, 571. Crucially, though, especially for what follows, Williamson concedes that that source must have been an Alexandrian.

23. Ellingworth, *Hebrews*, 699.

24. Philo, *De Confusione Linguarum*, 165.

God's generosity and willingness to provide what is needed are at issue. And even if it were the case that the thematic differences were significant enough to weigh against the author's knowledge of Philo, then it is not the common awareness of a tradition that is interesting here, but the lack of any attestation of it elsewhere, given that it was important enough to be committed to memory in such a way that it made sense to deploy it in contexts as diverse as some claim our two loci are.

But what does that mean? Many times, scholars who have argued that Philo and Hebrews are indebted to similar traditions have done it in order to push Philo and Hebrews quite far apart, so that Hebrews can be what it is essentially without reference to Philo. I do not see, given the above, how this can be the case. We have noted several apparent overlaps (again, strings of verbatim agreement, tropes that are common between them although unusual, and similar hermeneutic conventions) between Hebrews and Philo, and this is leaving aside entirely for the moment the data that Spicq examined. If we are to hold that there is no knowledge of Philo in Hebrews, each and every one of these overlaps must be a result of shared tradition, or else we have isolated a moment of clear dependence of Hebrews upon Philo. If, on the other hand, all three of these phenomena are attributable to common tradition, then Hebrews and Philo have to share (1) some work or collection of works in which the Esau tradition can be collated with the others, (2) some version of Deut 31:6 that is common to them but unpopular outside of Alexandria, and (not or) (3) some other work that describes compassion for others in the terms of and in an analogous context to Heb 13:3, again in a way not found elsewhere in ancient literature. We are talking about a substantial series of third terms here, something almost requiring the two authors to have either an overlapping library (in the event that two or less of those the works are the same) or a truly remarkable omnibus third term document that both Philo and Hebrews choose to use in ways that demonstrate literary dependence upon it. Such an overlap almost guarantees the author's presence in Alexandria's Jewish community at a time roughly contemporary with Philo if not just after it. In that case, the knowledge of Philo's work becomes more likely than not, and here we are again. For the author of Hebrews not to have known the work of Philo, we have to assume a fairly widespread distribution of Philonic ideas. We have no reason to think this is the case and many reasons to think that it was not (as we will consider directly). Moreover, even if we had nothing to consider on that score, the wider a dispersion we hold for traditions we find in Philo and Hebrews, thus making Hebrews and Philo possibly independent reproducers of a third tradition, the more remarkable it becomes that we see some of these traditions nowhere else at all, given (again) how eager Christians were to borrow traditions and how popular certain strands of Alexandrian Judaism were in the wider world. The more we allow their relative scarcity to discipline us into thinking such ideas were not terribly widespread, the more difficult it becomes to believe that our author did not know Philo: this, again, without even considering the data Hurst is eager to wave away.

Thus, there are hard data that seem to prevent a hasty separation of Hebrews from Philo. Rather, these data suggest that where there are questions concerning the presence in Hebrews of concepts or terminology adapted from Philo or Alexandrian Judaism, the absence of similar hard data from other contexts such judgments should bias towards an answer in the affirmative. And once that is done, the terminology that Hurst attempts to evacuate of Platonic or Philonic content makes a reappearance for fresh consideration. Where such terminology appears to overlap Philo, we should assume that it does so *because* of an awareness of Philo and of some traditions that Philo also knew. Terms like *hypodeigma* (or the related *paradeigma*)[25] and *skia*, whose meanings in Philo might well connote a Platonic worldview, must be seen in light of the foregoing to be engagements with Philonic concepts and context. Judgments made on internal grounds about the slightly different ways such words are used in Hebrews from Philo become not arguments in support of ignorance of Philo but the contours of a disagreement.[26] The author of

---

25. Hurst argues that Philo almost never uses *hypodeigma*, instead favoring *paradeigma*. But I think he forgets his argument, for three pages later, when he wants to relate *hypodeigma* to an OT context, he notes the etymological relation of *hypodeigma* to *paradeigma*, allowing 1 Chr 28 to be a source of *hypodeigma* language in the book. See Hurst, *Hebrews*, 13, 16–17.

26. See MacIntyre, *Whose Justice?*, 326–69, esp. 326: "The relationships which can hold between individuals and a tradition are very various, ranging from unproblematic allegiance through attempts to amend or redirect the tradition to large opposition to what have hitherto been its central contentions. But this last may indeed be as formative and important a relation to a tradition as any other." Scholars, when trying to evaluate the potential relationships of Hebrews to Philo, have simply not kept in mind the degree to which inheritors of common traditions often contend for the meanings of that tradition. Hurst dismisses any idea of robust engagement of Hebrews with Philo and philosophy because the terminological overlap does not seem to carry through into a shared conceptual universe: as if the profession of faith in Jesus Christ, risen and exalted, could leave that conceptual universe untouched!

Hebrews thought Jesus of Nazareth had risen from the dead and ascended to Heaven to appear before God as the High Priest of the whole earth! Ought there really to be any surprise, then, if Hebrews shows traces of a debate with the author's philosophical sources about the nature of time and space? Would not the resurrection and ascension of Jesus force a rethinking of philosophical traditions and ontologies in exactly the kind of ways that we see in Hebrews?

The collocation of terminology common to philosophical contexts, then, *in light of* the other, harder data, must contribute to a sense of the text of Hebrews as drenched in the language, thoughts, and ideas of Alexandrian Judaism. This judgment is furthered by the many *kinds* of engagements with Philonic material seen in Hebrews. There seems to be at some points direct indebtedness to Philo, at others development in different directions of the same traditions, and still at others contest over notions apparently common to both authors. This multi-level engagement has all the marks of a moment in the development of (or contest over) a tradition. Given that Philo has basically *no* first-century reception history, and a second-century showing mainly among Christian writers, the tradition that he represents in first-century Judaism is best understood as a *local* variation upon Alexandrian Judaism.[27] If the author of Hebrews is familiar with Philonic material, far and away the easiest way to account for familiarity is that the author of Hebrews is himself someone from Alexandria. And thanks to the wealth of what is shared between them (and how long it is before anybody else knows about Philo), this conclusion changes barely at all if it is determined that Philo is reproducing traditions not his own that the author of Hebrews appears also to know. In either case, when we review the author's use of Philonic conceits, of textual traditions only found in Philo (or Alexandria), and of exegetical

---

27. See Runia, *Philo in Early Christian Literature.* Both Runia and Najma understand Christian reception of Philo to begin with Clement of Alexandria, who cites Philo only four times even though various phrases and Scriptural catenae from Philo appear throughout his work. Najma does not address the question of Hebrews, while Runia asserts that Hebrews and Philo represent the same intellectual milieu rather than any dependence. Like that of Hurst, however, Runia's account begins on the wrong foot, addressing and dismissing conceptual parallels while giving basically no attention to harder data. Jewish tradition largely ignores Philo, so Hebrews, if indeed it shows influence of Philo, can be acclaimed the earliest extant Philonic tradition. Crucially, the next two earliest moments of Philonic reception are themselves *both* Alexandrian. Arguably, the preservation of Philo's work owes to the catechetical school of Alexandria, which makes knowledge of Philo by the author of Hebrews a fact of geographical, as well as intellectual, significance.

traditions found only in Philo, we are right to conclude that the person whose work we read in Hebrews is a Jew trained as Philo was—in Alexandria. Whether their overlaps are due to personal knowledge of Philo or common use of a tradition only they inherited turns out, in the end, to make little difference at all.

But if an Alexandrian context is the best explanation for the letter to the Hebrews, how is one to explain the fact that Alexandrian church fathers seem to be among the last to accept it as Scripture? Would they not recognize the writings of one of their own? In fact, would they not have seen it before? These questions compel us to look closely at another influence often detected in the letter, one as commonly noted in the early church as it is confidently dismissed in modern times: namely, the influence of Paul of Tarsus.

(b) Paul of Tarsus

The earliest manuscript of Hebrews circulated among the Pauline epistles, as P46 attests, reflecting judgments of Pauline provenance from at least the turn of the third century. Clement of Alexandria and Origen also thought Hebrews to be Pauline in origin, if Eusebius is to be believed, although each of them imagined different ways to account for significant differences between the other Pauline letters and Hebrews. Clement imagined that Luke was the actual hand, translating what Paul wrote in Hebrew,[28] while Origen supposed an eager disciple produced Hebrews, calling to mind "the acknowledged writings of the apostle."[29] The modern history of this discussion seems to have gone through phases. Hurst observes that the introduction in the late nineteenth century of the Alexandrian background "made it fashionable to see little if any connection between Hebrews and Paul."[30] But other modern scholars have witnessed to the presence of significant overlaps between Paul and Hebrews.[31] Windisch itemizes some fifteen apparent parallels, to which Hurst adds even more, even though Hurst himself chalks these overlaps up to a common

---

28. Clement of Alexandria, *Hypotyposes*, preserved in Eusebius, *Hist. Eccl.* 6.14.2. Cf. Attridge, *Hebrews*, 1–2.

29. From a fragment of his *Homilies on Hebrews* preserved in Eusebius, *Hist. Eccl.* 6.25.12.

30. Hurst, *Hebrews*, 107. Ménégoz and Manson are among the adherents to this scholarly fashion.

31. Hurst, *Hebrews*, 108.

inherited tradition.³² Keeping in mind judgments made in the previous section, however, concerning the difficulties of parallelism, it may be most helpful to search for evidence anywhere of direct dependence.

In this vein, chapter 13 cannot fail to escape notice as a passage peculiarly Pauline both in style and in various particulars. Overbeck famously asserted that chapter 13 was in fact an amendment to Hebrews, which was meant to bring the whole document into conformity with the Pauline corpus.³³ Certainly the news of Timothy's release (Heb 13:23) bespeaks a direct familiarity with at least some of the Pauline circle. Moreover, "The God of peace" is a unique phrase among early Christian writers, common only to Hebrews and to Paul.³⁴ And the final greeting of the epistle, "grace be with all of you," is also a fairly likely Pauline echo.³⁵

Formal overlaps like this, suggesting familiarity not only with at least some of Paul's associates but almost certainly with Pauline letters themselves, make terminological or conceptual overlaps much more likely to need accounting for in terms of Pauline literature. When Hebrews configures Christ's death (2:14) as the defeat of evil powers, the distinctive Pauline voice can be identified,³⁶ as it can in the case of "the

---

32. Hurst, *Hebrews*, 124.

33. Franz Overbeck, *Zur Geschichte des Kanons*, 16. Other scholars have suggested rather that chapter 13 is a Pauline text appended to the end of Hebrews (so Simcox and Jones; see Attridge, *Hebrews*, 384).

34. Johnson, *Hebrews*, 354. Cf. Rom 15:33; 16:20; Phil 4:9; 1 Thess 5:23; Heb 13:20.

35. Johnson (*Hebrews*, 359) cites the appearance of a grace wish at the conclusion of all thirteen letters attributed to Paul in the NT.

36. Hurst, *Hebrews*, 108. Clare Rothschild argues that this adoption is meant to "imply Pauline authorship of a message intended to stand in continuity with esteemed Pauline traditions" (Rothschild, *Hebrews as Pseudepigraphon*, 9–10; cf. 67–81). But this judgment has a few problems. First, Rothschild concedes reliance upon other traditions (p. 10); why not argue that the letter is meant to "imply" authorship along the lines of those traditions? Secondly, to suggest that the imitation of Paul is meant to *imply* authorship requires some account of why that would be. There are certainly records within the first century of contexts in which a letter supposed to be by Paul might not be all that helpful to gain one a hearing. Paul was not always as esteemed as he was in the era of many of the Apostolic Fathers. If in fact the letter *was* written to anyone for whom Pauline authorship would be persuasive, is it not quite likely that those very people would also know that the Apostle was dead? Finally, as Rothschild herself observes, we have evidence of a lot of Pauline pseudepigraphy (cf. letters between Paul and Seneca, 3 Corinthians, the so-called letter to the Laodiceans, etc.). She sees this as evidence for the plausibility that Hebrews is meant to be a Pauline pseudepigraph. But in light of the "numerous witnesses to Pauline imitation among early Christians" (p. 10), we must ask why the author does not employ the most *obvious* mechanism

righteousness which is according to faith" in Heb 11:7 (cf. Rom 4:13–25) and the identification of the hearers as "seed of Abraham" in Heb 2:16; cf. Rom 9; Gal 3:7). The earlier verses (1–7) of Heb 13 also seem to suggest a dependence upon a Pauline letter. Luke Johnson has argued that Heb 13:1–7 bears striking similarity to Rom 12:9–21.[37] Rom 12:9a and Heb 13:1 both seem to have an injunction to love that is followed by several explicating statements, probably meant to flesh out what the content of *agapē* and *philadelphia* are.[38] Among those clarifications are the command to contribute to the material needs of others (Rom 12:13; Heb 13:1),[39] to extend hospitality to strangers (Rom 12:13b; Heb 13:2), and the command to show honor when appropriate (Rom 12:10; Heb 13:7).[40] Stylistic parallels are also apparent, in that the first three words of both 12:9 and 13:1 consist of a terse, three-word imperative concerning the ongoing practices of love among the hearers. Given the combination of explicit indicators of Pauline influence in both the earlier and later parts of the passage (vv. 1–7 and 18–25), and given the stylistic similarities noted, it seems reasonable to conclude that it was not for no reason that earlier readers suggested a Pauline or Paulinist amendment to Hebrews meant to bring it into accordance with Paul.

Since such an amendment would render most of this material useless to the question of Hebrews' origin, it may be helpful to address this

---

for having the letter attributed to Paul, namely, the use of Paul's *name*? Rothschild is aware of the problem and attempts to dispense with attribution as a relevant criterion for proposing pseudepigraphy (pp. 123–32). But her attempts to depose this criterion on the basis of only one extant example (Hebrews) is unconvincing against the obvious fact that when people wanted their writings understood as Pauline, they explicitly proclaimed that Paul wrote them.

37. Johnson, *Hebrews*, 338.

38. The differences in terminology are probably not significant *in this case*, given that Paul supplements *agapē* with *philadelphia* immediately in Rom 12:10.

39. Johnson sees the practice of contribution to the needy brother implicit in the term *philadelphia* itself, as it refers to "a complex set of dispositions and practices" above all involving "mutual sharing of possessions and activities" (Johnson, *Hebrews*, 339).

40. The contexts here are somewhat different. The command in Romans seems to commend mutual honor while Heb 13:7 exhorts the hearers to honor those who spoke the word to them. But at least one manuscript of Heb 13:7 seems to have replaced the dominant *"hegouménōn"* with *"proegouménōn,"* reflecting an attraction to a parallel context in Rom 12. Johnson notes, "The original version of D has a singular reading here; instead of *hēgoumenōn* ("leaders"), it has *proēgoumenōn* perhaps influenced—since so much else in the first verses of Heb 13 resembles Rom 12—by the presence of *proēgoumenoi* in Rom 12:10" (Johnson, *Hebrews*, 338).

question a little more substantively. Almost every scholar that I can find notes the common assumption in late nineteenth-century Hebrews studies that chapter 13 was added on to the rest of Hebrews at a later time. Attridge notes no fewer than eight significant studies, although it is perhaps suggestive that every one of those studies dates from between 1890 and 1940, when partitioning NT epistles was something of a scholarly knee-jerk reaction.[41] Among these studies, Overbeck's seems to be the most plausible motivation for the addition of chapter 13. But all of these studies fail to process properly the importance of several factors. First, there are significant connections between chapter 13 with the foregoing (see esp. μενέτω in 13:1 and 12:27, the exhortation to suffer alongside those who suffer or are in prison in 13:3; cf. 10:33–34, and even more continuity in 13:7–17). Secondly, differences of vocabulary based only on a single letter are far too difficult to identify to be convincing, especially when one considers the continuities noted above. There are only twelve chapters of writing in existence for the author. As such, there are basically no parallel contexts with which we can compare Heb 13 in order to see whether differences of vocabulary do in fact exist.[42] Thirdly, although I judge Overbeck's thesis to be a response to language inflected by Paulinism in chapter 13 (about which, see below), it would require a demonstration that Heb 1–12 are themselves clearly *un*-Pauline to establish any sense of subsequent Pauline "correction." This seems at least debatable and, in light of phrases common in the Pauline corpus that appear in the main body of Hebrews (2:14, 16; 11:7—see above), unlikely. But fourthly, and most importantly, as will be explored in much of what follows, Heb 13:7–18 integrates themes of the entire epistle in one tight paraenetic section that also reprises both previous paraenetic sections in the epistle and the material in the sections that seem more obviously under Pauline

---

41. Attridge *Hebrews*, 384nn5–6. Vanhoye argues for continuity on the grounds that 13:1–6, 7–19, constitute paragraphs 2 and 3 of a section that begins with 12:14. This proposal seems to ignore a real change in tone and style at 13:1, which, while it may not be sufficient grounds for partition, distinguishes what follows 13:1 in *some* way from what precedes it. Clare Rothschild has proposed this thesis again in recent years, and her proposal will be addressed is addressed mainly in the footnotes above (n39) and below (nn68, 79). See Rothschild, *Hebrews as Pseudepigraphon*.

42. In order to make a strong judgment on differences of vocabulary, it is methodologically unsound to compare chapter 13 with the majority of the letter, since the discursive registers are quite different in, say, the defense of Jesus' priesthood from the paraenetic rhetoric deployed here. One could mark that there are parallels between chapter 13 and other paraenetic sections in the Heb 1–12, but I suspect that in those sections the overlap with chapter 13 is far more impressive than any differences.

influence. It is no more reasonable in my judgment, then, to conclude for pseudepigraphic amendment than for some other explanation of this chapter's Paulinism.

Most importantly, however, these arguments render the Pauline influence on chapter 13 significant for judgments about the provenance of Hebrews. What it seems must be accounted for, in any question of authorship, is the evidence in the letter that it was written by someone deeply steeped in specifically Alexandrian Judaism, of the kind that is seen reflected in Philo (inclusive of, but not nearly explained by, "wider" Jewish tradition). The kind of familiarity with Philo's traditions required would just about necessitate that the author have come from Alexandria himself. And hailing from or having come from Alexandria, the author would have to be somewhat familiar with Paul's letters (at least the letters to Corinth, Rome, and possibly Galatia and Philippi) within the first generation after they were composed, and at most within the first century CE. This would almost certainly require having traveled into the regions of the empire where Paul was or had been operative. On these two considerations alone, it should be clear that at least the most convincing candidate of whom the NT or early Christian literature give us *any* knowledge at all is the Apollos mentioned in Acts, 1 Corinthians, and briefly (perhaps) in Titus. Acts relates that Apollos is an Alexandrian Jew, eloquent and well-versed in the Scriptures, and prone to wander. He enters the scene in Acts 18:24 in Ephesus, but eventually arrives at Corinth (18:27). This arrival seems to be corroborated by Paul's own explicit mention of him in 1 Corinthians (3:5, 6, 22; 4:6). Apollos comes to know Paul at least before 1 Corinthians, and hence (probably) before 2 Corinthians, Romans, Galatians, and Philippians.[43]

It seems, then, that Apollos is the most likely candidate, about whom we have any knowledge at least, to have been capable of writing Hebrews. He seems to be the character most elegantly poised to fit the description proposed above, a description that (it should be stressed again) *any* proposed author will need to be able to fit. Of course, it is always true that the writer may be someone of whom we simply have no knowledge, either from the NT or elsewhere. Although this possibility is simply not as important as some might think,[44] it does require a certain reserve at

---

43. For the chronology understood here, see Campbell, *Framing*. Regardless of the merits of Campbell's proposal, however, most scholars would at least date Philippians, (parts of) 2 Corinthians, and Romans after 1 Corinthians.

44. There is a certain wearying circularity to much of the critical despair

this point about Apollos, despite the ease with which he satisfies the conditions named above. At this stage of the argument, then, Apollos must remain a highly plausible hypothesis, one capable of answering questions that must be answered if any author is to be proposed: hence, a hypothesis worth adopting and trying out. The next section will therefore test this hypothesis on the reading of Hebrews itself, to see if it can shed any light upon the rest of the letter. And while the data analyzed above must figure into any reconstruction of Hebrews' provenance, many of the data below do not necessarily imply anything about authorship. Instead, I will evaluate the data under the tentative assumption of Apollan provenance for Hebrews, to see whether that assumption makes any of the letter more intelligible. This will require importing into the discussion of Hebrews such information as we can glean from the rest of the NT concerning Apollos, but there is nothing at all remarkable about that. All historical reconstructions must make similar moves; the strength of any given hypothesis is the fit between data imported and the surface of the object under analysis. To that we now turn.

II. Trying Apollos on for Size

The New Testament is relatively spare in its account of Apollos and his movements through the early church. On the one hand, it is clear that Apollos traveled through the early Christian communities, apparently with the intent to convert Jews to the Messiah (Acts 18:26) and (possibly) to strengthen the assemblies he met along the way. The New Testament definitely locates him in Ephesus (Acts 18:24; 1 Cor 16:12), likely more than one time. His closest associates in Ephesus, Aquila and Priscilla (so it seems, anyway; Acts 18:26), moved to Rome late in Paul's ministry (Rom 16:3), and it is quite reasonable to think that Apollos would have visited them there, given the opportunity. Additionally, Aquila and Priscilla seem to have recommended Apollos to the Corinthian assembly, thus gaining him his first audience there (18:27). Thus, Ephesus, Corinth,

---

surrounding the background of Hebrews. Questions raised on internal evidence are quickly met with the objection that the writer is or could be unknown to us. And the fact that the writer is or could be unknown to us is then used to dismiss suggestions that internal evidence is significant. One begins to get the impression that the only convincing piece of evidence concerning the authorship of Hebrews would be a first verse that read "Apollos, a slave of God and of Jesus Christ," as if such greetings weren't dismissed all the time and with extreme confidence!

Apollos and the Pauline Influence on Hebrews

and Rome, places where the ministry of Apollos is known or is likely to have taken place, are initially plausible candidates for shedding light on Hebrews. Parallels between Hebrews and those contexts, if available, may shed more light on the origins of Hebrews and confirm or change the hypothesis here adopted. Here, I will limit my discussion to the Corinthian and Roman contexts. This is, in part, due to the contested nature of supposed Ephesian evidence,[45] and in part due to a judgment reached on the basis of Hebrews' own reception.[46]

(a) Do Not Forsake the Gathering

For a composition that so strongly emphasizes pilgrimage, moving on, and going to Jesus "outside the camp" (13:13), the places where paraenesis is most explicit in Hebrews seem to say a lot about gathering in. "Do not forsake the gathering of yourselves together" (10:25), "Keep on loving one another as brothers" (13:1), "Remember your leaders, who spoke the word of God to you" (13:7), and "Submit to leaders" (13:17). If, according to common practice in deliberative rhetoric, the intended action is hinted at early in the letter but becomes clearer as the letter goes on, then all of this "together" rhetoric cannot be insignificant. Luke Johnson argues (rightly, I think) that the sermonic character of Hebrews shows itself in an interlacing of exposition and exhortation, in which

> the author puts forth themes that are only later developed more fully, thus creating a wavelike, cumulative effect. Thus Jesus' fellowship with humans (2:14-18) is made thematic in 5:1-10; his faith (3:1-6) is made explicit in 12:1-3; his role as priest (4:14; 5:1-10) is developed more fully in 7:1—9:28; and the pilgrimage of the people to God's rest is stated in 3:7—4:11 and brought to a magnificent climax in 11:1—12:29.[47]

---

45. There are any number of questions concerning 1 and 2 Corinthians and Romans. But Ephesians is unique among letters attributed to Paul in that there are serious questions about who the letter's actual intended recipients were, i.e., whether they were Ephesians. This evidence therefore must be bracketed, at least until more conclusive evidence about the nature of Ephesians can be discovered. See Campbell, *Framing*.

46. This will be discussed at length below, but I regard it as significant that Hebrews' first known reception is in 1 Clement, a letter from Rome to Corinth dated probably to about 90 CE.

47. Johnson, *Hebrews*, 10.

If indeed deliberative rhetorical techniques are operative here, then it is arguable that the more cryptic imperatives ought to be interpreted in light of the clearer versions of them later on. Is "drifting away" (2:1) a drift away from the gathering church (10:25)? Is the "turning away from the living God" (3:12) a turning away from the *ekklēsia* to which the readers are all summoned? Is the "falling short of God's rest" a typological reading of an on-the-ground reality of pulling away from a united church? It is crucial to remember that the clearest hortatory discourse in the letter (13:1–6) agrees with this reading, commanding the continuance of *philadelphia*, the remembrance of the brothers in prison, and care for the suffering as though the hearers "were in one body with them" (13:3).[48] But can this reading be sustained? What is it about Christian disunity that merits such extreme rebuke? And if the warnings do not refer to schism, to what great sin do the warning passages refer?

The Corinthian correspondence is of course the *locus classicus* for Paul's insistence that the believers are one body (1 Cor 12:12–27; Heb 10:17). While Calvin speaks for a patristic commonplace when he supposes that "as if in one body with them" (Heb 13:3) refers to the church as Christ's body (cf. 1 Cor 12:12), Ellingworth and Attridge both reject that interpretation, Ellingworth without further comment and Attridge with an emphasis that the conjunction *hōs kai* functions hypothetically (*as if* . . .). Their judgments seem to be based on a mistake, however, in that they read later sacramental theology onto what is in Paul arguably an analogical description of the body meant specifically to fund an exhortation (i.e., you are members of one another, so live *as if* that were true). Hebrews' way of putting it is comparable; you *have been* sharers of the sufferings of others (the *hōs kai* being implied here), so *keep* doing that (Heb 13:3; cf. 10:33). And similar convictions seem to underlie the paraenetic turn in Paul's letter to the Romans. Before beginning the set of instructions whose influence was traced above in Rom 12:10–21, the

---

48. Moule and Ellingworth agree that the author intends by "those in prison" a group of Christians undergoing persecution, and this would seem to follow from the short imperative that begins this section (Ellingworth, *Hebrews*, 695). But the exhortation to care for those in prison remembers the congregation's own former practice (10:34). Johnson sees the problem as one of temptation, i.e., the hearers do not need to be talked *into* a practice; they need to be talked into maintaining it (Johnson, *Hebrews*, 340). There is a temptation to abandon those with whom they have been in solidarity formerly. But theirs is supposed to be a love that *cannot* be shaken. They have been faithful before. Now, *hē philadelphia menetō*, as if each believer were in the position of the neediest among them.

Romans are exhorted to humility with one another, since "we, though many, are one body in Christ, and individually members of one another" (Rom 12:5). Although the fellowship is endangered seemingly by difficulties between Jews and gentiles (1:16; 2:10–11; 12:10), Paul commands that the Romans remember that they are members of one another. To my mind, then, there is nothing said or implied in Paul's "body" ecclesiology that does not map quite easily onto what Hebrews says. In fact, the author incites the Hebrews to continue in actions that make *no sense* unless the ὡς καὶ is a hypothetical that is tacitly affirmed.[49] A tradition at both Rome and Corinth of conceiving the church as one body whose members are mutually dependent, then, explains very well Hebrews' exhortation to maintain fellowship with suffering brothers and sisters in terms of a single body.

(b) Foods: Pauline Context as Suggestive for Idol-Meat

In a brief excursus on the question of what Heb 13:9's denunciation of "dietary regulations" precisely refers to, Attridge observes a number of possibilities.[50] Such regulations may refer, he notes, to (a) prohibitions about meat sacrificed to idols (cf. 1 Cor 8–9), (b) the Eucharist (hence involving Hebrews in disputes about the sacramental presence of Christ in the early Christian rite), (c) various Jewish quasi-sacramental meals known throughout the diaspora.[51] Alternatively, they may be a kind of synecdoche for the entire observance of Torah.[52] The features of the passage that assist interpretation seem also to obscure it. The halakhic language ("Teachings" that do or do not profit "those who walk [*hlk—to walk!*] in them") suggests the teachings to be concerned with Jewish

---

49. There are other considerations, of course, that would corroborate this argument. The Pauline influence on this entire passage has already been observed, yielding confusion and open questions on many other points. But chapter 13, which Overbeck *inter alia* thinks was added to Hebrews *specifically* to bring Hebrews into line with Paul, is probably not the place where exegetes should commit too strongly to arguments about the irreconcilability of Hebrews to Paul.

50. Attridge, *Hebrews*, 394–96.

51. Cf. 1QSa 2.17–22; Josephus, *Ant.* 14.10.8 § 213–16; Philo *Vit. cont.* 64–82; *m. Ber.* 6–8.

52. Johnson, *Hebrews*, 347: "In the same way, 'dietary regulations' may stand for the whole complex of laws dealing with material things that the author regards as ineffective for the perfection of persons (see 9:9–10; 10:1–4). That this is likely is shown by the contrast."

obedience. The opposition of teachings concerning foods to "grace" as ways of strengthening the heart and conscience (cf. Heb 10:1-2) has convinced some interpreters that what is at stake is the relative worth of physical regulations and observances. And the subsequent verse, if it is meant to explicate v. 9, raises the question of cultic eating, either Jewish practices themselves, which case the author counsels refraining from them in favor of a "better (Eucharistic?) table" or Jewish prohibitions from impure meat (cf. perhaps Acts 15:29), in which case the hearers are being advised not to heed those prohibitions.

The problematic assumption is that these options must be exclusive. And it is just here that the Pauline context helps us. Chapters 8-10 of 1 Corinthians find Paul engaged in a delicate discussion over questions of conscience. The sight of their brothers and sisters eating meat sacrificed to idols, he observes, afflicts the consciences of some members of the Corinthian assembly (1 Cor 8:7). Paul's advice is an abstention from *known* instances of idol-meat, not because idol-meat itself defiles (8:8) but because the weak consciences of some are to be treasured as the presence of Christ in the assembly (8:12-13). Paul proceeds to warn that just as those who participate at the Jewish altar partake of the sacrifices (10:18) and those who participate in the Eucharistic table share in Jesus' body (10:16), those who eat food sacrificed to idols unite themselves to demons (10:20). Instead, believers ought to prefer the table of the Lord, which is also the table of the weak. Paul's discussion here is instructive in that nearly all of the features that supposedly make Heb 13:9-10 difficult to interpret are present in Paul's discussion. The relative unimportance of food regulations is emphasized, as is a preference for the Lord's table, the instructive value of Jewish *cultus*[53] and an account of just how dietary regulations may strengthen the conscience. The Corinthian context reveals that there is nothing inherently implausible about Heb 13:9-10 referring to disputes of conscience over meat sacrificed to idols. It is clear that the adoption of regulations against idol-meat will strengthen the consciences of some in the Corinthian assembly. The question is whether the Corinthian context provides the best narrative fit.

What is missing in Hebrews from the Corinthian context is any obvious sense that the regulations being adopted are *Jewish* regulations although those can be discerned eventually, as in chapter 2. But the internal

---

53. Admittedly, the instructive value of the Jewish table in Hebrews is, like the entire *cultus*, negative; the instruction comes in the distinction of the new order from the old rather than in their comparison.

evidence of the rest of Hebrews suggests that the "dietary regulations" in view in Heb 13:9 are Jewish, as the only other mention of "foods" in Hebrews seems to be in a list of the first covenant's ordinances that are to be left behind in the new order. Even this does not preclude the Corinthian context, since the NT preserves a strong witness of a specifically Jewish concern. But in Corinth, those whose consciences are offended by the practice of eating idol-meat seem to be recent converts who can still remember thinking idols represented real gods (1 Cor 8:7). Hebrews seems to worry that at least some of the hearers might be tempted to embrace dietary regulations as part of a wholehearted defection to the first covenant. This entire dynamic recalls not so much 1 Corinthians as Gal 2:12–16, with Jews separating from the gentile believers and returning to Jewish dietary practices. In the sphere of Apollos' influence, a similar dynamic seems to be in play at Rome. A letter that at various points has charted the difficulties of fellowship in a congregation with apparently significant numbers of Jews and gentiles also contains instructions about conscience and the consumption of or abstention from meat, presumably that sacrificed to idols although this is not specified (14:1–4, 13–23). That this difficulty maps onto Jewish and gentile issues seems confirmed by the fact that the climax of this section of Romans (15:7) immediately precedes a discussion of how the gospel is given as "a servant of the circumcised" (15:8) in order that "the gentiles might glorify God" (15:9).

It appears, then, that the opposition in Heb 13:9 of *charis* to dietary regulations as a means to strengthen the conscience has a strong echo with particular struggles that plagued Pauline churches, where at least some of those struggles were due to the difficulties of Jewish Christians to live alongside their gentile brothers and sisters. The witness of Acts 15 suggests, in fact, that the sensitivity in the early church over idol meat and the temptation on the part of Jewish Christians to withdraw from their gentile brothers are in fact dimensions of the same problem. Paul's insistence upon the body of Christ as the place where grace destroys the dividing wall between Jews and gentiles and makes them one family of God seems, therefore, to have a strong ally in the letter to the Hebrews. His pastoral application of that conviction in the case of Rome seems to be the most likely analogue for the temptations faced by the hearers of Hebrews, who are reminded in Heb 13:9–10 that grace does more for the heart than Torah, and that those who eat at the table of the Lord are not moving forward if they turn away.

(c) Meat and Maturity

Hebrews exhorts its hearers on to maturity and away from basics of faith (6:1) via an analogy of maturity with adulthood and the eating of solid food and a corresponding assimilation of those who turn from the Lord to infants who still need milk. As Luke Timothy Johnson notes, the contrast is a Hellenistic commonplace, found in Epictetus, Philo, and Seneca, *inter alia*.[54] But in the New Testament, Heb 5 has only one echo, namely, that in 1 Cor 3. In 1 Cor 2:6, Paul apparently defends himself against a charge that he has not delivered the goods: "yet among the mature we *do* impart wisdom."[55] After giving an account of the nature of true wisdom, he continues in 3:1–2: "I could not address you as spiritual men, but as men of the flesh, as babes in Christ. I fed you with milk, not solid food; for you were not ready for it; and even yet you are not ready."

That these two accounts run in parallel probably cannot be proven entirely. But several considerations merit their consideration alongside one another. The first such consideration is that in Heb 5, the author rebukes his audience in terms similar to 1 Corinthians. Luke Johnson notes as a striking feature of Hebrews' discourse that this Hellenistic commonplace is deployed not merely in terms of the relationship between basic ideas and more complicated ones, but in terms of moral capacity.[56] For the author, maturity is demonstrated specifically in the capacity to judge good and evil (5:14). The idea is that having been instructed in the basics of faith, the hearers should be equipped to move on (*pherōmetha*) toward perfection. Similarly, in 1 Cor 3, Paul rebukes the Corinthians as those whose lack of morality reveals them to be infants (3:3–4). Secondly, Heb 6:3 gives the impression that solid food is what will occupy the remainder of the letter. In other words, there is a claim to be giving solid food even though there is a hesitation over whether the audience is quite ready for it. They will demonstrate their fitness for solid food, the author continues, in their love for one another and their mutual provocation to continue gathering together (10:24–25). Paul, on the other hand, defends a decision *not* to give solid food in 3:1–2, as was noted already. Paul asserts that it was the infancy of the Corinthians that prevented his giving them meat and that their factiousness reveals they have not grown.

---

54. Johnson, *Hebrews*, 156.

55. Emphasis added to RSV's translation to reflect the posture Greek syntax suggests Paul to be taking.

56. Johnson, *Hebrews*, 156.

They are "still not" ready. It is worth noting that Paul is *defending* himself here.[57] Thirdly, that Paul does not use the trope of milk vs. solid food in other contexts where he is dealing with conspicuous recalcitrance *may* suggest that the discourse is imported.[58] Paul's frustration here seems to be matched at least by the tone of 2 Cor 10–13, parts of the Thessalonian correspondence, and (most obviously) Galatians; but Paul never mobilizes this discourse in any of those contexts. Lastly, the one with whom the Corinthians are comparing Paul in 1 Cor 3 seems to be Apollos! Apollos had given them meat and Paul had not, and Paul's withholding is (so they say) the source of their formation into various parties.[59] This argument may appear circular, so it may help at this point to restate our position. Apollos has already been suggested on other grounds, explored in section I. In trying out this hypothesis, we are able to discern a powerful explanation for Paul's use of the milk/meat contrast in 1 Cor 3 but not in parallel contexts. As discussed already, it is likely that Hebrews' author

---

57. His defense of a course he did not take, when combined with a repeated insistence that the Corinthians are immature, seem to suggest that his posture here is reactive, probably to a charge they had made, "that *at the level of rhetoric* his discourse is mere milk-and-water" (Thiselton, *First Epistle to the Corinthians*, 292). It seems to me that given Paul's reply, Thiselton is right to note the accusation but wrong to note that it refers only to rhetoric.

58. To be sure, this is an argument from silence on an admittedly small collection of samples (i.e., between seven and thirteen letters). However, this is where Johnson's insight concerning the relative commonplaceness of the metaphor is helpful to remember. If Paul does *not* get the contrast of milk and solid food from the discourse of the person against whom the Corinthians are unfavorably comparing him, then he likely gets it from one of those other sources as a consummate label for the kind of behavior he names. If that contrast is a conventional trope for that kind of behavior, the relative probability that it would be deployed again increases. On the other hand, if the author of Hebrews is the source of the milk/meat discourse, it makes sense, given its commonness, to assume that the author of Hebrews will have used that discourse on several occasions.

59. So Thiselton approvingly quotes Witherington: "Apollos had a following among some Corinthians. He had affected some Corinthians in the matter of *Sophia*, both in its rhetorical form and as esoteric content. These influences had managed to stir up the pot" (Thiselton, *First Epistle to the Corinthians*, 124). Although space does not here permit, it should be said that the logic of this defense can be traced through the entirety of the letter. In 1 Cor 14:20, for example, Paul exhorts the Corinthians not to be "children" in their thinking but rather "adults" (*teleioi*). Once it becomes clear that *teleioi* here corresponds to *pneumatikoi* in 3:2 (as evidenced by the opposition to *nēpios* in that text), vast stretches of the letter become intelligible as Paul thematically deconstructs the Corinthians' perception of themselves as mature/spiritual/capable of discerning good from evil ("we all possess knowledge").

will have used that discourse many times before. This possibility allows us to posit influence of Hebrews' author on Paul at some point in time without needing to argue for literary dependence of 1 Corinthians upon Hebrews as some scholars have.[60]

(d) Those from Italy and the Letter from Italy

"Those who come from Italy send you greetings": most scholars think that not much can be established on the basis of these words.[61] As conclusive evidence, this point must be granted. But as corroborative evidence, Italy is quite suggestive. On the one hand, "those from Italy" may refer to the letter's being written *from* Italy and that the greetings of those who are with the author travel with the letter.[62] This would agree with Paul's sending of greetings to Corinth from Ephesus on behalf of the churches in Asia (1 Cor 16:19). On the other hand, the phrase may refer to those who are with the author, outside of Italy, sending greetings along presumably to some other place, or even back home. On the adoption of Apollos as a hypothesis, given the post-Pauline date of the letter,[63] the two most likely options are that the letter would be written from Rome to Corinth or vice versa. On the former construal, those from Italy may include Aquila and Priscilla, with whom the Corinthians are quite familiar already. On the latter construal, the greeting may refer to Roman Christians who have made their way to Corinth (and points east and south) at some point. Either of these is quite possible, as the path between the Corinthian assembly and that of Rome is one of the

---

60. Both Spicq and Montefiore argue for Hebrews to be the explanation for the formation of the so-called Apollos party of 1 Cor 3:4. As will be discussed below, there seem to be good reasons to date Hebrews in later, post-Pauline Christianity. See Montefiore, *Hebrews*, 21.

61. Johnson, *Hebrews*, 358; as well as Attridge, *Hebrews*, 409–10, citing half a dozen or so arguments for different construals of the meaning of the phrase and concluding that none are decisive. He does concede, however, that the thesis that the writer is with Italians somewhere other than Italy is the more natural reading, even if it is not unassailable (Attridge, *Hebrews*, 410). My own reading agrees with what Attridge takes to be more natural. It can hardly claim to be decisive, but in the kind of argument mounted here, it need not be.

62. So Montefiore, noted in Ellingworth, *Hebrews*, 735.

63. About which, see below.

most well-traveled in early Christianity.[64] In either case, the letter would travel one of the most popular routes in early Christianity.

The choice between these two construals, even if it is impossible to rule for either, is still quite informative for the study of Hebrews' place in early Christianity. Hebrews, if this understanding is correct, is best read as the contribution of Apollos of Alexandria to ongoing developments in the churches of Corinth and/or Rome. The hypothesis of Apollos' authorship arose in answer to features of the letter that any account of authorship must answer. Apollos, once proposed as an author, makes a number of interpretive difficulties in the letter intelligible. And, on the basis of Apollos as a proposed author, it becomes possible to propose a "theater" of action for the letter, between Corinth and Rome. The hypothesis receives a tremendous boost, however, by external evidence confirming exactly the theater of influence for the letter that the proposal of Apollos as its author led us to expect. Sometime in the last two decades of the first century CE,[65] the first letter of Clement of Rome shows extensive engagement with the letter to the Hebrews.[66] This letter is the first known reception of Hebrews, and Clement clearly receives the letter as authoritative, quoting it alongside Old Testament and other early Christian writings[67] without distinguishing between them. Intriguingly, Clement's letter from Rome is addressed exactly where we might expect based on our investigation so far: namely, to Corinth.[68] In the extant writings of the Apostolic Fathers,

---

64. See, e.g., Paul's list of greetings in Rom 16. That Paul could write from Corinth (Rom 16:23) and greet that many people by name at a church he had not yet been to personally suggests that Christians from Rome made their way at least to Corinth quite frequently.

65. See Holmes, *Apostolic Fathers*, 35–36.

66. See citations or allusions in 1 Clem 9:3, 4; 10:1–7; 12:1–7; 17:1; 36:2, 3, 4, 5; 43:1. For an argument against what seems a quite unreasonable skepticism in the case of 1 Clement's use of Hebrews, see Attridge *Hebrews*, 6–7.

67. Alongside Hebrews and a couple other sayings of Jesus (in different form from those found in the Synoptic Gospels), Clement quotes 1 Corinthians and Romans and no other early Christian writings. See Holmes, *Apostolic Fathers*, 37: "It is virtually certain that he used 1 Corinthians, and very likely Romans and Hebrews as well (beyond these, however, no firm conclusions may be drawn regarding the other writings that came to be included in the New Testament." See also Gregory, "1 Clement."

68. Rothschild contends that Clement's use of Hebrews alongside Paul indicates his understanding that Paul wrote Hebrews (Rothschild, *Hebrews as Pseudepigraphon*, 6, 19, 30). Yet while Clement attributes Paul's own letters to him in the letter, Hebrews is used without comment on authorship. Rothschild's is an argument from silence. She cites Charles Anderson approvingly: "'Otherwise we have to suppose that he [the

no other clear allusions to Hebrews exist. These facts suggest, then, that the reason Clement quotes the letter is because he has a copy of it. And he quotes it in a letter to Corinth without comment, very likely because they know of the letter too.

External evidence, then, little as there is, seems to corroborate the judgments we have reached on internal grounds, namely, that Hebrews was originally sent between Rome and Corinth. But will that judgment about 1 Clement, or indeed any other judgments reached in our examination to this point, assist us at all in deciding which was the origin and which the destination? While I acknowledge that perhaps none of the following will be decisive, there may in fact be reason to suspect Rome as the letter's destination. First, while various parts of Hebrews are well-explained by the Corinthian and Roman contexts, there are texts in Hebrews that seem to require a community at least parts of which are tempted to embrace a Jewish way of life. Although some of this might be explained by the fact that at least some of the Corinthians seemed to want to obey Jewish food laws, it seems hard to imagine that the Corinthian church could ever to be tempted to Judaize in the way that the Galatians did.[69] Romans, on the other hand, seems to address a community in which Jewish and gentile Christians are struggling to know how to live together in Christ. Some are tempted to observe dietary regulations (Rom 14:2) and observe Jewish feast days (v. 5), while others are not. Some seem to be convinced that there are significant privileges attached to being Jewish, or even to being circumcised (3:1). While 1 Corinthians does seem to alert us to the presence of Jews in the Corinthian assembly

---

author of 1 Clement] had access to some of Paul's letters—Romans, 1 Corinthians, and perhaps several others—and also to Hebrews as an independent document *known not to be Pauline*, and still chose to make use of the letter in the closest association with authentic Pauline letters' ('The Epistle to the Hebrews and the Pauline Letter Collection,' 435; emphasis original)." Not only is this what I will argue, but I shall attempt to give reasons *internal to the letter* why that should be the case. I am confirmed in these judgments by (a) the implausibility on other grounds of the thesis Rothschild advocates, and (b) the fact that before I discovered her work I had formulated just such a case as she understands to be the only (and unlikely) alternative to her own thesis.

69. So argues Johnson: "Although Acts supports the picture of a strong Jewish community in Corinth and of conflict between the synagogue and Pauline foundation (18:5–17), neither Acts nor 1 Corinthians supports other elements in the rhetorical situations suggested by Hebrews (public humiliation and affliction, imprisonment, expropriation of property, the danger of apostasy) or some of its major themes, above all the sustained *synkrisis* between the sacrifice of Jesus and the Jewish sacrificial system" (Johnson, *Hebrews*, 44).

(1 Cor 1:13; cf. Acts 18:8), in the Roman church it appears that someone was boasting of the relation that the Jews have to God. Thus, it would seem that Hebrews maps a little more easily onto the struggles known to have arisen in Rome. Secondly, the evidence from 1 Clement seems also to corroborate this judgment. In many of its references to Hebrews (17:1; 36:2, 3, 4, 5; 43:1), 1 Clement seems to be directly quoting Hebrews. In other places (9:3-4; 10:1-7; 12:1-7), we see what seem to be Clement's own compositions written heavily under the influence of Hebrews' catalogue of the faithful in chapter 11. It seems, then, that Clement has not only read the letter but has had his way of seeing Christian faith deeply *shaped* by Hebrews. The complexity of Clement's engagement with Hebrews suggests that it has been handed to him as important for his own context. The internal and external considerations, taken together, seem to favor an origin in Corinth and a destination in Rome.

Significant questions remain, however. The tone of Paul's letter to Rome is positively irenic towards Jews and gentiles in the community. While he does counsel the Roman assembly concerning how to live as Jewish and gentile brothers and sisters in Christ, he does not seem to envision the possibility that schism would actually happen. The letter to Hebrews, if written to the same assembly, gives advice in the direst of terms. What happened between Paul's and Apollos' letters to merit such a change in tone? To answer this question, I will proceed (in the next section) to give as full an account as possible of the letter's occasion. Before doing so, it may be helpful to sum up the argument so far. The presence of both Alexandrian/Philonic tradition and Pauline influence in the letter urged a hypothesis of Apollos as the best candidate for the letter's authorship. The hypothesis of Apollan authorship was then tested on various difficult questions in the letter's interpretation. The urgency of the exhortations to unity was mapped onto a particularly Pauline way of understanding the church as Body of Christ, such that fracture of that body was a sin against Jesus himself. The interpretive difficulties surrounding the opposition between grace and "foods" in Heb 13 became intelligible in light of the Pauline trouble with food sacrificed to idols. The exhortation to partake of the "meat" that follows Heb 5 made excellent sense of a Pauline *hapax*. And external evidence corroborated judgments reached so far. The success under wide internal examination of a hypothesis reached on broadly inductive grounds constitutes strong evidence that our hypothesis concerning the origin of Hebrews is correct. The further corroboration of judgments reached on the basis of that hypothesis by external evidence seems only to strengthen the case. It remains to give as full an account as possible of the letter's occasion, in order to elaborate the significance of judgments about authorship on the letter's interpretation.

III. The Purpose of Hebrews

Clement's letter to Corinth within the last years of the first century sets a *terminus ad quem* for the letter's composition. And if the Pauline influence upon Hebrews argued for above is correct, there is reason to suspect that the letter is written after Paul has been martyred.[70] Thus, the late 50s, by earliest estimates for Paul's death, provides a *terminus a quo*. Between them, judgments are difficult to make. Clement's letter suggests a deep familiarity with the letter, and his ad-hoc deployment of its terms and arguments alongside Scriptural exegesis and other arguments may indicate partial or full memorization of Hebrews. It appears the letter has been in the hands of the Roman church for a sizeable interval of time. Moreover, although we cannot be too sure of when Timothy died, his accompanying Paul for so much of Paul's ministry suggests that he was near adult age at least by the 40s.[71] Thus, that he is in traveling shape after an imprisonment implies that Hebrews is written closer to the early side of the window in which it must have been written. Finally, although dating early Christian literature with reference to the destruction of the temple is notoriously difficult, in a letter that dedicates so much time to showing the supremacy of the "true tent" the lack of reference to the destruction of the temple is striking. It seems therefore appropriate to constrict our window to some interval between the late 50s and the destruction of the temple in 70. And at just this point, a rationale for Hebrews begins to suggest itself.

An odd facet of the brotherly love commended in 13:1 is the mandate to care for those in prison.[72] Moule and Ellingworth agree that the author intends by "those in prison" a group of Christians undergoing persecution, and this would seem to follow from the short imperative

---

70. The judgment about a post-martyrdom writing is the result of the fact that a letter bearing the influence of Romans and mentioning Paul's favored associate does not mention Paul at all.

71. Again, here, following a judgment of Douglas Campbell concerning the years in which Paul's ministry commenced.

72. But cf. Voulgaris, "Hebrews," 199–206.

in 13:1 that begins this section.⁷³ But the exhortation to care for those in prison remembers the congregation's own former practice (10:34). Johnson sees the problem as one of temptation, i.e., the hearers do not need to be talked *into* a practice; they need to be talked into maintaining it.⁷⁴ There is a temptation to abandon those with whom they have been in solidarity formerly. But theirs is supposed to be a love that *cannot* be shaken. They have been faithful before. Now, "let brotherly love continue," as if each believer were in the position of the neediest among them. The injunction to remember that one is in one body, that is, explicates another command to remember the imprisoned brothers and sisters as if one were imprisoned alongside them (*syn-dedemenos*).⁷⁵ Similarly, the exhortation not to give up gathering together is paired with reminders of the community's former persistence to gather, even though some were in prison (10:34). In this case, then, the exhortations to unity that have already been examined at length seem to be threatened by the possibility of suffering persecution and imprisonment.

But this reading raises another question. If imprisonment and persecution are the main motivators for some to abandon the assembling of themselves together, how is the extended *synkrisis* that occupies the body of the letter to be accounted for? Here is where an occasional reading of the letter is most helpful. We have roughly dated the letter to a window between the late 50s and the destruction of the temple, that is, during the reign of Nero. Under Nero, J. B. Lightfoot argues that there was a longstanding, strict regulation of assemblies as Imperial security risks. And while Jews had an official exemption as *religio licita*, that exemption was subject to inconsistent enforcement. A letter found in Josephus' *Antiquities*, for example, notes that in Delos under Julius, local leadership had forbidden Jews the right to assemble. A praetor wrote the letter to the magistrates of the Parians, reminding them that "*even in Rome*" [i.e., where one might expect security to be tightest and assembly to be most highly regulated], Jews were not prevented from assembling.⁷⁶ Still,

---

73. Ellingworth, *Hebrews*, 695.

74. Johnson, *Hebrews*, 340.

75. The wordplay here (dede-*menos*) is worth noting for two reasons. First, the root of "remain" in the description of those who are imprisoned is meant, probably, to show just what Apollos means by imploring that brotherly love continue (*menō*). The second reason is that a later suggestion will depend for its plausibility on the fact that Apollos knows how to play with words.

76. Josephus, *Ant.* 14.10.8 § 213–16.

on the basis of reports from Tacitus and Suetonius (whose sources he finds to be reliable at other points), Lightfoot suggests that it is quite possible that "a certain number of Jews, from malice or ignorance on the part of the officers who conducted the persecution, suffered in its earlier stages."[77] But that confusion would soon be cleared up, because the Jews had a powerful advocate at Rome:

> If Nero ruled the world, Poppœa ruled Nero. Her power with the emperor was never so great as it was about the time when these incidents occurred . . . she would certainly have cared to save the Jews. She herself was a proselytess. She had intimate relations with Jews resident in Rome. Through one of these, an actor Aliturus by name, the historian Josephus obtained access to her, apparently in the very year of the fire; and through her intercession with the emperor he secured the release of certain Jewish priests on whose behalf he had undertaken his journey to Rome, while the empress herself loaded him with presents.[78]

There is, then, a plausible external account of a situation in which a stark differentiation between Jewish and gentile Christian identity would tempt Jewish Christians to withdraw from their gentile brothers and sisters. And this situation takes place more or less exactly when our hypothesis would lead us to date the letter. From an Imperial perspective, the Christian assemblies were recognizable and dangerous, and unlike Jewish assemblies they were treated as threats to the emperor. Paul (and apparently Peter) had paid quite a price for their association with the new assemblies. And the temptation to withdrawal of Jews from their gentile brothers would create a situation of real urgency and dire consequence for gentile believers, in that such a withdrawal would make explicit the illegal nature of the Christian assembly. This possibility renders intelligible the urgency with which Hebrews speaks of this abandonment (neglecting so great a salvation, drifting away, and crucifying Jesus afresh) as well as the letter's statement that the Jewish Christians have not yet resisted to the shedding of blood. But they are summoned to risk bloodshed in solidarity with those who have been persecuted, to be imprisoned in the bodies of their brothers and sisters, and to suffer as if in one body with those who suffer. In so doing, they affirm with their lives the surpassing greatness of the new covenant in Christ and share in a table from which

---

77. Lightfoot, *The Apostolic Fathers*, 2.1.10.
78. Lightfoot, *The Apostolic Fathers*, 2.1.11.

those of the Jewish assembly have no right to eat. Hebrews thus affirms a union of Jewish and gentile believers that is more primary and ultimate than the bonds that Jews share with one another.

In light of these proposals, yet one more feature of Hebrews may admit of an explanation. The anonymity of the letter is perhaps the most vexing feature of all. And that vexation may become more acute in light of the fact that while Clement knows the origin of the Pauline letters he has in his possession, he either does not know who sent Hebrews or thinks it was Paul. Clement's ignorance or mistake concerning the letter's author suggests that the letter was anonymous from the beginning. The letter may indeed have arrived at Rome with no name, "without father, without mother, without genealogy," the literary figuration of a Christ presented in exactly this way. This *Christos agenealogētos* is a Christ shorn of his pedigree, a Christ who will pay any price to be "made like his brothers in every way" (2:17). Many critics have treated the letter's anonymity as an unfortunate accident; but perhaps the letter's anonymity is part of the intended effect, part of its summons of the Roman Jewish Christians to join themselves entirely to their gentile brothers and sisters, to refuse the prerogatives of their status as Jews. They are invited to embrace a kind of indistinguishability from their imprisoned brothers and sisters. Timothy is an imprisoned Jew, and the author expects he will soon journey to Rome, as a model of those who suffer for the unity of the body.

Finally, the Pauline imprint upon the letter can likely be explained in quite similar terms. The Roman Christians may not know who wrote the letter. But they can scarcely be uninformed about Paul's fate (cf. 1 Clem 5:5). The Pauline echoes of the letter, then, are meant not to fake Pauline authorship[79] but to recall the apostle to their memories. The anonymous evocation of Paul, like the mention of Timothy, may in fact be part of the presentation as well: a reminder analogous to that found in 10:34, that some Jewish Christians have paid an enormous price for the gospel to the gentiles. Some, that is, have suffered to the point of pouring out their own blood in order to be made like their brothers in every way.[80] And

---

79. Again, I had reached this conclusion prior to discovering Rothschild's work. Even so, I take it that this is the best way to explain the Pauline voice in a letter almost certainly written to people who knew Paul to be dead.

80. It may also be worth recalling that Paul declares his attentions along the very same lines: "Though I am free and belong to no one, I have made myself a slave to everyone, to win as many as possible. To the Jews I became like a Jew, to win the Jews. To those under the law I became like one under the law (though I myself am not under the law), so as to win those under the law. To those not having the law I became like

Hebrews presents Jesus as the pioneer and perfecter of a faith that saves to the uttermost those who come to God through him. Of that gospel, Timothy and Paul are examples to be followed, much like the saints rehearsed in chapter 11. If these suggestions are on the mark, the letter to the Hebrews relates a testimony to the influence of Paul in earliest Christianity, an indication that at least one early Christian remembered Paul as he hoped to be remembered. The remembrance of Paul in Hebrews, then, commends an imitation of his behavior to those who may fear paying the price he did to welcome their imprisoned brothers and sisters into the assembly of God.

IV. Conclusion

Corroborative arguments are devilishly tricky, but this essay has been an exercise in the value of a cumulative case. There are certain features of Hebrews that any exploration of the letter's origin and occasion must answer. I have taken as of primary importance the common scholarly observation of the letter's Alexandrian flavor and the ancient attribution of the letter to Paul. I then suggested Apollos as the most likely candidate to explain both of these features. The hypothesis that Apollos wrote Hebrews was then tested against the rest of the letter, as the traces of spheres of Apollan influence in the NT were allowed to illuminate interpretive difficulties in Hebrews itself. That a hypothesis reached on the basis of the letter's own features also illuminated difficult parts of the letter was reckoned as strong evidence that the hand behind the letter is that of Apollos. That suggestion was then further strengthened by external evidence that linked Hebrews to spheres of likely Apollan influence. The Apollan hypothesis was then developed into a more complete account of the letter's occasion that connected with another piece of external data. Finally, the occasional reading there pursued illuminated a facet of the text that has bedeviled interpreters since antiquity, namely, the rationale for its anonymity and corresponding similarity to Paul's letters. The mixture of direct and corroborative evidence, and the fit between them, displays that this account of the letter's origins is probably accurate and that Hebrews

---

one not having the law (though I am not free from God's law but am under Christ's law), so as to win those not having the law. To the weak I became weak, to win the weak. I have become all things to all people so that by all possible means I might save some. I do all this for the sake of the gospel, that I may share in its blessings" (1 Cor 9:19–23).

testifies to the reception of Paul in the generation immediately after the Apostles (Heb 2:3).

Many questions remain. The successful derivation of an occasion for Hebrews is not the end but the beginning of understanding the letter and its place in the New Testament church. First, there are interesting historical questions yet to be explored. If the hypothesis developed here is correct, for example, how does the apparent reconciliation of Paul and Apollos compare to the irenic account of Pauline and Apollan relations given in 1 Cor 3:5-9, an account of which many scholars have been quite suspicious? Secondly, there are many particularities of Hebrews that I have passed over here in the interest of space. But many of them may be due for a rethink. How, for example, do the spiritual gifts, signs, and wonders mentioned in Heb 2:3 compare to those in 1 Cor 12 and 14? How do Christology and ecclesiology relate? What is the current shape of Jesus' priestly ministry in the one community of Jews and gentiles? How does the judgment that the letter's occasion is an exhortation to maintain ecclesial unity affect the interpretation of texts in Hebrews that seem to point to early Christian practices (e.g., baptism and Eucharist)? Thirdly, there are other background questions that could occupy further research. Hurst makes a convincing case, for example, that the polemic of Stephen against the temple has affinities with Hebrews' demotion of the tabernacle.[81] How will our hypothesis concerning the occasion of Hebrews inform further work on other background questions? Such work may further confirm or challenge the hypothesis explored here, but the strength of the evidence collected here suggests that we can be more confident than many scholars have thought about the origin and occasion of Hebrews. To be sure, Hebrews conceals itself well; in the nature of the case, many of these judgments cannot be decisive. But if the strength of this hypothesis shifts the burden of proof to those who would deny Apollan authorship, this chapter will have done its job.

---

81. Hurst, *Hebrews*, 94-104.

5

"What Is Born of Spirit Is Spirit"
Paul's "Spiritual Body" in Luke and John

Brendan Case

In the ninth of his *Lectures on the Doctrine of Justification*, St. John Henry Newman "comment[s] on several important texts of Scripture," which conspire to show that "our ascended Lord, in ascending, has returned to us invisibly in the attributes of a Spirit."[1] Newman goes on to highlight several important parallels between Christ's "Bread of Life" discourse in John 6 and St. Paul's account of the "spiritual body" in 1 Cor 15:35–50.[2] Newman's interest in this passage is only in the combined

---

1. Newman, *Lectures* 9.3, 209.

2. "The second Man is not merely living, but life-giving; He is a 'quickening or life-giving Spirit;' the very words (be it observed) which our Saviour had used in His discourse at Capernaum. He is life-giving; and what He is, such are His followers; 'as is the Heavenly, such are they that are heavenly.' As Adam diffused death, so the life-giving Spirit is the seed and principle of spiritual bodies to all who are His. 'Flesh and blood,' says the Apostle, 'cannot inherit the kingdom of God;' here, too, is a parallel to our Lord's words, 'The flesh profiteth nothing.' And further, as our Lord referred to His ascension and exaltation, so here again the life-giving Spirit is said to be 'the Lord *from heaven*.' Thus this passage, equally with the foregoing, speaks of our ascended Lord as a Spirit present in His people, and that, apparently, *because* He has ascended" (Newman, *Lectures* 9.5, 212).

authority of these texts, and so he merely juxtaposes them, presupposing, if anything, Paul's awareness of the Johannine material.

In fact, however, John seems not merely to have known, but indeed to have been fascinated with this short Pauline passage: at least four times—in the third, sixth, twelfth, and twentieth chapters of his Gospel—he alludes to it in the course of discussions of Christ's descent from heaven, of the resurrection which transfigures his corruptible flesh into a glorious Spirit-giver, and of the new birth "by water and the Spirit," which assimilates humanity to him. This chapter considers the influence of Paul's treatment of the "spiritual body" in the Gospel of John, along with the decidedly more anxious treatment of it given in the Gospel of Luke.[3]

Luke appears to have regarded Paul's notion of the "spiritual body" with some concern; at any rate, the resurrected Lukan Christ seems to go out of his way to forestall his disciples from interpreting his resurrection along Pauline lines (Luke 24:39). John, by contrast, while every bit as solicitous as Luke to affirm the identity of the crucified Christ with the resurrected Christ (cf. John 20:27), nonetheless seems to have adopted 1 Cor 15:35–50 as a crucial inspiration for one of his key themes, namely Christ's descent into the flesh, making possible the ascent of flesh to spirit.

This early reception of Paul is interesting for several reasons. Luke's apparent willingness to part ways with Paul attests to the fact that robust and committed communion within the earliest church in no way prevented sharp disagreement. Conversely, John's deep interest in this Pauline passage provides additional evidence that the Fourth Evangelist was no isolated sectarian, but was instead firmly embedded in the Mediterranean churches depicted in, e.g., Acts and the epistles of Ignatius of Antioch. And finally, as we'll see below, both Luke and John provide extremely early support for the "compositional" (as opposed to the "instrumental") interpretation of the "spiritual body."

---

3. I'll have little to say in this chapter about the dating, authorship, purpose, or original language of 1 Corinthians, Luke, or John, apart from the view that Luke and John both post-date and depend on 1 Corinthians. There is of course much more that could be said about the dating and authorship of the Gospels in particular (and a good deal about the background of 1 Corinthians can be found in ch. 2 above), but I skirt those discussions here simply to avoid multiplying the issues at play in an already expansive chapter.

"A Life-Giving Spirit": Paul's "*sōma pneumatikon*" in Current Debate

With what sort of body do the dead rise? (1 Cor 15:35) As Joshua Matson has shown ("Anthropological Crisis and Solution," *NTS* 2016), Paul's account of the "*sōma pneumatikon*" is fundamentally exegetical, a meditation on Ezekiel's vision in "Valley of Dry Bones" (37:1–14) of Israel's resurrection by the Spirit from the death of exile. While our present bodies are "*psychikos*," "animate," living by virtue of the soul, the resurrected body is "spiritual"—but in what sense? Does this adjective simply mean that the resurrection is brought about by the Spirit, or does it indicate that those who are resurrected have in some sense become spirit themselves?

Much of the lively and ongoing recent debate about the "*sōma pneumatikon*" has turned on whether Paul means here that the resurrected body is somehow the *instrument of* the Spirit, or is rather *composed of* spirit (or even "the Spirit"). Most commentators have opted for the former position not least because it is clear that, for Paul, not merely bodies, but indeed also anything docile to the Spirit is "*pneumatikon*," whether the Torah (Rom 7:1), charisms (1 Cor 12:1–11), or human judgment (1 Cor 2:15). Indeed, the very contrast between "*psychikon*" and "*pneumatikon*" reaches back to 1 Cor 2:12–15, where "the spiritual man," having *received* the Spirit of God (cf. 2:12),[4] "judges all things" (2:15), whereas, "the psychical man does not receive the things of God's Spirit" (2:14). This explanation satisfies Wright: "The contrast of the *psychikos* person with the *pneumatikos* goes back to an earlier passage in the letter, where both categories of persons are just that, persons, not one category of ordinary people and another of stars in the sky."[5]

Nonetheless, as Wright's own comments suggest, Paul's discussion of the resurrection body in 1 Cor 15 does seem to suggest, not merely docility to the Spirit, but also a particular kind of body which is fitted for that docility. The most energetic contemporary advocate for the view that the resurrection body is, not merely "animated by" the Spirit (an odd idiom anyway, given that Paul is expressly contrasting "animate" [*psychikos*] with "spiritual" bodies), but indeed composed of spirit, is Troels Engberg-Pedersen, for whom Paul's cosmology and anthropology are fundamentally marked by Stoic thought-forms. For Engberg-Pedersen,

---

4. "But we have not received the spirit of the world but the Spirit which is from God, so that we might see the things which have been given to us by God" (1 Cor 2:12).

5. Wright, *Paul and the Faithfulness of God*, 1399.

the whole contrast between an "instrumental" and "compositional" reading of "*pneumatikon*" is ill-conceived, since the former depends, in Paul's thought, on the latter: only what is remade as spirit, and so escapes the corruption and lusts of flesh, can be truly docile to the Spirit.

Engberg-Pedersen's "compositional" reading of *pneuma* relies on the parallelism among a series of contrasts which Paul develops in 1 Cor 15:35–50. First, there is the contrast between the body that is sown unto death and the body that sprouts unto life (15:37), and then between the distinct kinds of body, first divided between the earthly and the heavenly, but then divided further among the various kinds of heavenly bodies, each of which differs in its glory (15:39–41). As Paul continues, we meet new contrasting pairs, most importantly that between the corruptible "*sōma psychikon*" and the incorruptible, glorious "*sōma pneumatikon*" (15:42–44), which Engberg-Pedersen understands as a body *composed* of *pneuma*.[6] There's also the contrast between "the first man, Adam," who "became a living soul (*psychēn zōsan*)," and was "from the earth, earthy," and "the last Adam," who "became a life-giving Spirit (*pneuma zōopoioun*)," and who was "from heaven" (15:45, 47). The last clause is the linchpin for Engberg-Pedersen, as it ties the *pyschikon/pneumatikon* contrast to the prior contrast between earthly and heavenly bodies.[7] Paul's thought shifts from heavenly bodies in 15:41 to pneumatic bodies in 15:42, and then reverses direction, shifting from pneumatic bodies in 15:45 to heavenly bodies in 15:47, because for him, as for the Stoics, the paradigmatically pneumatic bodies are heavenly ones,[8] and it's into this sort of body that the resurrected saints, following Christ, are to be transformed.[9]

Perhaps most importantly of all, Christ himself is said to be, not merely "*pneumatikon*," but a "life-giving *spirit* (*pneuma zōopoioun*)" (1 Cor 15:45). It's striking how little this crucial statement figures in the defense mounted on behalf of the "instrumental reading" of the "*sōma pneumatikon*." After all, the one claim that reading is tailored to rule out—that the resurrected are properly "spirits" rather than merely "spiritual"—appears on the surface of 1 Cor 15:45!

6. Engberg-Pedersen, *Cosmology and the Self*, 30.

7. Cf. also 15:48, where Paul applies the contrast between the two Adams to the rest of humanity.

8. Cf. e.g., Cicero, *De Natura Deorum* 2.15.39, 160); Engberg-Pedersen, *Cosmology and Self*, 20.

9. Engberg-Pedersen, *Cosmology and the Self*, 27–28.

"A Spirit Has Not Flesh and Bones": Luke's Uneasiness about the "Spiritual Body"

In any case, this seems to have been the interpretation of the "spiritual body" which provoked Luke's sense of unease. The Gospel of Luke is also among the earliest Christian texts to receive 1 Cor 15:35–50, and it displays a distinct discomfort with Paul's notion of the resurrected Christ as himself a "life-giving spirit" (cf. esp. Luke 24:39). Before we consider that point of contact, however, it is worth noting that there are a number of affinities between 1 Corinthians and Luke's Passion Narrative. As we discussed in chapter three, Paul's "Institution Narrative" is strikingly "Lukan" (cf. p. 8bove), as is his description of Christ's post-resurrection appearances: only Luke and Paul mention that Christ appeared to Peter before the Twelve as a group (cf. Luke 24:34; 1 Cor 15:5), and only Luke and Paul omit Jesus' earliest resurrection appearance to Mary Magdalene, whether alone (John 20:11–17) or in a group (Matt 28:9).[10]

Now, if, as seems likely, Paul knew something like (an early version of) the Passion Narrative that eventually appeared in Luke (cf. esp. his explicitly flagging this material as traditional in 1 Cor 15:3), it is not hard to imagine how it might have stimulated his reflections on the "spiritual" character of the resurrected body: Jesus seems somehow to elude recognition even by those who know him well (Luke 24:16; cf. John 20:14), and can vanish and appear without warning (Luke 24:31, 36). The general intimacy between 1 Cor 15 and Luke's account of Christ's resurrection makes the discord between 1 Cor 15 and Luke 24 all the more striking. When Jesus suddenly appears in the midst of the gathered Eleven, they "became afraid and thought they were seeing a spirit (*pneuma*)" (Luke 24:37). His reassurances echo 1 Cor 15:45, 50: "See my hands and my feet; it is I. Touch me and see that a spirit (*pneuma*) does not have flesh (*sarka*) and bones, as you see that I have" (Luke 24:39).[11]

---

10. One detail included in Paul's account but absent from Luke (as from the other canonical Gospels) is Christ's appearance to James (1 Cor 15:5). Interestingly, Jerome mentions that *The Gospel of the Hebrews* also narrated a post-resurrection appearance of Christ to James (*Vir. Ill.* 2, quoted in Edwards, *The Hebrew Gospel*, 280). Even this story, however, might have some distant connection to Luke: Edwards speculates, on the basis of some lexical and thematic overlaps, that it "may be related to Jesus' appearance to Cleopas and a fellow disciple on the way to Emmaus in Luke 24:13–27" (*The Hebrew Gospel*, 81).

11. Paula Fredriksen flags the tension between these passages, though without making any definite claim regarding literary dependence: "What did [the apostles]

How can we best explain the disciples' concern that Jesus might be a "spirit," and Jesus' own protests that he *cannot* be a spirit, since he still has "flesh and bones"? In the broader context of the Gospel, "*pneuma*" does not, of course, only refer to the Holy Spirit, but equally often to "unclean spirits" (cf. Luke 4:36; 6:18; 7:21; 8:2), with whom Jesus is at war throughout his ministry. Perhaps more relevant still is Luke's remark that, when Jesus raised the synagogue ruler's daughter, "her spirit turned back to her" (8:55), a usage which perhaps trades on analogous anthropological presuppositions to those implied in Paul's division of the human person among "the spirit and the soul and the body" (1 Thess 5:22).[12] In context, the point of Jesus' comment seems to be that he is not a shade, a leftover fragment of a human being, but rather the same human person who had been crucified (what purpose could his gesture toward his feet serve (cf. Luke 24:39), except to point out his nail wounds?),[13] capable of being touched, and indeed even of eating some broiled fish and honeycomb (Luke 24:42).

Nonetheless, 1 Cor 15:45 and 50 certainly suggest that the "Lukan" traditions about Christ's resurrection appearances which Paul summarizes in 1 Cor 15:5 did not include Christ's simultaneous denial that he was a spirit and affirmation of his fleshliness—at the very least, it seems unlikely that the Apostle would have contradicted a dominical word so directly. And indeed, we find some striking evidence for the secondary character of the wording of Luke 24:39 in Ignatius of Antioch's *Epistle to the Smyrneans*, written to combat those who denied the full humanity of Christ. Ignatius insists,

> I know that after [Christ's] resurrection also he was still possessed of flesh, and I believe that he is so now. When, for instance, he came to those who were with Peter, he said to them, "Lay hold, handle me, and see that I am not a bodiless demon

---

see? Christ in a spiritual body, Paul insists, and definitely *not* in a body of flesh and blood (1 Cor 15.44, 50). Christ in a flesh-and-blood body, some later evangelists insist no less strongly (Lk 24.39–40; Jn 20.27)" (Fredriksen, *Paul*, 4). As we will see below, Fredriksen is right to see John as sharing Luke's concerns for the continuity of Christ's natal and resurrected flesh, but wrong to see him as a critic of Paul's "spiritual body."

12. Irenaeus draws on this Pauline passage, which he takes to indicate that flesh, as much as spirit and soul, is essential to human nature, in countering the Valentinian interpretation of 1 Cor 15:50 as teaching that all flesh is left behind in the resurrection (cf. Irenaeus, *Adv. Haer.* 5.9.1).

13. Many thanks to the Rev. Brandon Walsh for pointing this out to me in a fine sermon on Luke's resurrection appearances.

(*daimonion asomaton*). And immediately they touched him, and believed, being convinced both by his flesh and blood (*sarx kai haima*)." For this cause also they despised death, and were found its conquerors. And after his resurrection He ate and drank with them, as being possessed of flesh, although spiritually He was united to the Father.[14]

Ignatius here is recognizably describing the scene narrated in Luke 24:38–41, but in terms that are slightly but significantly different from canonical Luke. Particularly important here is Jesus' claim, "See that I am not a bodiless demon," or "incorporeal divinity." Jerome later identified this passage as a quotation from a text called *The Gospel of the Hebrews*, which he identified as having been written in Hebrew (or perhaps Aramaic) by the apostle Matthew.[15]

I won't here enter into the complex debate over the relation between *The Gospel of the Hebrews* and the canonical Gospels, except to observe that Ignatius provides clear evidence that an alternative version of Luke 24:39 was in circulation in the early second century, one which, while agreeing in substance with the canonical formulation, strikingly differed in its wording in such a way that Paul himself very likely would have endorsed it as well: after all, 1 Cor 15:35–50 was written to maintain that the resurrected Christ was precisely a *corporeal* spirit. And if the phrasing—if not the substance[16]—of Jesus' words in Luke 24:39 is a secondary addition to the tradition, then it seems hard to avoid the conclusion that it was crafted in part to address Luke's concerns over Paul's understanding of the resurrected Christ as a "*pneuma zōopoioun*" (1 Cor 15:44).

We should, nonetheless, consider an important objection to reading Luke 24:39 as in opposition to 1 Cor 15:45, 50. This is the fact that, in Paul's appearance before the Sanhedrin in Acts, the sequel to the Gospel of Luke, we find the narrator explaining that "the Sadducees say that

---

14. Ignatius, *Ep. Smyr.* 3.1-3, in Holmes, *The Apostolic Fathers*.

15. Jerome, *Vir. Ill.* 16, quoted in Edwards, *The Hebrew Gospel*, 45–46, 281.

16. In my view, it's generally a mistake to go looking in (or behind) the Gospels for the *ipsissima verba* of Jesus, not least because the Evangelists themselves seem not to have troubled themselves about minor variations among reports of Jesus' sayings. (And of course there's no reason that Jesus couldn't actually have uttered both versions of, e.g., the Beatitudes, at different points in his ministry!) Rather, it makes more sense to see the Gospels as attempting to reproduce what Pitre has called Jesus' "the substance of Jesus' words (*substantia verba* [sic] *Jesu*)," albeit shaped in indefinitely many ways by the experiences and debates which intervened between the ascension and the composition of the Gospels (Pitre, *Jesus and the Last Supper*, 47).

there is no resurrection, neither a spirit nor an angel (*mēte angelon mēte pneuma*)" (23:8). This verse has often been translated as simply offering a list of three disconnected things in which the Sadducees disbelieved: "the Sadducees say that there is no resurrection, nor angel, nor spirit" (23:8 RSV). On this reading, no special connection is drawn here between the resurrection and spiritual or angelic modes of existence.

However, as David Bentley Hart has pointed out, the idea that a sect of first-century Jews denied the existence of angels outright is hard to swallow, while "it seems natural to read the more typical formula of '*mēte . . . mēte . . .*' as forming a couplet distinct from the subject of the immediately preceding *mē . . .* as an elucidation thereof."[17] That is, "resurrection" here seems to be clarified by appeal to the concepts of "spirit" and "angel"; the Sadducees deny "both" modes of resurrection. The sentence is somewhat gnomic (indeed, in Acts 19:16, Luke seems to use "*ta amphotera*" to mean "all" rather than "both"), and no further interpretation is given in context. Nonetheless, it is at least plausible to see it as presupposing an interpretation of the resurrection body as a kind of celestial spirit, in broad continuity with 1 Cor 15:35–50.

Can we resolve the apparent conflict between Acts 23:8 and Luke 24:39? One possibility is that it is an effect of the editorial seam dividing a section of the "we-source" (Acts 20:5—21:26) from Acts 21:27—27:1, a purely third-person account of Paul's arrest, imprisonment, and trials in Judea, which gives way once again to the we-source beginning with Paul's sea voyage to Rome (27:1). The ultimate source of Acts 21:26—27:1 is very likely Paul himself, and so convergences between its theology of the resurrection and that of 1 Cor 15 are no great surprise. The canonical revision of Luke 24:39, by contrast, perhaps more clearly reflects Luke's own theological concerns.

And to be honest, those concerns are understandable. After all, as Irenaeus complained, "all the heretics always introduce this passage" in justifying their rejection of bodily resurrection as such.[18] *The Treatise on the Resurrection*, which survives only in a Coptic version recovered at Nag Hammadi, represents the "Valentinian" position that the general resurrection has already occurred,[19] and appeals to 1 Cor 15:35–50 in

---

17. Hart, *The New Testament*, 401.
18. Irenaeus, *Adv. Haer.* 5.9.1–4; 5.13.1–2, quoted in Pagels, *The Gnostic Paul*, 85.
19. "Therefore, do not think in part, O Rheginos, nor live in conformity with this flesh for the sake of unanimity, but flee from the divisions and the fetters, and already you have the resurrection. For if he who will die knows about himself that he will

defense of this view: "This is the spiritual resurrection (*tanastasis enpneuma*), which swallows up the psychic (*ent-psychikē*) in the same way as the fleshly (*tke-sarkikē*)."[20]

As Elaine Pagels summarizes their views, "the Valentinians claim that Paul shows that the 'first Adam' must put off the material bodies which bear the 'choic image,' and be transformed. They insist that Paul states this clearly in 15:50 when he declares that 'flesh and blood cannot inherit the kingdom of God, nor can corruption inherit incorruption.' They consider this decisive evidence against the church's claim of bodily resurrection—resurrection 'in this flesh,' as Tertullian says."[21] Indeed, Peter might well have had this verse in mind as one of those "things which are hard to understand" in Paul's epistles, "which the unlearned and stiffnecked distort, like the rest of the Scriptures, to their own destruction" (2 Pet 3:16).

John's Spiritual Bodies: 1 Cor 15:35–50 in the Fourth Gospel

If the Gospel of Luke betrays a certain anxiety over Paul's talk of a "spiritual body," the Gospel of John indicates a pervasive, if subtle, enthusiasm for it. Indeed, despite the scant attention paid by commentators at least since Bultmann to the possibility of literary dependence between Paul and John,[22] 1 Cor 15:35–50 plays a fundamental role in shaping at least two and perhaps four seminal passages in the Gospel: certainly the promise of a "new birth" in John 3 and the "Bread of Life" discourse in John 6, and arguably also the "dying seed" in John 12:24, and the new Adam

---

die—even if he spends many years in this life, he is brought to this—why not consider yourself as risen and (already) brought to this? If you have the resurrection but continue as if you are to die—and yet that one knows that he has died—why, then, do I ignore your lack of exercise?" (Robinson, *Coptic Gnostic Library* 1,4: 49.9–30). For the treatise's Valentinian milieu, cf. Malcolm L. Peel, "The Treatise on the Resurrection." Peel compares this view to the position condemned in "Alexander and Hymenaeus" at 2 Tim 2:17.

20. Robinson, *Coptic Gnostic Library* 1,4: 45.39—46.2.
21. Pagels, *The Gnostic Paul*, 85.
22. "It is clear: John does not belong in the Pauline school and is not influenced by Paul, but rather is an original form and stands in another atmosphere of theological thinking (Es ist klar: Johannes gehört nicht in die paulinische Schule und ist durch Paulus nicht beeinflußt, sondern er ist eine originale Gestalt und steht in einer anderen Atmosphäre theologischen Denkens)" (Bultmann, *Theologie des Neues Testaments*, 9, quoted in Hoegen-Rohls, "Johanneische Theologie," 593.

typology in John 19:41; 20:15, 22. A subterranean Pauline stream runs throughout the Gospel, periodically surfacing in Johannine springs, welling up to eternal life.

Exegetical attention to John's relation to Paul has been scant, but not total; Troels Engberg-Pedersen in particular devotes a brief section to it in his recent study of John, and concludes that John drew on Paul in developing his understanding of "believing in Jesus Christ, receiving the *pneuma* in baptism, being 'in' Christ, and living a life of mutual love (and then also being resurrected by the *pneuma* into eternal life together with Christ)."[23] Engberg-Pedersen cites a number of Pauline passages as possible influences on John (e.g., Rom 8:10; 1 Cor 6:9; 2 Cor 3:17; Gal 4:23, 29). Curiously, he does not consider the possible influence of one of his favorite Pauline passages, which, as we'll see below, was also crucial for John, i.e., 1 Cor 15:35–50.

Engberg-Pedersen is right to see some relation of dependence between Paul and John for these ideas—but why assume that John is borrowing from Paul, rather than Paul drawing on Johannine dominical traditions? As we'll see, the dispersion and variety of the echoes of 1 Cor 15:35–50 in John are the fundamental reason for seeing Paul as influencing John rather than vice versa. The former explanation is more parsimonious: it's more likely that John's interest in this short Pauline passage (a mere fifteen verses) explains its literary echoes throughout the Gospel than that Paul knew and collated at least four Johannine traditions which, in their eventual literary setting, are widely separated. And (as I noted above17), the fact that Jesus' wording in John is influenced by later developments is not, in itself, a reason not to take John to be a faithful witness to the *substance* of Jesus' teaching and ministry.

---

23. Engberg-Pedersen, *John and Philosophy*, 324. As Hoegen-Rohls notes, prior to Bultmann, much German scholarship influenced by F. C. Baur similarly took it "that John took the Pauline thought-world as his premise (daß Johannes die paulinische Gedankenwelt zur Prämisse habe)," or that "Pauline thought" played a "catalytic function for Johannine theology (paulinische Denken ... katalysatorische Funktion ... für die johanneischen Theologie)" (Hoegen-Rohls, "Johanneische Theologie," 598, 599). As Julius Wellhausen put it, "John stands upon Paul (Johannes fußt auf Paulus)" (*Das Evangelium Johannis*, 721, quoted in Hoegen-Rohls, "Johanneische Theologie," 599).

Born of Water and Spirit

The first place in John where echoes of 1 Cor 15:35–50 begin to sound is Jesus' nighttime conversation with Nicodemus about the necessity, for entering "the kingdom of God," of being "born again" or "born from above" (John 3:3), which Jesus then glosses as being born "of water and of the Spirit." Now this slogan seems, on its face, to be a shorthand reference to a pair of passages which we'll call "Ezekiel's Diptych" (Ezek 36:22—37:14), both concerning the LORD's redemption of Israel from her bondage in exile. In Ezek 36:22-26, the LORD depicts this saving action both in terms of washing and in terms of the Spirit's indwelling:

> I will take you from among the heathen, and gather you out of all countries, and will bring you into your own land. Then will I sprinkle clean water upon you, and ye shall be clean: from all your filthiness, and from all your idols, will I cleanse you. A new heart also will I give you, and a new spirit will I put within you: and I will take away the stony heart out of your flesh, and I will give you an heart of flesh.

Then, in Ezek 37:1-14, we hear of the LORD's resurrection of exiled Israel from their graves by the power of the Spirit: "I will open your graves, and cause you to come up out of your graves, and bring you into the land of Israel. . . . And shall put my spirit in you, and ye shall live, and I shall place you in your own land: then shall ye know that I the LORD have spoken *it*, and performed *it*, saith the LORD" (37:12, 14). Israel will be reborn by water and the Spirit, that is, by baptism and by the Spirit's indwelling.[24]

Now, as Joshua Matson has recently shown, Paul's account of the "*sōma pneumatikon*" is also fundamentally a meditation on Ezekiel's vision in "Valley of Dry Bones" (37:1-14) of Israel's resurrection by the Spirit from the death of exile.[25] Given that Paul has already primed his readers to expect a scriptural framework for the resurrection of the dead ("according to the Scriptures," 1 Cor 15:4; cf. also 15:54), and given his deep and repeated engagement with Ezek 37 elsewhere in his letters,[26]

---

24. Cf. Brown, *The Gospel according to John*, 140.
25. Matson, "Anthropological Crisis and Solution," 533-48.
26. Cf. esp. 1 Thess 4:8 (Ezek 37:6), 2 Cor 3:6 (Ezek 37:5), and Rom 8:2, 10 (Ezek 37:5). On 1 Thessalonians, cf. Rudolf Hoppe: "Particularly close is the statement of Ezek 36:27, 37:14, 37:28, where the Spirit of the LORD equips the people for obedience and reconstitutes it (Besonders nahe kommt der Aussage Ez 36,27; 37,14; 37,28, wo

it would be no great surprise if a text such as Ezek 37:1–14 formed the subtext for 1 Cor 15:35–49.²⁷

And indeed, the link between these passages is straightforward: Ezek 37:1–14 is the Old Testament text which most clearly links resurrection—here employed as a figure for the LORD's bringing Israel out of the death of exile (Ezek 37:12–14)—to the Spirit, whom God sends to revive the reconstituted corpses: "I will put my Spirit within you and you will live (*dōsō pneuma moue is humas kai zēsesthe*)" (Ezek 37:6, with similar formulations at 37:10, 14). Moreover, Ezekiel figures resurrection as a new creation, by echoing the creation of humanity in Gen 2 (cf. Gen 2:7; Ezek 37:5).²⁸ It's no surprise that when Paul describes the resurrected body, the paradigmatic new creation (cf. Rom 8:19–23), he chooses "*pneumatikos*" as a summary term for the human being as revived and transformed by the divine Spirit.

Of course, Paul's most explicit engagement with the Old Testament in this section of 1 Cor 15 is with Gen 2:7 (1 Cor 15:45), but this is equally one of the verses in which the influence of Ezek 37 in this chapter is clearest. Paul in fact seems to be reading Gen 2 through Ezek 37. (The noisy echo of Gen 2:7 (LXX) in Ezek 37:5 (LXX) perhaps creates some exegetical pressure in that direction quite apart from Paul's own interests: the re-creation of Israel from her death in exile naturally draws upon

---

der Geist JHWHs das Volk zum Gehorsam befähigt und neu konstituiert)" (Hoppe, *Der Erste Thessalonikerbrief*, 244). Cf. also Shogren, *1 and 2 Thessalonians*, 167; Green, *The Letters to the Thessalonians*, 200–201; Marshall, *1 and 2 Thessalonians*, 114–15. For Paul's allusive use of Ezek 36–37 in 2 Cor 3, cf. esp. Hays, *Echoes of Scripture in the Letters of Paul*, 122–53. And on Rom 8, notwithstanding Gordon Fee's arguments to the contrary (*God's Empowering Presence*, 553), cf. esp. Cranfield: "In the OT Ezek. 37.14 is of course relevant, and relevant also is the Rabbinic teaching derived from it, e.g., *Exod. R.* 48 (102d): 'In this world my Spirit has given wisdom within you, but in the future my Spirit will make you alive again'" (Cranfield, *Epistle to the Romans*, 392n2). Schreiner as well: "Fee's (1994: 553) contention that the Spirit is not elsewhere the agent of the resurrection is unpersuasive, for Ezek. 37 conveys this very idea, and verse 10 probably teaches that the resurrection is due to the Spirit" (Schreiner, *Romans*, 417). And finally, Wright's comment: "The echoes of Ezekiel 37 in Romans 8:9–11 . . . make clear what this is about: resurrection indicates covenant restoration and renewal" (Wright, *Paul and the Faithfulness of God*, 720).

27. "Ezekiel 37 is perhaps the most famous of all 'resurrection' passages in the Old Testament" (Wright, *The Resurrection of the Son of God*, 102).

28. Another text that connects resurrection to the gift of the Spirit and to re-creation is 2 Macc 7:23: "Therefore the Creator of the world, who shaped the beginning of man and devised the origin of all things, will in his mercy give (*apodidōsin*) life and breath (*to pneuma*) back to you again."

the original creation of humanity in Genesis.)[29] Fee proposes that Paul, in 1 Cor 15:45-49, offers "a kind of midrashic interpretation of Gen. 2:7 in light of the resurrection of Christ."[30] That's true, but incomplete, for, as is common in midrash, Paul here reads Genesis in concert with another, related text, namely Ezek 37.[31] Indeed, it seems at least possible that Paul's "it is written" encompasses both Gen 2:7 ("living soul") and Ezek 37 ("life-giving Spirit") at once.)

Paul develops a contrast in this passage between the "psychical body" of the first Adam, and the "spiritual body" of the last Adam. As a warrant for the first claim, Paul quotes from Gen 2:7, where "God . . . breathed (*enephusēsen*) into his face the breath of life (*pnoēn zōēs*) and, the man became a living soul" (1 Cor 15:45). Adam is a "*psychē*," and so possesses a "psychical body (*sōma psychikon*)." But if Gen 2 is all that Paul has in view in 1 Cor 15:45-46, then two things are still puzzling:

First, since the "breath of life" (which Fee, for instance, proposes as the basis for Paul's saying of the second Adam, "he became a life-giving Spirit")[32] is both logically and temporally prior to the "living soul," why does Paul immediately insist that the "psychical" comes first, and then the "spiritual"? (1 Cor 15:46) Indeed, Gen 1-2, on its face, lends itself more readily to Philo's figural reading, according to which bodily creatures (represented by the "living soul" of Gen 2:7) are modelled after a prior creation, which is "heavenly (*ouranios*)" and "according to the image of God" (*kat' eikona theou*; cf. Gen 1:26).[33]

Paul is clearly reading Gen 2:7 in a way quite different from (if not contradictory to) Philo, and he might be marshalling that reading to contradict the Corinthians' overly "realized" eschatology.[34] Nonetheless, neither of those observations clarifies his exegetical *warrant* for claiming

---

29. Cf. the "*pneuma zōēs*" in Ezek 37:5 with the "*pnoēn zōēs*" in Gen 2:7.

30. Fee, *First Epistle to the Corinthians*, 788.

31. For a parallel case in the New Testament, cf. Daniel Boyarin's reading of John 1:1-18 as a midrash on Gen 1, read in concert with Prov 8 (Boyarin, "Gospel of the Memra," 243-84).

32. Fee, *First Epistle to the Corinthians*, 788-89.

33. Cf. Thiselton, *First Epistle to the Corinthians*, 1283. Cf. Philo, *Leg.* 1.12.

34. Cf. Fee: "Against the Corinthians, who assumed that they had already entered into the totality of pneumatic existence while they were still in their *psychikos* body, Paul insists that the latter comes 'first,' that is, that they must reckon with the physical side of their present life in the Spirit" (Fee, *First Epistle to the Corinthians*, 791). Cf. also Sampley, *First Letter to the Corinthians*, 988; Thiselton, *First Epistle to the Corinthians*, 1284; Hays, *First Corinthians*, 273.

that "psychical" precedes "spiritual." However, his reasoning comes into focus if we imagine him as interpreting the state of the "last Adam" principally through Ezek 37's revision of Gen 2: in Ezekiel, Israel is "dead" in exile, already east of Eden, but God promises, "I will bring into you the Spirit of life" (Ezek 37:5). (The key phrase in this verse is also verbally closer to Paul's "life-giving Spirit" (1 Cor 15:45) than is Gen 2:7.[35] And, as we saw above137n27), Ezek 37:5 is also likely a source for Paul's Spirit-talk in Rom 8:2.) It's only in the re-creation envisioned by Ezekiel that the "Spirit of life" enters and transforms humanity; the "spiritual body" is last because it's the result of the Spirit's action at the end of all things.

And second, Gen 2 alone doesn't explain why it is only at the *resurrection* that the second Adam becomes "spiritual." Just before his discussion of Gen 2:7, Paul writes, "It is sown a psychical body, it is raised a spiritual body; if there is a psychical body, there is also a spiritual one" (1 Cor 15:44), and it seems clear that he intends this same logic to apply in the following verse ("thus also"). Gen 2:7 doesn't include any indications of either death or resurrection, for the obvious reason that death is still in Adam's future. But if Ezek 37 is on Paul's mind as a kind of post-lapsum recapitulation of the creation narrative from Gen 2, then Paul's reasoning is clear and cogent: only once humanity has suffered the exile of sin and death does God send his Spirit upon them, to raise them to new life.

John and Paul not only have a shared interest in the resurrection as figured by Ezek 37, but John 3 is also rife with more specific echoes of Paul's treatment of the resurrection body. For instance, Jesus says, "Truly, truly, I say to you, unless one is born of water and the Spirit (*pneumatos*), he cannot enter the kingdom of God (*ou dunatai eiselthein eis tēn basileian tou theou*). That which is born of the flesh is flesh (*sarx*), and that which is born of the Spirit is spirit (*pneuma*)" (3:5–6). This is strikingly similar to Paul's declaration, "The spiritual is not first but the psychical, and then the spiritual," for "flesh and blood cannot inherit the kingdom of God (*sarx kai haima basileian theou klēronomēsai ou dunatai*)" (1 Cor 15:46, 15:50). If John is in fact thinking about 1 Cor 15 in this passage, that has

---

35. Andreas Lindemann (*Erste Korintherbrief*, 361) notes, as another possible parallel, Wis 15:11: "they failed to know the one who formed them and inspired (*empneusanta*) them with active souls (*psychēn*) and breathed a living spirit (*pneuma zōtikon*) into them." This verse shares Paul's re-ordering of the creation account, so that "spirit" follows "soul," but, unlike Ezek 37, it doesn't re-read Gen 2 in connection with resurrection from the dead as God's action to save his elect.

the interesting consequence that the only two occurrences of "kingdom of God" in the Gospel of John (cf. 3:3, 5) are under the influence, not of the Synoptic Gospels, but rather of Paul!

And the volume of this echo is amplified two others a few verses later: Paul writes that there are "both heavenly (*epourania*) bodies and earthly (*epigeia*) bodies," the former of which, though largely unknown to us, somehow mysteriously anticipate or reflect humanity's true destiny (1 Cor 15:40); similarly, Jesus tells Nicodemus, "If I speak earthly things (*epigeia*) to you and you do not believe, how will you believe if I speak heavenly things (*epourania*) to you?" (John 3:12). Likewise, Paul describes Jesus as "the second man [who is] from heaven (*ex ouranou*)" (1 Cor 15:47); Jesus declares "no one has ascended into heaven except the one who descended from heaven (*ex ouranou*), the Son of Man" (John 3:13).

For John, as for Paul, impotent flesh must give way to the Spirit if we are to enter the kingdom of God, and this metabolism of flesh by Spirit somehow occurs in and through the "descent" of the heavenly man, Jesus. Importantly, John's appropriation of 1 Corinthians here braids together both the "instrumental" and "compositional" aspects of Paul's "spiritual body": what is born *by means of* the Spirit *is itself* Spirit (John 3:6).

The Man from Heaven

A second allusion to Paul's account of the resurrection arguably appears in Jesus' "Bread of Life" discourse in the Capernaum synagogue (John 6:22–71). After crowds come to Capernaum to ask Jesus for an encore of the Feeding of the five thousand, which they liken to "the bread of heaven" given by Moses (6:31–32), he scandalizes them by telling them that he himself is "the bread of life" (6:35), the "bread descending out of heaven" (6:51), and that they must even "eat [his] flesh" and "drink [his] blood" (6:53).

That these commands are expressly Eucharistic becomes clear if we look back to the beginning of the story, the miraculous feeding itself from the first twelve or so verses of John 6, which John shares with the Synoptic tradition. John subtly alters the Synoptic (likely Markan)[36] account of this

---

36. John and Mark share a reference to two hundred denarii (Mark 6:37; John 6:7) which is absent from Luke and Matthew; for John's knowledge of Mark more generally, cf. Bauckham, "John for Readers of Mark," in *Gospels for All Christians*). I should emphasize, however, that this need not mean relegating John to a series of theological glosses on the Synoptics—as Bauckham himself has emphasized, there is

story to assimilate it to the Synoptic Institution narratives: he exchanges the Synoptic *eulogesō* for *eucharisteō* (so moving it toward at least the Lukan-Pauline "institution narrative," cf. Luke 22:17, or 1 Cor 11:24) and *airō* for *sunagō* (a term that, at least by the early second century, had acquired a technical relation to eucharistic gatherings; cf. Didache 9:4; Ignatius, *Ep. Poly.* 4:2; 1 Clem 34:7).

Further, John alone notes that the miracle occurs "near Passover" (6:4), with its immediate association to the Last Supper and Jesus' Passion. Finally, John makes this act the occasion for a debate about eating Jesus' flesh and his blood: Ignatius, in the *Ep. Phil.* 4 employs the paired "*sarx/haima*" to describe the Eucharist (see also Ignatius's *Ep. Smyr.* 6:2); and the near parallel of *sōma* and *haima* of course occurs in the Institution narratives. These parallels account for the paired appearance of "flesh and blood" more fully than the does the manna tradition alone. These textual indicators strongly suggest that we should read this passage as a commentary of sorts on Eucharistic practice, one that, in its use of the manna traditions, recalls the imperfect hints of the Church's practice (and contemporary failures) in the wilderness wanderings, and that, in its use of Ezek 37 (see below), proleptically points to the eschatological feast of heaven.

Surprisingly, however, when challenged by the disciples to explain this teaching, Jesus offers a clarification which has seemed to many to be a contradiction: "The Spirit is the life-giver (*to pneuma estin to zōopoioun*); the flesh profits nothing. The words which I have spoken to you are spirit and life" (John 6:63). Interpreters at least since Zwingli have seen here a decisive rejection of "Eucharistic" reading of the foregoing, in favor of a command to feast on Jesus by feasting on his words.[37] (The triumph of the Liturgy of the Word over that of the Table!) And some modern interpreters, beginning with Bultmann, have argued that the tension within

---

abundant evidence that John in fact provides the comprehensive chronological framework within which the Synoptic evidence ought to be fitted, rather than vice versa (cf. Bauckham, *Jesus and the Eyewitnesses*; Bauckham, *The Testimony of the Beloved Disciple*; cf. also Robinson, *The Priority of John*). Some cases of apparent contradiction between John and the Synoptics are in fact scholarly chimeras—the best instance is doubtless the date of the Last Supper, about which there is a long running debate over whether John or the Synoptics have it right. As Pitre shows, however, John, properly interpreted, in fact reflects the same chronology of the Passion week as do the Synoptics (Pitre, "The Date of the Last Supper," in *Jesus and the Last Supper*, 251–373).

37. Cf. Zwingli, *Commentary on True and False Religion*, 208–9.

the passage runs along a poorly-hid editorial seam, disclosing John's contradictory and shambolically-reconciled sources.

The coherence a unified "Eucharistic" reading of this passage is only saved if, as Brant Pitre emphasizes, we once again see how Ezek 37 forms the subtext for Jesus' words: "The number of parallels between Ezekiel's vision [in Ezek 37:1–14] and the response of Jesus to the disciples is striking. . . . Just as Jesus declares that it is the spirit that gives life, so too in Ezekiel it is 'the spirit' (*ruach*) that makes the dead 'live' (*chayah*) in the bodily resurrection (Ezek. 37:1–6)."[38] Indeed, Ezek 37 is doubtless already in the background of Jesus' earlier comment that, "The one who eats my flesh and drinks my blood has eternal life, and I will raise him up on the last day" (John 6:54)—the one who partakes of the Eucharistic flesh and blood will be raised up, because Jesus' ascended "flesh" is itself the bearer of the life-giving Spirit.

Pitre is doubtless right to emphasize the importance of Ezekiel in the Bread of Life discourse, but stronger still are the echoes in John 6 of Paul's own appropriations of Ezek 37. "The Spirit is the life-giver (*to pneuma estin to zōopoioun*)," Jesus declares; "the flesh profits nothing" (John 6:63): in background here are perhaps both 1 Cor 15:45 ("the last Adam [became] a life-giving Spirit (*pneuma zōopoioun*)") and 2 Cor 3:6 ("the letter kills, but the Spirit gives life (*to pneuma zōopoiei*)").nd a further echo appears still earlier, in John's repetition of the trope (which appeared already in John 3) of Jesus as the "man from heaven," now likened to the heavenly manna (cf. Exod 16:4): "I am the living bread which comes down from heaven (*ek tou ouranou*)" (John 6:50a). Outside of John, this idea—of Christ as "from heaven"—appears only in 1 Cor 15:47. While Pitre is right to see Jesus' predictions of his impending *ascent* to heaven (cf. John 6:62) as allusions to Dan 7:13–14, where "one of like a Son of Man" comes on the clouds into the presence of the Ancient of Days, that passage doesn't itself account for Christ's *descent* as straightforwardly as does 1 Corinthians.

Particularly once we see it against the backdrop of 1 Cor 15:35–50, the "Institution Narrative" of John 6 begins to look like an extended meditation on the purpose of the Incarnation as a bid to infuse dying flesh with the life-giving Spirit, so as to transform the former into the latter. Jesus is the man from heaven, whose resurrection transforms his flesh to be a life-giving Spirit; John 6 specifies that it is precisely the Eucharist,

---

38. Pitre, *Jesus and the Last Supper*, 218.

where this flesh is given to us, in which and by which the Spirit carries out this strange metabolism. As Augustine puts it in *Confessions*: "I heard this voice of Yours from on high: *I am the food of strong men; grow, and you shall feed upon me; nor shall you convert me, like the food of your flesh, into you, but you shall be converted into me.*"[39]

The Dying Seed and the New Adam

The most decisive and evident influences of 1 Cor 15:35–50 in John appear in chapters 3 and 6. However, two other Johannine passages arguably betray the influence of Paul's discourse on the "spiritual body." The first is the strange account of Philip's being approached by "some Hellenes from among those who ascended to worship at the feast," who ask to see Jesus (John 12:20–21). We never actually find out what happened to these eager pilgrims, who play no further role in the Gospel.

Presented with their request, however, Jesus darkly replies, "Truly, truly, I say to you, unless a grain of wheat (*ean mē ho kokkos tou sitou*) falls into the earth and dies (*apothanē*), it remains alone; but if it dies, it bears much fruit" (John 12:24). The likening of human death-and-resurrection to a seed's "dying" and "rising" finds a close parallel in Paul's declaration, at the opening of his discussion of the resurrection body, "You fool! What you sow does not come to life unless it dies (*ean mē apothanē*). And what you sow is not the body which is to be, but a bare kernel (*kokkon*), perhaps of wheat (*sitou*) or of some other grain" (1 Cor 15:36–37).[40]

Further, John's account of Christ's resurrection develops, in narrative form, the same "new Adam" typology which Paul deploys in 1 Cor 15:21–22, 45–49. Jesus is buried in a "garden" (John 19:41), and raised on the first day of the week (20:1), on which creation began. Mary mistakes Jesus for "the gardener" (20:15)—but of course, he *is* the gardener, the new Adam, raised in a new Eden on the first day of a new creation. (A "new Adam" typology is also no doubt present in the Synoptic accounts of Christ's temptation,[41] but only John and Paul link the new Adam typology to resurrection in this way.)

39. Augustine, *Confessions* 7.10.16.

40. Brown acknowledges the close parallels between Paul and John in these verses, but rejects the possibility of literary influence without argument (Brown, *The Gospel according to John*, 473).

41. Cf. Joel Marcus notes the parallel between Mark's temptation narrative and "a Jewish legend [which] depicts 'ministering angels' (*ml'ky hsrt*) preparing food and

A further apparently Pauline element in John 20 is Jesus' giving—or rather, "breathing"—the Spirit upon the disciples: "And when he had said this, he breathed (*enephusēsen*) on them, and said to them, 'Receive the Holy Spirit (*pneuma hagion*)'" (John 20:22). This verse almost certainly echoes Gen 2:7, where "God . . . breathed (*enephusēsen*) into [Adam's] face the spirit of life (*pnoēn zōēs*)." But this is the very passage which, as we saw above, forms the basis for 1 Cor 15:45.

Paul declares that while the first Adam received the breath of life, and so became a living soul, the second Adam is himself a life-giving spirit (Spirit?) (1 Cor 15:45), and so able to give the life-giving Spirit (cf. Rom 8:9; 2 Cor 3:6). John dramatizes this exegesis: after the resurrection, Jesus no longer needs to receive the "breath of," but himself breathes out the Holy Spirit, the agent of resurrection prophesied in Ezekiel's vision (cf. 37:5, 9). In this passage, that is, John brings together Gen 2 and Ezek 37 in a way paralleled in the NT only in 1 Cor 15.

The Solidity of John's Spiritual Body

As in Luke, John's resurrected Jesus is clearly related to space and time in a different way than other humans; in John too, he simply appears among the disciples, despite their having locked the door (20:19). And, also like Luke, John is keen to emphasize Jesus' resumption of his former body—indeed, only John notes that Christ still bears the wounds of the crucifixion (20:27, though cf. again "see my hands and feet" in Luke 24:39). However, where Luke seems to reflect a worry that a Pauline "spiritual body" would be somehow *less* than the fleshly bodies with which we're familiar, John's reception of 1 Cor 15:35–50 demonstrates a clear confidence that what Paul has in mind is a body which is somehow realer and more solid than flesh and blood ever could be.

John's account of the resurrection invites us to experience, in reading 1 Cor 15, a sudden reversal of perspective, like that described in C. S. Lewis's *The Great Divorce*:

> Then some re-adjustment of the mind or some focusing of my eyes took place, and I saw the whole phenomenon the other way round. The men were as they had always been. . . . It was the light, the grass, the trees that were different; made of some

---

drink for Adam in Eden (*b. Sanh.* 59b)" (Marcus, *Mark 1–8*, 168).

different substance, so much solider than things in our country that men were ghosts by comparison.[42]

Perhaps Jesus passes through the closed door, not because he had become insubstantial in comparison with it, but because it had become insubstantial in comparison with him, no more a hindrance than a fogbank would be to us.

---

42. Lewis, *The Great Divorce*, 22.

7

In Memoriam

The Influence of Paul and Peter on the New Testament and the Early Church

THE FIRST CENTURY CHURCH left a two-fold inheritance to those who would attempt to understand it: the New Testament and the second-century church. Yet by an odd scholarly fashion, these two portions of the inheritance were split into discrete fields of study in the modern period, arguably to the impoverishment of both fields. At least one shortcoming of this phenomenon is that exegesis of the New Testament often proceeds as though the judgments of those who first received the writings that compose it had never occurred. Mercifully, recent years have seen a sea change on this score, as historians have begun to investigate memory as a vehicle of historical significance. Scholars as diverse as James Dunn, Anthony LeDonne, and Chris Keith (in Jesus studies), Marcus Bockmuehl (in the Petrine field), and Richard Bauckham (in Johannine research) have begun to investigate historical figures by examining the contours of their "footprints" in subsequent life of those who knew them.[1]

---

1. Dunn, *Jesus Remembered*; LeDonne, *Historical Jesus*; LeDonne, *Historiographical Jesus*; Bockmuehl, *Simon Peter in Scripture and Memory*; Bauckham, *The Testimony of the Beloved Disciple*.

In some ways, this investigation may help to compensate in cases where direct sources are scarce or lacking (so, e.g., Bockmuehl's work on Peter). But in cases where direct sources are somewhat more plentiful, such study may assist in either fleshing out historical reconstruction or adding interpretive weight when multiple options exist. Doubtless, there is a need for caution on this score, as "footprints" are not themselves obvious in either presence or meaning. Nevertheless, for at least a couple reasons, allowing the two parts of the earliest church's historical bequest to interpret one another may prove fruitful for scholarship. First, the difference between direct sources and subsequent "indirect" ones can easily be overestimated. All of the sources for history are *stricto sensu* indirect. Paul's letters are themselves interpretations of the events they report, and it is at least possible that less "direct" observation may better present the meanings of certain events than direct reportage. Secondly, it is descriptively true that all interpreters of history allow *some* indirect evidence to have a shaping effect on the data they interpret. One would never guess, for example, how small the actual New Testament testimony is to the relationship of Paul to Peter, after seeing how voluminous the writing on the topic has been and how sweeping the judgments. In response to some of those judgments, I will contend below (I) that many reconstructions of the relationship of Paul to Peter have been unduly influenced by the indirect evidence of Protestant and Catholic polemics in which the two apostles have been interpreted as figurations for one or the other side. Such influence, I will suggest, has actually distorted the evidence itself. I will then examine earliest Christian portrayals of the relations between them (II), to argue that they are of such a character as to exert interpretive pressure on the New Testament evidence itself. In light of the early patristic evidence, I will reexamine the Pauline (III) and Petrine (IV) evidence, in order to contend that the relationship between Paul and Peter is much more constructive and cooperative than has often been supposed. Indeed, I will conclude, the best historical judgment about their relationship consists in the presence of writings attributed to both apostles in the New Testament canon itself.

I. A Conflicted History[2]

It is hard to overestimate the significance of F. C. Baur upon subsequent investigation of the New Testament. Virtually every arena of NT study is influenced in one way or another by his view of Christian origins. For Baur, the fault line in early Christianity finds its origin not in Paul's innovations but in a siege of contraries within the person of Jesus himself.[3] Peter and Paul, then, are each legitimate heirs to Jesus, but each to a different Jesus. Many of the nineteenth and twentieth century's great scholars advanced this thesis even as they modified it in particular ways. Bockmuehl observes that Wrede, Bultmann, Käsemann, and Campenhausen furthered the Tübingen project in Germany, while Goulder and Barrett lent their support to it in the English-speaking world.[4] For some of these scholars, early Christianity consisted of polarized factions of charismatic freedom versus hierarchical institutionalism, the latter represented by Jewish Christians and the former by Paul and the Pauline circle, who militated against those institutions.[5] And the later developments both of Marcionite Christianity and of the Christian movement responsible for the *Pseudo-Clementine Recognitions* testify to a largely continuous network of developments of these two factions from their conflictual NT beginnings.

Congruent with this hypothesis is a deep suspicion of the historical value of Acts. "Major commentators on the book of Acts routinely dismiss signs of accommodation between Paul, Peter, and Jerusalem as Lukan

---

2. I am heavily indebted in what follows to the work of Markus Bockmuehl, whose relation of this debate can be found in Bockmuehl, *Seeing the Word*. It was Bockmuehl, years ago, who got me reading F. C. Baur, and I was entranced by what I found there. In the main, however, my own criticisms of Baur largely echo those of Bockmuehl. There is no point, then, in reconstructing what he has so ably done. We have engaged and evaluated this debate from other angles throughout this book, and interested readers can pick up the rest of our perspective on these developments there.

3. Baur, *First Three Centuries*, 49: "Here, however, we shall do well to attend to the two elements which we found in the person of Jesus, and to their relation to each other. First, there was the moral universal in him, the unconfined humanity, the divine exaltation, which gave his person its absolute significance. On the other side there was the cramping and narrowing influence of the Jewish national Messianic idea. The latter was the form which the person of Jesus was obliged to assume if the former element was to have a point of vantage from which to go forth into the stream of history, and to find the way on which it could pass into the general consciousness of mankind." Cf. Bockmuehl, *Seeing the Word* 127.

4. Bockmuehl, *Seeing the Word*, 125.

5. See Campenhausen, *Ecclesiastical Authority*.

wishful thinking—just as to German writers of an earlier generation they were unmistakable symptoms of the cancer of 'early catholicism.'"[6] Baur concludes that Acts owes its existence to the attempt of a later church to come to terms with the real and permanent feud between Peter and Paul, which bears fruit in the dispute at Antioch and leaves traces as well in 1–2 Corinthians.[7] For Baur, the factions at Corinth (specifically, the Cephas and Christ party) are mirrors of the opposition Paul faced at both Antioch and Galatia, Petrine advocates of a fully Jewish Christianity that pressed "the claims of Jerusalem over against Paul's Law-Free Gospel."[8] E. P. Sanders, likewise, expresses a deep suspicion that behind the mask of Acts are fierce and ongoing disagreements.[9]

As will become clear later, however, these claims seem to me to be overcooked. For one thing, there is only one clear testimony in the entire New Testament of any such struggle between Paul and Peter as these scholars note—namely, Gal 2. Hints in the rest of the New Testament are entirely ambiguous and depend for their plausibility, in any account of inter-apostolic rivalry, on interpretation of the Antioch episode. Bockmuehl cites Weschler's view that one's exegetical view of the relationship between Paul and Peter—and especially of the significance of the confrontation in Gal 2—depends largely on one's view of Christian history as a whole.[10] Indeed, although it can scarcely be denied that Baur

---

6. Bockmuehl, *Seeing the Word*, 125. We have already noted a deep suspicion of Acts in the work of Knox, Hurd, and (of course) Käsemann.

7. See Baur, *First Three Centuries*, 132: "How could Jewish and Gentile Christians draw closer to each other and join in one and the same religious and ecclesiastical community, how could the Christian Church which arose out of their union regard itself as a Church built on the foundation of the apostles, if it could not get rid of the consciousness that the two apostles who had stood at the head of the two great parties had held such antagonistic views and principles, and if it was impossible to think of these apostles without remembering the conflict which had arisen between them, and which had never been reconciled? It is evident that any agreement which Jewish and Gentile Christians might desire to form could only be regarded as well founded, if the relation now actually subsisting between them could be regarded as one which the two apostles had themselves contemplated, and could be traced to their mutual agreement. This is the point where the Acts of the Apostles not only finds its place as a literary product, but also plays its part as an independent factor of the history in the development of these relations." On a Petrine origin for the "Peter party" at Corinth, see Goulder, *Paul and the Competing Mission*.

8. Bockmuehl, *Seeing the Word*, 128.

9. Sanders, *Paul*, 22.

10. Bockmuehl, *Seeing the Word*, 126.

was significantly influenced (like most German thinkers of the twentieth century) by G. W. F. Hegel, he himself makes explicit the relationship of the Peter/Paul feud to later Catholic and Protestant polemics.[11] Weschler notes that Bultmann's students made the influence upon them of post-Reformation polemics even clearer: "This interpretation seems also dominated by the hermeneutical presuppositions of Protestantism, in that it positions itself to one side, behind Paul, yet runs the risk of becoming subordinate to Luther's second-hand reading of Paul."[12] Eduard Lohse notes Baur's influence on interpretation of the Antioch incident: "Although these ideas have been very stimulating for historical research one may raise the objection as to what extent these perspectives have been of a special Protestant character seeing Protestantism as a later branch of Paulinism and Catholicism as an expression of what could have been called Petrinism."[13] The paucity of actual data, when compared to the elaborateness of these theories, urges a determination that Reformation church politics have exerted a strong hermeneutical leverage on the data themselves. A tradition is at work here.

And that tradition is especially remarkable for going virtually unattested in the second-century church.

II. A Straighter Line through the Early Church: Re-evaluating a Tradition

The tradition that *does* assert itself in the immediate aftermath of the first-century church, however, witnesses to a complex and hard-won unity between Paul and Peter. Nor does this tradition reveal the kind of hagiographic gushing that would be expected in the case of a fabrication. The witness of the NT and those who first received it testifies both to complexity and to practices of unity that serve to bind together in

11. Baur, *First Three Centuries*, 112: "It is indeed in the renewal of its youth, when it developed into Jewish Christianity, that Judaism appears before us in the full splendor of its historical significance. For whence were all those theocratic institutions and aristocratic forms derived, in which the Catholic Church found ready to her hand the elements of her future organization, and which contained in themselves all the conditions of a power that should conquer the world, whence but Judaism?"

12. Weschler, *Geschichtsbild und Aposteltreit*, 285 ("Diese Auslegung scheint auch durch hermeneutische Voraussetzungen des Protestantismus geprägt, weil sie sich einseitig hinter Paulus stellt und Gefahr läuft, dem Paulus-Verständnis Luthers untergeordnet zu werden").

13. Lohse, "St. Peter's Apostleship," 433.

Christian fellowship those who otherwise would surely have little to do with one another.[14] To demonstrate this, we will analyze the relation between apostles Peter and Paul as understood in Acts, 1 Clement, Ignatius, Polycarp, and Irenaeus.

Acts (in the latter half of the first century) does portray an agreement to have taken place that many scholars find incredible, between Paul and Jerusalem.[15] It also, as Baur rightly notes, delivers a Petrinized Paul and a Paulinized Peter. Paul, after fleeing Damascus, visits Jerusalem (Acts 9:26–30) specifically to have an audience with the apostles and (presumably) to show himself to them. This is the first of no less than five visits (Acts 11:30; 12:25; 15:2; 18:22; 21:17), which serves to give the impression that Paul's ministry was regularly punctuated by such trips even though Paul seems to contradict this in Galatians. In echo of Peter's miraculous escape from prison (12:5–7), Paul has his prison door opened by an earthquake (16:26). Both Peter and Paul preach long sermons intended to make clear something that is misunderstood (2:15; 17:23). And, finally, Paul and Barnabas heal a man born lame (14:8–9) recalling Peter and John as they heal the lame man at the Beautiful gate (3:6–7). So much for a Peter-shaped Paul.

Alternatively, it is clear even in Acts that the apostle called to the gentiles is Paul (9:15; 13:2) and that problem of gentile Torah observance arises in the context of Paul's ministry (15:1–2). Yet before Paul's gentile mission inaugurates, Peter receives instruction from the Lord to preach to the gentiles (10:19–20) in terms that seem specifically to violate the Torahic purity codes (10:13–15). Peter's actions, like those of Paul, elicit dissent and necessitate something of a proto-conciliar meeting (cf. Acts 15) in which Peter has to give an account of the Spirit's work among the gentiles (11:4–17). Peter defends his gentile mission on the basis of a vision from God rather than from any personal memory of Jesus, thus mirroring Paul's call on the road to Damascus. Whatever the merits of his other judgments, then, it cannot be denied to F. C. Baur that Acts narrates the ministries of Peter and Paul in such a way as to make the agreement

14. What else would one expect to be the practical equivalent of a gospel that, as Paul insists, has broken the barrier of hostility between Jews and gentiles, between (analogously) master and slave, female and male? Cf. Gal 3:28; Eph 2:11–14.

15. Knox famously maligned the Council along with much else in Acts as a Lukan error. See Knox, *Chapters*, xii ("there is apparently some confusion in Acts concerning this visit"), 44 ("There can be little doubt that the meeting in Jerusalem that Luke represents as an impressive apostolic council in Acts 15:1–29 is the same meeting that Paul has more accurately described in Gal. 2:1–10").

at Acts 15 intelligible and credible. A Peter who does not disagree *fundamentally* with Paul is the Peter who can testify to the validity of gentile Christianity at the Antioch conference (15:7–11).[16]

Still, the resemblances draw the episodes together, so that their differences are luminous. Peter's sermon in Acts 2 explains a mysterious charismatic occurrence in which God is being made known in history, as Jesus pours forth "this that you see (*"blepete"*) and hear." For Paul, it is precisely the *ignorance* of God's action within history that is to be overcome (17:23). Similarly, Peter is sprung from prison by the agency of an angel that he sees and interacts with (12:7–11), while Paul's prison doors are opened by an earthquake and without any visible manifestation. In Acts 3, the lame man sees Peter and John about to enter the Beautiful gate, and is further told "look (*blepson*) at us" (3:4). At Lystra, however, the lame man merely listens to Paul and gets healed. And the people, when they do see what has happened, draw the wrong conclusion. What is to be made of these differences becomes clear in the prison scene, where Peter is imprisoned between two thieves (perhaps recalling Luke's passion narrative; cf. Luke 23:32), while Paul remains in prison with Silas after the earthquake. Luke's remembrance in Acts of the two thieves beside Jesus agrees with the emphasis on what is seen in the Pentecost and the Petrine prison episodes. Peter's ministry is the ministry of one who saw the Lord in his life and crucifixion and who was chief among the eyewitnesses to the resurrection. And when we recall that one of the criteria of apostleship in Acts 1 was that the person had to have been with them "during all the time that Lord Jesus went in and out among us" (v. 21), the rationale for the distinction Luke draws becomes quite clear. The significant distinction between Paul and Peter, from the perspective of Acts, seems to be that Paul did not accompany the historical Jesus in his earthly ministry. That this becomes a cause for suspicion of Jewish Christians seems borne out by Paul's own letters.[17] But that Luke preserves this

---

16. This line of reasoning presses the question, of course, whether Peter can possibly be the one who would then make the mistake at Antioch after the incident. The question is valid and will merit some discussion below.

17. 1 Cor 9:1. See also Brown, "The Gospel Takes Place." In 1 Cor 9:1 and 15:8, Paul seems to speak of sight of the Lord as a condition for apostleship. And in Galatians, it might be argued that Paul makes a virtue of necessity, claiming that his gospel was not given to him by human beings but by direct revelation of God's son *in* him (Gal 1:16). Yet his apostleship is everywhere under fire, which may suggest that a significant part of the challenge to Paul was that he did not follow Jesus in his earthly ministry and was thus a second-class apostle.

difference suggests indeed that his presentation is no shallow hagiography. Rather, Acts remembers a Peter and Paul whose distinct roles in the church reflect differences in the nature of their experiences of Jesus, but whose differences are held together by a choice to follow Jesus into the complexities of unity between the Jewish and gentile missions.

Written at some point during the last two decades of the first century,[18] 1 Clement also testifies to that unity, less extensively and without the same complexity as Acts, but even so along more or less the same lines. In a rebuke of the jealousy and factiousness that has arisen at Corinth, Clement states the consequences of such a failure of love in the starkest possible terms. Jealousy, he argues, is at the heart of the death of at least some of the apostles, namely the *styloi*. Clement may be referring here to Gal 2:9 (his knowledge of other Pauline letters is clear; cf. 1 Clem 47:1). Or he may be referring merely to a tradition of referring to Peter, James, and John in this way; Paul's own use of the word seems to refer to a pre-existent tradition. In either case, he qualifies his reference to the pillars by exhorting the Corinthians to remember Peter, as we would expect (5:4) but also Paul (5:5–7) as pillars of the church. Peter, so argues Clement, suffered "unrighteousness neither once nor twice, but many times" before he was martyred (5:4); likewise Paul was in chains seven times, was exiled and stoned, and eventually departed from the world as an example of holy suffering and endurance. If Clement is referring here to Galatians, then he clearly has access to the uncomfortable Antioch events that have energized the imaginations of modern scholars. If not, he still has access to a testimony about Peter that emphasizes the centrality of his position as one of Jesus' inner circle. In either case, Clement shows awareness of all the traditions that have motivated scholarly hypotheses concerning the long-term division between Peter and Paul, yet he names them both good apostles and pillars (expanding Peter's place in Jesus' circle to include Paul). Clement, for whom Paul's authority is clearly important, feels no tension about receiving Peter's testimony as central to the life of the church.[19] Indeed, the parallel description of the two apostles in 1 Clement, as faithful witnesses to the same gospel, as patient

---

18. See Holmes, *The Apostolic Fathers*, 35–36, reflecting a broad (though not total) consensus.

19. Holmes notes that, outside of Hebrews, the only NT writings Clement makes use of are Pauline letters. See Holmes, *The Apostolic Fathers*, 37. The significance of his usage of Hebrews occupies a previous chapter in this book.

sufferers of jealousy and factiousness, and as those who themselves were not possessed of such vices, mirrors what we found in Acts.

Ignatius' letter to the Romans,[20] from the first decade of the second century,[21] also testifies to a common reception of the co-apostleship of Peter and Paul. As Ignatius contemplates his impending martyrdom, he exhorts the Romans to pray for him, qualifying that exhortation with a reminder about Peter and Paul, and the insistence that Ignatius does not, like them, give orders to the Romans (4:3). Ignatius, then, agrees with Clement about the cooperation of the two apostles, remembering a time when each of their orders would compel obedience from the Romans. Ignatius' use of so much of the Pauline corpus makes the reception of Peter more remarkable than that of Paul. In Pauline churches (at least Antioch), Ignatius can recall the witness of Peter as co-equal with that of Paul in a non-polemical, matter-of-fact way, which testifies strongly against any "guilty memory" of an enduring family feud between them. Ignatius' contemporary Polycarp likewise remembers Paul "*kai tois loipois apostolis*" as a coordinated group in which Paul is worthy still of distinction (Polycarp, *Phil.* 9:1).

Finally, in *Adv. Haer.* III.3 (written in the mid- to late-second century), Irenaeus speaks of the church at Rome as the cooperative effort of Peter and Paul (III.3.2). Irenaeus distinguishes their work in the church (III.3.2), with (presumably) Peter as foundation and Paul building up the church, but he then testifies to their cooperated action in the commission of the church to the bishop Linus. He may mean to identify Peter as the *actual* founder of the church. But, just as reasonably, he may refer here to Peter in terms common to early Christianity: as the foundation and head, along the lines reported by Jesus in the gospel traditions. In either case, it must not be overlooked that Irenaeus is countering heretical teaching here by speaking of a common and public doctrinal inheritance from the bishops that succeed Paul and Peter. Although their roles are distinct,

---

20. Assuming the authenticity here of the middle recension. Agreement between scholars generally in quite substantial disagreement, namely Harnack and Lightfoot, testifies to an emergent and rarely challenged consensus on this score. See, in comparison, Zahn, *Ignatius von Antiochen*; Harnack, *Die Zeit des Ignatius*; Lightfoot, *The Apostolic Fathers*, pt. 2.

21. Certainly some scholars, of whom Harnack is chief, guess that Ignatius' letters are written much later. For our purposes here, it turns out not to matter too much where we place Ignatius, although I suspect that critical indigestion about the date of Ignatius arises from not having metabolized Lightfoot's arguments concerning Eusebius' sources on the relevant dating questions.

that is, Irenaeus understands them to be the sources of a common and identifiable tradition. And Irenaeus' opponents, promoting occult traditions based on private encounters with the apostles, confirm by their own argument the basic truth of Irenaeus' claim to public tradition, at least as it was received in the late second century.

This foray into early Christianity is not sufficient to address the nearly endless contentions made about various parts of it. Nevertheless, it is hard to avoid the conclusion that there is a basically continuous line of testimony from the first recipients of the apostolic testimony to Irenaeus that both does justice to the distinct roles Peter and Paul played in apostolic Christianity and affirms a unity between them, a unity that bears its strongest fruit in the unified witness of the church at Rome.

The scholars noted in section I are not ignorant of this tradition but skeptical of it. They suspect that the early church's insistence upon the unity of Peter and Paul is a simple case of protesting too much. The divisiveness of early Christianity, they maintain, required a polemical spin upon the tense relationship between the two apostles, and that polemic makes any recognizable unity in history quite unlikely. I have already contended that such scholarship may have been unduly influenced by post-Reformation polemics. Nothing in the skepticism of such scholars about the early Christian traditions about Paul and Peter merits much reconsideration of this view, since they merely buttress such skepticism by playing New Testament traditions off against the emerging post-apostolic tradition. This choice seems incoherent as Paul writes his letters in the midst of struggles of which the letters themselves do not relate the outcome! In the nature of the case, those who come *after* the apostles are in the best position to testify to the endurance or change in the state of affairs visible in the letters. Thus, to read the NT writings with a hermeneutic of historical trust while applying a ruthless suspicion to its first recipients merely begs the historical question, marginalizing the evidence by assertion of a theory the evidence alone can prove or disprove.

Taken on their own terms, however, the "early catholic" writers reveal no trace of an enduring schism between Peter and Paul. Clement, for example, urges the example of Peter and Paul as an antidote to divisions in the Corinthian assembly (47:1-2), divisions that Clement explicitly denies have anything to do with the apostles: "but that partisanship [i.e., that between the parties in 1 Cor 1:12] brought less sin on you; for you were partisans of the *well-reputed* apostles, and of a man approved by *them*" (47:4). In other words, the Corinthians in Clement's day are tearing themselves from each other in allegiance to a minority of far less impressive people (hence the diminutive 47:6: "a mere one or two persons"). The example of Peter and Paul, then, functions as an example of unity to those who are inciting rebellion against the Corinthian presbyters. The polemical deployment of their example would have no force except that not only Clement but also the Corinthians remembered Peter and Paul as cooperative rather than competitive. Similarly, while Valentinus does seem to refer to Paul as the head of his particular tradition,[22] the Nag Hammadi scrolls have shown that gnostics claimed a secret heritage from all of the apostles rather than any one or other of them as would almost certainly have been the case had there been living memory of factions between them.[23] And Irenaeus makes specific mention of the distinct but cooperative work of Peter and Paul in establishing the Roman assembly. What scholars who are skeptical of that cooperation have failed to note is that Peter and Paul are remembered as unified not in arguments about their unity but in *other* cases of schism. Their unity is not argued *for*; it is argued *from*.

There is then a compelling historical reception of the unity of Peter and Paul as a fact that could be used in discussion of other problems in the early Church. Irenaeus' memory of the unity of Peter and Paul depends upon the testimony of their successors, testimony that Clement's own letter from Rome corroborates. This tradition is not haphazard and polemical; it is tight and unified and bears the marks of responsible historical memory. To be sure, this tradition does not establish beyond doubt that the memory of unity between the two apostles is historically reliable; but in the absence of contradicting testimony, responsible historiography compels at *least* that we give the benefit of the doubt to the early tradition that remembers them as those who participated variously in a unified witness to Jesus. This evidence has an integrity, and this integrity demands a hearing. And in our attempt to allow the joint inheritance of the first century church to cohere, it seems reasonable to try out on the primary evidence (the letters of Paul and, if authentic, of Peter) a hypothesis that between Peter and Paul the differences were far less significant and numerous than the agreements.

---

22. Pagels, *The Gnostic Paul*, 2.
23. See, especially, *The Letter of Peter to Philip*.

III. Rereading the Pauline Evidence

(a) Galatians

As has been noted above, a significant part of the scholarly tendency to see Paul and Peter as perpetually in conflict with one another comes from judgments about Galatians. In Gal 2:1–10, Paul narrates what most scholars see as his own version of the Jerusalem council found in Acts 15.[24] Paul's own version of the story seems combative compared to what is found in Acts, which is admittedly quite Synodic. But Paul's own account raises questions. Paul narrates the trip to Jerusalem as the simple conclusion to a catalogue of trips to Jerusalem, which seems meant to counteract the idea that he is a client of Jerusalem. He emphasizes that God shows no partiality and that he is not in any sense inferior to the pillars (2:6); he stresses also that the "pillars" added nothing to him. But in Paul's presentation, there is a detail that suggests the matter-of-fact way in which he presents that trip may not do justice to what has actually happened. First, Paul went up to Jerusalem "according to a revelation," in keeping with his rhetorical posture throughout the letter of independence from the pillars at Jerusalem. But one wonders why, if he really is independent from them, he should have chosen to go at all? What did their opinion matter to him that he should, in the midst of his own missionary journeys, suddenly go up to Jerusalem, specifically to have something adjudicated ("I laid before them the gospel I preach among the gentiles ... lest somehow I should be running or had run in vain" [Gal 2:2])? One can scarcely imagine that their opinions kept him up nights. His course of action *does* make sense, however, if people Paul cares about suddenly have doubts about his gospel and its pedigree.

There is also a question whether Paul's own story in Galatians actually makes sense. How likely is it, that is, that a meeting in which "they added nothing" to Paul's practices among the gentiles would immediately precipitate a crisis of the very same kind between two of the primary parties to the agreement made there? Titus, brought into the midst of a gathering (*ho syn emoi, Hellēn ōn*) of the pillars, is not compelled to undergo

---

24. I am aware, of course, that that certain readers would try to place the visit reported in Gal 2 as a visit *before* that reported in Acts 15. This seems implausible to me for a number of reasons. The first is the implausibility of a Paul-friendly conclusion to the visit to Jerusalem reported in Galatians, followed by a dispute over exactly the same problem supposedly solved in Gal 2 that was big enough to require a subsequent trip to Jerusalem to sort it out! See also Campbell, *Framing*, 181.

circumcision. Is Peter, who does not require Titus to be circumcised in Jerusalem, in the very shadow of the temple, going to level tougher regulations later, in Galatia? This difficulty presses questions about Paul's report, which, at the very least, make the reliance upon it that has been seen among NT scholars a curious thing.

On this score, the most recent work of Douglas Campbell is quite helpful. He notes the question among some scholars concerning the chronology of the events narrated in Gal 2.[25] On the standard view, Campbell argues, difficulties also arise for details within the Pauline corpus. In 1 Cor 15:1–11, for example, Paul seems to be at pains to tie his ministry and message as closely as possible to that of Peter and the Jerusalem church.[26] His witness to the resurrection stands in total continuity with that of Peter, to whom Jesus appeared alive first (15:5–8). Campbell argues that 1 Cor 15:1–11 "is one of Paul's most ecumenical passages, affirming in the strongest possible terms that his gospel and the gospel of the apostles and the Twelve are part of the same tradition. It therefore presupposes a fundamentally resolved relationship between Paul and Jerusalem." And a sequence in which the agreement at Jerusalem is not enough to resolve a later conflict between Peter and Paul has a hard time making sense of Paul's sanguinity about his relation to Jerusalem.[27]

On the other hand, as Campbell (following Luedemann) observes, ancient rhetors could change the narrative order of events in order to bring thematic focus to various parts of their narratives. It is worth considering, then, that Paul has inverted the episodes for some rhetorical reason and that the conflict between Peter and Paul in Antioch is the occasion for the Jerusalem Council (Gal 2:11–14; Acts 15:1–2).

This suggestion, once adopted, not only resolves the tensions in the text we have already observed; it also explains a few tensions not yet noted. For one thing, Paul's own narration of the trip to Jerusalem as

---

25. E.g., Lüdemann, *Paul, Apostle to the Gentiles*, 61–62.

26. Campbell, *Framing*, 180.

27. Campbell's own version of this argument (Campbell, *Framing*, 180) compares the confrontation with an emerging chronology in which Galatians is written shortly after 1 Corinthians, making the tension between the two accounts of Paul's relationship to Peter acute. But whatever the relationship of Galatians to 1 Corinthians in time, a feud between Peter and Paul that even an amicable end to the Jerusalem council is not able to fend off is unlikely to be resolved by any other means (thus the perception, based almost wholly on Gal 2, that the rivalry between Peter and Paul continues unabated). So the tension between 1 Corinthians and Galatians remains, whatever the conclusions about Campbell's own work.

one meant to adjudicate something makes sense if there was a conflict between him and another apostle. Additionally, the confusion in the Antiochene congregation and even of Barnabas (Gal 2:13) makes perfect sense as an occasion for the normally independent Paul suddenly to leave the mission field and turn to Jerusalem. Finally, as is probably obvious, the agreement that concludes the conference inaugurates the collection that becomes so important for Paul's later career and (most importantly) affirms the Christian *bona fides* of uncircumcised gentiles. How could that not confirm Paul's sense that he and the Jerusalem pillars are one in mission and message (1 Cor 15:1–11)?

Two powerful corroborative arguments also serve to cement the hypothesis explored here. First, Acts 15 reports that Barnabas and Paul both enter into dispute with those in Jerusalem who would compel the gentiles to be circumcised (15:1) in order to follow Jesus. If we read Galatians as though the two episodes of Gal 2:1–14 are reported in chronological order, we would (a) have no sense that Barnabas was a part of the problem that needed adjudication in Jerusalem, and (b) have to believe (assuming any reliability at all for Acts) that Barnabas was part of that meeting, witnessed the agreement reported in Gal 2:9, and *even so* subsequently fell under the sway of the men from James (Gal 2:12). Read the other way, Barnabas is involved in the problem at Antioch and so would quite reasonably accompany Paul to Jerusalem for the decision. A second corroboration occurs in Paul's testimony (2:12) that "certain men from James" were the reason for the conflict. Similarly, Acts 15:1 sets the scene for its own version of the council by reporting that "certain men came down from Judea" and troubled the Antiochene believers.

It remains to examine whether any difficulties arise on this hypothesis. One potential problem might be Paul's apparent statement of his own reasons for going to Jerusalem in Gal 2:2a: "I went up by [because of/according to] revelation." Many translators render it that Paul goes to Jerusalem at the instigation of a revelation, implying that Paul had been told by the Lord to go to Jerusalem.[28] "Revelation" (*apokalypsis*), however, is an extremely pregnant word in Paul, both in Galatians and in non-Galatian literature. In Gal 1:12, he insists that the gospel that he preaches came "through a revelation of Jesus Christ," *di' apokalypseōs Iēsou Christou*. In that gospel of Jesus Christ, the righteousness of/from God "is revealed, *apokalyptetai* (Rom 1:17). And Paul proclaims that gospel according to

---

28. Cp. NRSV: "I went up in response to a revelation"; ESV and NASV: "I went up because of a revelation."

revelation, *kata apokalypsin* (Rom 16:25). *Apokalypsis* may refer, then, to something about the way the gospel is made known (cf. also Matt 16:17), such that it serves as a shorthand for a making-known not by flesh and blood and human practice or initiative. This certainly seems to be the case in Gal 1 and Rom 16:25. When Paul relates that he goes to Jerusalem *kata apokalypsin*, it need not imply that he goes in response to a revelation that he should go to Jerusalem; rather, it might mean that it is on account of (or in defense of) the gospel that was revealed to him not by flesh and blood that he goes to Jerusalem. The council of Acts 15 becomes not a failed, perhaps naïve, venture in unity but rather a resolution in earliest Christianity of a concern we have already discovered in Acts, namely the congruence between Paul's gospel and that of those who had known Jesus personally during his earthly ministry.

But why does Paul reverse the narrative order of the episodes to begin with, leaving to readers the possibility that he and Peter remain in conflict? Campbell suggests that "the arrival of the enemies" explains the rhetorical reversal of these events, since the reversal then leaves Paul "courageously standing for the Gospel—if necessary, *contra mundum*—just the impression the Galatians need to gather."[29] It seems obvious based on the rest of the letter that the subsequent arrival of the enemies to Galatia angers Paul enough to configure the reversal in just that way. But Paul seems to think the enemies come from James (2:12). Why, then, would he narrate the conflict with Peter as the decisive event rather than with James? It may be that Peter's authority over the church was already recognized in a trans-local way, so that there is no bigger person to confront. Alternatively, however, it may be that Paul, by focusing on Peter, rhetorically triangulates the people who seem to be the real source of the problem out of the discussion: namely, those who came from James (Gal 2:12). By narrating the confrontation with Peter, then, Paul implicitly affirms the position, authority, and responsibility of the prince of the apostles precisely to marginalize the men from James and their (possible) Jacobite pedigree. The confrontation with Peter then would raise Paul to that level of conversation, above squabbling with the Jacobites.[30] That

---

29. Campbell, *Framing*, 181.

30. It should be said that Paul notes "men from James" as the cause of disagreement and not James himself. For some, this prospect may be a bridge too far. But if, as we discussed in a previous chapter, the men from James are zealous and bad interpreters of James (applying his distinction between faith and works of charity to faith and performance of works that identify one as Jewish—e.g., circumcision), it makes sense

Peter's testimony occasioned the deal that maintained fellowship between Paul's churches and Jerusalem (Acts 15:6–11) suggests that Paul had grounds to think this strategy might work. On this reading, then, Paul portrays himself as someone of comparable stature of Peter, one of the pillars, in order to neutralize the influence of those who once came from James (Gal 2:12) and seem to have come again (Gal 1:6; 6:12).[31]

If the reading of Galatians pursued here is correct, and if Campbell is also right that the events are reversed, then Paul's conflict with Peter establishes Paul as fit to converse and disagree with Peter. And his subsequent conciliation with the rock of the church justifies the portrayal of Paul in early Christian literature as a cooperative but distinct collaborator in the trans-local coherence of the church. If Acts can be condemned for Petrinizing Paul, then one must also condemn Paul himself. To be sure, even on this account, Acts reflects a concern to involve the apostles in dispute as little as possible. Peter is not mentioned among those at Antioch, and Luke renames the "certain people from James" as certain people from Judea. But this stylized account may reveal not an embarrassment about the conflict but Luke's reflection, in a favorable year, of the meaning of Peter's

---

for Paul to be mistaken (because misled) about the extent to which James' own wishes authorize the men from Judea.

31. What Baur and those who follow him rightly saw was the strength of opposition that left Paul so often in an embattled state. By this point in our investigation, one mounting objection may well be that in arguing for an understanding of Peter and Paul as fundamentally unified in mission and message, I have papered over the real evidence throughout Paul's letters for an ongoing rivalry with *someone*. Paul states that he confronted Peter over the influence of "some men from James," and we have shown already that the fruit of that confrontation was the Council at Jerusalem. Paul's deployment of the consent to his gospel by "the pillars" Peter, James, and John, operating in tension with his insistence that his gospel does not depend upon them, seems to suggest that Paul fears an apostolic source for the current resistance. If the men from James have returned to Galatia, even after the Jerusalem conference that included them (Acts 15:1, 5?), we may conclude that here at last are enemies whose consistent, ongoing opposition to Paul can make sense of what we see in his letters. Peter cannot be the source of that opposition, as we have already discussed. James may or may not be involved, but the men from Judea seem to have opposed Paul before the Jerusalem council and not to have let up afterward (which argues against their actual, and in favor of pretended, authorization by James). That they are the source of the opposition confronting Paul at every turn is further attested by Paul's worry in Rom 15:30–32 that the trip to Jerusalem may endanger him. The mistake of Baur and subsequent scholarship in his vein may then be identified as the ascription to Peter of the activities of these men, whom Lou Martyn called "the Teachers" and Douglas Campbell, in the idiom of Philippians, has recently named "the enemies." See Martyn, *Galatians*; Campbell, *Framing*, 134–35.

and Paul's deep acts of ecumenical savvy, which early Christians termed "holiness" (1 Clem 6:1) and Paul himself named "*agape*" (1 Cor 13).

(b) Corinth.

As Bockmuehl notes, Baur held that the factionalism of early Christianity bears fruit at Corinth in opposition of Paul's party by the "Petrine" and "Christ" parties, so that the Petrine party at Corinth echoes the concerns of similar parties in Galatia and Macedonia.[32] Likewise, Goulder identifies a unified, Petrine and anti-Pauline front in Corinth.[33] Paul's portrayal of himself as fundamentally at one with Peter, for them, is merely an apologetic meant to calm the anti-Pauline voice at Corinth. Certainly, Baur's thesis cannot be said to have withstood subsequent inquiry. For one thing, none of the concerns that seem to be at issue in Galatia or Philippi are present in 1 Corinthians. Even if 2 Corinthians seems a little closer to the concerns found in other Pauline literature, the question of circumcision is absent there as well. Additionally, Paul's extended treatment of Apollos in 1 Cor 3:1–23 and 16:12 seem to suggest a particular concern with Apollos. Thirdly, the interpretation of Paul's language in 1 Cor as mere rhetorical posturing leaves the letter itself unaccounted for; certainly (as Galatians shows us) Paul can narrate his fundamental compatibility with Jerusalem without the slightest gushing. The flavor of his language in 1 Cor 15:1–11 is almost triumphalistic in its celebration of the unity Paul enjoys with Peter and Jerusalem.

One of Peter's concerns that seems quite obviously to be at issue in Corinth is the question of idol food, about which a previous chapter had a great deal to say. What is left is to note the conspicuous absence in the Pauline churches of any legacy of libertinism with respect to meat sacrificed to idols.[34] Although, as we said before, Paul seems himself to have held a relatively flexible view with regard to food sacrificed to idols (1 Cor 8:1, 7–8), in the years after the council in Jerusalem he embraced a

---

32. Bockmuehl, *Seeing the Word*, 126.
33. Bockmuehl, *Seeing the Word*, 126.
34. This is not to say there was no such legacy anywhere. Certainly, Revelation seems to imply that there were controversies concerning idol-meat in post-Pauline Asia Minor. Yet even that testimony agrees; the one church in Asia Minor that we know Paul to have founded is commended for *rejecting* the teachings of those who advocated the consumption of idol-meat, contrary to the others who were seduced by that teaching.

pastoral reversal of his previous position for the sake of compliance with the decree (10:20–21). That decree, even if it placed an apparent limit upon the *praxis* of Paul's congregations, nevertheless upheld the basic integrity of the gentile mission. Gentile Christians were to be recognized members of Christ *as gentiles*. They would not need to be circumcised, but they would be expected to engage in acts of self-giving love for the sake of their brothers and sisters in Christ. In his last written letter to a church, Paul continues to articulate both sides of the dialectic created for him by the council: "I know and am persuaded in the Lord Jesus that nothing is unclean in itself; but it is unclean for anyone who thinks it unclean. If your brother is being injured by what you eat, you are no longer walking in love. Do not let what you eat cause the ruin of one for whom Christ died" (Rom 14:14–15). He could not be faithful to the honest transcendence of Christ over the dividing walls between Jew and gentile without the first half of the statement; he could not embody the love in which that transcendence bears fruit without abstaining from what he was free to do.

Modern scholarship, exaggerating the difference between Paul and Jerusalem on this score, has tended to portray Paul as basically libertine about the practice of idol-food, with certain pastoral exceptions.[35] On this view, Paul is responding to an internal problem only, dealing with how the "strong" at Corinth relate to the "weak."[36] I have already affirmed that Paul's emphasis on liberty in Christ affirms the view modern scholars have attributed to him. But there are significant problems in suspecting that Paul is affirming a libertinistic participation in meals where idol-food is served while only commending abstinence when some weaker brother *in the congregation* is offended (i.e., if there were a congregation where nobody in the congregation were offended, Paul would allow the practice to go on). First, it is difficult to imagine (given the ongoing presence of the "weak" in the congregation on this view) that there would ever be a time when the "strong" would be able willfully to eat idol-meat.[37] Second,

35. Alex Cheung observes the "common view" that "Paul agrees in principle with the 'strong' that the issue of idol food is an *adiaphoron*. He urges abstention from idol food only when there is the danger of causing the weak to stumble" (Cheung, *Idol Food in Corinth*, 16).

36. Cheung, *Idol Food in Corinth*, 85. See also Barrett, "Things Sacrificed to Idols," 40–59. See also Martin, *Corinthian Body*.

37. It is worth observing though that Paul *does* imagine the possibility of believers' *unknowingly* eating idol-meat, even if that ignorance is planned. But willful consumption is ruled out anyway.

Paul writes about idol-meat along similar lines to other congregations, testifying against the interpretation of this as a *merely* local problem. And thirdly, there are significant witnesses in the rest of the New Testament that idol-meat is an issue of contention (Rev 2:14, 20; and, of course, Acts 15:29). These other NT witnesses speak in unremittingly negative terms about idol-meat.[38] But the possibility that commentators would interpret Paul along lines so divergent from what is found in Acts and in Revelation suggests that Paul is a problem case. We have explored the problematic nature of Paul's teaching on this in a previous chapter. But accounts of just how problematic Paul is have been exaggerated.

For this reason, it may be helpful to survey the attitudes towards idol-meat of those who received Paul. The early Christian attitude towards idol-meat (outside Paul and, maybe, Hebrews) is universally negative.[39] First Clement, a letter written *to* Corinth and demonstrating extensive knowledge of at least two Pauline letters (Romans and 1 Corinthians, both of which address idol-meat), is pregnantly silent about idol-meat as any source of controversy. If the many scholars who have identified the teaching of the Nicolaitans with (among other things) the eating of idol-meat are correct,[40] Ignatius' commendation of the Ephesian church for rejecting false teachers (*Ig. Eph.* 9:1; cf. 6:2; 8:1) seems significant on this score.[41] And Polycarp's acquaintance with the Johannine tradition (directly, as in Irenaeus, Eusebius, and Tertullian, or indirectly)[42] makes his reception of Paul remarkable if he actually understood Paul to condone eating idol-meat.

These judgments about the apostolic fathers are corroborated by external evidence in Pliny's letter to Trajan, where he notes the scarcity of anyone, before Pliny made a regular habit of putting Christians on trial, to buy idol-meat in Pontus and Bithynia.[43] And Irenaeus, who demonstrates

---

38. By contrast, possibly, with Heb 13:9, which, if it is about idol-meat, seems to counsel placing no weight on such prohibitions.

39. Cheung, *Idol Food at Corinth*, 278.

40. Cheung, *Idol Food at Corinth*, 201n109: "Note the emphatic parallel between Balaam and the Nicolaitans in 2:15 . . . (Hemer, *Seven Churches*, p. 88). Moreover, since 'Jezebel' teaches the same vices of which 'Balaam' is accused (2:14, 20), they probably belong to the same group."

41. Cheung, *Idol Food at Corinth*, 216.

42. Irenaeus, who thought the book of Revelation to be authored by John (*Adv. Haer.* 4.20.11), was a personal associate of Polycarp's.

43. "*Certe satis constat prope iam desolata templa coepisse celebrari, et sacra sollemnia diu intermissa repeti passimque venire carnem victimarum, cuius adhuc rarissimus*

extensive knowledge of the Corinthian epistles and Romans, denounces the libertinism of the Valentinians and their indulgence in deeds "about which the Scriptures assure us, those who practice them shall not inherit the kingdom of God."[44] Among the deeds that the Scriptures apparently condemn is the eating of idol-food, "from which they think they contract no defilement" (1.6.3).

It can thus be concluded that reception of Paul among early Christians coincided precisely with a rejection of idol-meat. Early Christian interpreters certainly understood the prohibition to apply universally rather than locally, suggesting the issue was not a local, congregational issue. Now, a previous chapter of this book showed how Paul's willingness to suspend his own freedom and conviction was an effort to bring the churches into compliance with the Apostolic Decree. Certainly the reception of Paul alongside the practice of abstaining from idol-meat suggests that Paul's own practices, subsequent to the Decree at least, were also in accordance with the Decree suggested by the council in Acts 15. Again, therefore, if Acts is to be accused of Petrinizing (or Judaizing)[45] Paul, Paul himself must stand accused of the charge as well.

IV. Petrine Evidence

(a) Establishing the Petrine Voice

What about the other half of Baur's charge? This will be difficult to assess, in large part because what literature in the NT *does* bear Peter's name is usually looked at with a great deal of suspicion. There will be a need, before we evaluate what is actually said in the Petrine letters, then, to probe briefly the reasons commonly given for holding 1 and 2 Peter to be forgeries.

---

emptor inveniebatur." (Certainly, it is clear that the temples are beginning to be crowded again, and that the sacred rites, long abandoned, are recommencing, and the flesh of the victims is being sold again, for whom buyers could not be found before.)

44. Irenaeus, *Adv. Haer.* 1.6.3: *"peri hōn hai graphai diabebaiountai, tous poiountas auta basileian theou mē klēronomēsein."*

45. Although James is the source of the compromise that ends the Council in Acts 15, it is worth saying that for most of the scholars who have written on Paul and Peter, Peter is the head of the Jewish Christian opposition to Paul. A Judaized Paul and a Petrinized Paul are essentially the same for our purposes, since a Peter who stands at distance from the Judaizers is exactly what we are arguing for.

Although most scholars seem to suspect that both 1 and 2 Peter are pseudonymous, 1 Peter receives more kindness from interpreters in general. Bockmuehl holds 1 Peter to be authentic and 2 Peter to be pseudonymous, in large part due to significant differences between them. He begins his analysis of 1 Peter with the statement that early Christian interpretation never doubted the provenance of 1 Peter (not so for its apparent sequel). He notes, first, the problem of language: "It is often taken as self-evident that the Greek in 1 Peter is too refined to have originated from the pen of a backwater fisherman from Bethsaida (cf. Acts 4:13, where Peter is described as *agrammatos*, i.e., illiterate, and *idiōtēs*)."[46] There is also the question of historical context: what is the "fiery ordeal" in 4:12–19? Third, Babylon as a stand-in for Rome (5:13) to many critics indicates a post-70 origin, making Petrine authorship nearly impossible.[47] Fourth, the letter betrays none of the problems we know afflicted first-century Christianity, such as law observance or the validity of the gentile mission. Additionally, the church structure seems too developed for early Christianity. Finally, the author seems at points to refer not to Petrine eyewitness testimony of Jesus of Nazareth but rather to "quasi-Pauline tradition."[48] Other than the question of Greek capacity, none of the arguments seems convincing. The fiery ordeal is only problematic if imagined as State-sponsored, while there are clear indications both of localized persecution and at times of stronger enforcement of existing laws.[49] Other arguments about theology or ecclesiology merely beg the question; doubts about the authenticity of 1 Peter based on the absence of supposed first-century theological or ecclesiological concerns depend

---

46. Bockmuehl, *Simon Peter in Scripture and Memory*, 126. This challenge has been made much more forcefully, at about the same time as the release of Bockmuehl's book, by Bart Ehrman. As Brendan notes in the essay on the letter of James, Ehrman relies upon recent studies that place rates of literacy in ancient Palestine at 3 percent to cast what he takes to be inexorable doubt upon the possibility that the letters attributed to Galilean peasants could actually have been written by them. See chapter 2, above, as well as Ehrman, *Forgery and Counterforgery*, 246–47, 286–87. We will return to this objection below.

47. Bockmuehl *Simon Peter in Scripture and Memory*, 126.

48. Bockmuehl *Simon Peter in Scripture and Memory*, 126. Cf. Ehrman, *Forgery and Counterforgery*, 250–54, where Ehrman concludes that our "author is someone claiming to be Peter who is trying to sound like Paul" (p. 254).

49. Bockmuehl, *Simon Peter in Scripture and Memory*, 128. Cf. Lightfoot, *Apostolic Fathers*, 2.2.11, which impressively argues for how Christian ways of being might very well have run afoul of the law and brought Rome down upon them without there being, necessarily, any persecution of them as a named and known group.

for their force on a prejudice that 1 Peter does not itself represent an authentic witness free of those concerns.

While evidence *for* pseudepigraphy seems unimpressive, there is at least corroborative evidence against it. If 1 Peter were fully pseudepigraphical (composed by an anonymous person unconnected with the apostle), Bockmuehl concludes, it "would require an almost impossibly rapid process of acceptance as authentic by the group to whom it was sent."[50] This is problematic, given 1 Peter's probable appearance in 1 Clement and in 2 Pet 3:1.[51] And while 1 Peter may evince a use of language unlikely for Peter, the letter does not claim that Peter alone wrote it. There may, then, good reason for holding 1 Peter as a letter written by the assistance of a scribe (cf. 1 Pet 5:12).[52]

But this conclusion has received a strong repudiation by Bart Ehrman. In a recent work arguing that forgery is pervasive in the New Testament, Ehrman argues that low literacy rates preclude the possibility that Peter could have authored the epistles attributed to him.[53] And this argument is not challenged in the least, so Ehrman thinks, by the possibility that it was written by the assistance of a scribe. "There is nothing to suggest," he argues, "that it was an acceptable practice—or even a practice at all—for an 'author' to have someone else write a work for him."[54] And

---

50. Bockmuehl, *Simon Peter in Scripture and Memory*, 128.

51. Bockmuehl, *Simon Peter in Scripture and Memory*, 128. It is not clear internally to 2 Peter that 1 Peter is what is in view. But 1 Peter is alone among letters in the early period attributed to Peter. Additionally, 1 Peter was widely recognized from a very early date to be an authentic Petrine communication. The absence of other antecedents strongly suggests 1 Peter as the letter refered to in 2 Pet 3:1.

52. Cf. Bauckham, *James*, 23–24. Bauckham makes this case in response to similar arguments about James, and for the same reasons. There is nothing said there that would not apply just as usefully, in virtually every way, here. Thus: "Preaching the Christian message to these visitors must have been a significant part of the ministry of the Jerusalem church. James had every opportunity and very good reasons for acquiring good proficiency in Greek. He would be quite used to using the Septuagint Greek version of the Scriptures in evangelism, discussion and worship with Greek-speaking Jews. Finally, in the composition of his letter he could easily have had the assistance of a more Hellenized Jew than himself, a native Greek speaker with a good Greek education, since there were certainly such people in the Jerusalem church. Since Josephus employed assistants to polish his Greek (*Contra Apionem* 1.50)—not because he could not write Greek quite competently, but in order to give his work the extra literary flair and flourish he wanted—there is no reason why James should not have done the same" (p. 24).

53. Ehrman, *Forgery and Counterforgery*, 246–47.

54. Ehrman, *Forgery and Counterforgery*, 248.

while he does concede that in some contexts secretaries had more active roles in ancient epistolary literature,[55] evidence for this activity is limited to the upper classes. Moreover, Ehrman asserts that even if one could find the kind of secretary that would be required for 1 Peter to be in any sense Petrine, "Peter himself could not have dictated this letter in Greek to a secretary any more than he could have written in Greek. To do so would have required him to be perfectly fluent in Greek, to have mastered rhetorical techniques in Greek, and to have had an intimate familiarity with the Jewish Scriptures in Greek. None of this is plausible."[56]

At first blush, Ehrman seems quite persuasive. But his argument relies upon several flawed judgments that cause him to pass over evidence in key places. First among these judgments is that Peter could not really have known Greek well-enough to write it. Even if we grant that Peter could "have picked up a knowledge of Greek," Ehrman insists, in his missionary efforts, he could not likely have learned enough to produce a composition in literary Greek.[57] Of course, this judgment depends upon the conviction that Peter did not speak Greek, a conviction that is surely up for debate. Peter's hometown, whether it be understood as Capernaum (Mark 1:29; Luke 4:38) or as Bethsaida (John 1:44), is just a couple of miles from the more cosmopolitan Tiberias, where a sailor and fisherman like Peter would certainly have spent some time. Moreover, and far more significantly, the New Testament documents themselves witness to the importance of names for the children of Israel, even in Peter's time. It cannot be insignificant, then, that in a house where one brother was named Simeon the name of the other was *Andreas*. In almost any other case, if historians discovered evidence of a family in the Roman empire about which nothing was known except that one of their sons had a Hellenic name, they would quite rightly conclude (at least until given a conclusive reason to think otherwise) that that family spoke Greek.[58]

---

55. Ehrman, *Forgery and Counterforgery*, 220.
56. Ehrman, *Forgery and Counterforgery*, 248–49.
57. Ehrman, *Forgery and Counterforgery*, 247.
58. This observation of course agrees with a wide swathe of more moderate opinion among historians. Cf. Crossan, *The Historical Jesus*, 19. Even the skeptical Dale Allison (*James*, 25) offers a far more temperate view of the problem than does Ehrman: "Given what we now know about the nature of first-century Judaism, it would be imprudent to insist that James of Jerusalem could not have composed a letter in Greek. Greek was spoken—and not just in upper circles—in Jewish Palestine, Nazareth was close to Sepphoris and its Greek culture, and there were Greek-speaking Jews in Jerusalem from the whom James, when he resided there, could have learned much were he so motivated."

Ehrman skates over this evidence, making judgments about Peter and his family without pausing at all over the fact that Peter's brother has a Greek name. This evidence, while not decisive, must surely challenge any easy certainty about the lack of familiarity with Alexander's language in Peter's house.

But even if Peter knew Greek from an early age, Ehrman might contest that such knowledge in no way qualifies him to have written 1 Peter. After all, how many native speakers of Greek still could not compose in literary idiom? But just here the secretary hypothesis, which was rejected by Ehrman in large part on the basis of Peter's apparent lack of Greek, reemerges as quite a plausible theory. Ehrman demands that readers attributing the high style of 1 Peter to the work of a secretary should "always try to think through how, exactly, the hypothesis is supposed to have worked in a specific instance."[59] But a Peter with at least a real knowledge of spoken Greek might easily have been able to work with a scribe to produce the first of the letters that bear his name. This suggestion of course depends, as did the argument for the authenticity of James in an earlier chapter, on the quite active role scribes could and did play in letter-writing.[60] Richards argues that when less-educated authors turned to scribes for help in composing a letter, "the form, syntax, vocabulary and style as well as specific pieces of content were contributed by the secretary, who was usually more experienced in epistolary expression, while the general content and perhaps argumentation remained the author's."[61]

---

59. Ehrman, *Forgery and Counterforgery*, 249.

60. Cf. Bauckham, *James*, 23–24. Bauckham makes this case in response to similar arguments about James, and for the same reasons. There is nothing said there that would not apply just as usefully, in virtually every way, here. Thus: "Preaching the Christian message to these visitors must have been a significant part of the ministry of the Jerusalem church. James had every opportunity and very good reasons for acquiring good proficiency in Greek. He would be quite used to using the Septuagint Greek version of the Scriptures in evangelism, discussion and worship with Greek-speaking Jews. Finally, in the composition of his letter he could easily have had the assistance of a more Hellenized Jew than himself, a native Greek speaker with a good Greek education, since there were certainly such people in the Jerusalem church. Since Josephus employed assistants to polish his Greek (*Contra Apionem* 1.50)—not because he could not write Greek quite competently, but in order to give his work the extra literary flair and flourish he wanted—there is no reason why James should not have done the same."

61. Richards, *Paul and First-Century Letter Writing*, 65. Cf. also: "Most typical letter writers from Paul's day did not have the educational training to compose a pleasing letter. These less literate writers likely wanted the secretary to improve the grammar, etc." (Richards, *Paul and First-Century Letter Writing*, 74–75).

Brendan noted that Josephus relied upon scribes to correct his style,[62] but early Christians clearly made use of them as well. Papias, for example, notes that Mark was Peter's interpreter and that the Gospel of Mark reliably passes on Peter's own preaching just because of Mark's relation to the apostle: this even though Mark's Gospel also bespeaks a competent literary stylist.[63] Thus, Brendan's conclusion about James can also be applied rightly in the case of Peter: nothing about [1 Peter] requires that its author himself have been a formally educated author; a literate, Greek-speaking Jew familiar with the OT and with access to competent scribes would have sufficed. And the fact that there is every reason to believe that Peter had access to such scribes supports that the all-but universal early reception of the letter as authentically Petrine.

Finally, as Brendan observes in the chapter on James, while it might be true that average Galilean peasants might not have had access to scribes to write their letters, the undisputed facts of Peter's life show at every turn that he was simply not an average Galilean peasant. Whatever the judgments about him reached by the Temple officials (Acts 4:13), Paul's letters and the witness of the first post-apostolic generation witness to a Peter who was head of a growing and diverse international community containing both peasants and the wealthy, both slaves and Roman citizens. These facts can hardly be debated, and if such a person wanted to communicate with those who were under his pastoral care, it would surely be more remarkable if he did *not* have access to effective scribal representation.

So much for the first letter, then. If 1 Peter is held to be authentic, 2 Pet 3:1 almost certainly appears to claim some kind of continuity with 1 Peter, especially given the first letter's wide and early popularity as Petrine. Some have argued that such continuity is unlikely and that 2 Peter is a different case than 1 Peter for a number of reasons. First of all, its use of Greek is truly remarkable; it has more rare words relative to the size of the letter than any NT document.[64] Additionally, 2 Pet 3:3–4 seems to imply that the letter was composed late in the first century. Lastly, 2 Peter has quite a complicated reception history: modern interpreters were not the first to doubt its authenticity. Richard Bauckham notes that although "there is better evidence than is sometimes admitted for the fact that

---

62. Josephus, *Ag. Ap.* 1.50.

63. Eusebius, *Hist. Eccl.* iii.39.15. Cf. Bauckham, *Jesus and the Eyewitnesses*, 217-21. See also Witherington, Review.

64. Bauckham, *Jude, 2 Peter*, 135.

2 Peter existed in the second century"⁶⁵ (it *may* be attested in Shepherd of Hermas, 1 Clement, 2 Clement, Epistle of Barnabas, Theophilus, and Irenaeus),⁶⁶ none of these possible allusions is certain. Rather, the *Apocalypse of Peter* seems to be the first clear use of 2 Peter (c. 110–40 CE). Even so, it was not widely used. Bauckham suspects that the churches that first received it knew it not to be Peter's own letter and so did not use it. Origen records doubts about it, even as he is one of the first to refer to the letter by name.⁶⁷ But Jerome's advocacy all but guaranteed the letter's eventual canonicity.

In my opinion, despite the apparent force of Bauckham's linguistic and reception-historical arguments, several pieces of evidence related to 2 Peter's authenticity have not been processed sufficiently. First, 2 Peter likely demonstrates awareness of 1 Peter, but just so it makes a pretty bad stylistic sequel to it. Given 2 Peter's awareness of 1 Peter, the lack of echoes between them is conspicuous. If 2 Peter is a forgery, it is unique among such literature. Several pieces of Christian biblical pseudepigraphy have come to us. And a common, necessary feature of pseudepigraphy is *imitation*. Third Corinthians and Laodiceans are both hodge-podge arrangements of Pauline phrases known in the undisputed letters. *The Letters of Paul and Seneca* likewise consist of common Pauline phrases scattered throughout. Petrine pseudepigrapha imitate the language of 1 and 2 Peter. And *Acts of* John attributes appropriate Johannine vocabulary to its hero.⁶⁸ But 2 Peter simultaneously demonstrates familiarity with 1 Peter and yet does not in any discernible way imitate it. It is so bad as an imitation that if some other explanation surfaces that can explain its relation to 1 Peter, that relation would almost perforce have to be adopted. A forger who knew 1 Peter would surely do a better job!

But have I not just made Bauckham's other case for him? By arguing for a dissimilarity that rules out imitation, have I not conceded Bauckham's argument that the *difference* between the letters makes common authorship unlikely? Bauckham's argument that style and vocabulary seem sufficiently different to justify the assessment that "common authorship is very improbable"⁶⁹ must be called into question, however; a

---

65. Bauckham, *Jude, 2 Peter*, 162.
66. Bauckham, *Jude, 2 Peter*, 162.
67. Bauckham, *Jude, 2 Peter*, 163.
68. Bauckham, *Jude, 2 Peter*, 147.
69. Bauckham, *Jude, 2 Peter*, 146.

sample size this small can hardly justify judgments of comparative style or vocabulary. Additionally, there does at least seem to be one thematic commonality between the two. Both seem to show a familiarity with Enoch's Book of the Watchers (1 Pet 3:19–20; 2 Pet 2:4).[70] This is not an attempt to have it both ways; the fact of *some* commonality between two letters written by the same person is not the same as imitation, as a comparison of any of the pseudepigraphs noted above with authentic documents will show. There is quite a difference between consistency (i.e., a coincidence that would not *justify* ascribing different authors) and imitation (i.e., a coincidence that would not, except in the case of external evidence, *allow* ascribing different authors). The two petrine letters are thus not different enough to justify a judgment of differing authors and not similar enough to compel judgment of the same author, which would be a forger's goal).[71] The easier way to account for all of this is that the two letters represent two successive communications by one author (and, probably, his scribes).[72]

Second Peter 3:3–4 seems to be for Bauckham a "smoking gun" concerning the dating of the letter. This verse seems to presuppose that "the fathers" have already died, and on that basis predicts that scoffers will come, to mock believers over the tarrying of the Lord. This indicates to him that the letter could not have been written except during the post-apostolic generation.[73] But Bauckham forgets here, it seems to me, that the letter is a testament (1:14–15) and the author's death is imminent.[74] The author has a sense that his death will cause a significant problem for his audience, and the letter is meant to assist them in recalling the blessing that has come to them in Jesus. As the author claims to be an (independent) eyewitness to the Transfiguration of Jesus (i.e., his earthly life), his death would be a significant moment of change for the community, especially if it had been formed by a strong sense of eschatological

---

70. It could of course be argued that 2 Peter merely lifts this out of Jude. But it could just as easily be suggested that Jude lifts it from Peter, unless some decisive evidence pushes judgment one way rather than the other. This will be addressed below.

71. Except, of course, for Peter's name on both of them.

72. See the discussion of the Petrine "authorial community" in Greene, *Vox Petri*, 5–6, 93–100, 304, 403.

73. Bauckham, *Jude, 2 Peter*, 157–58.

74. Cf. Rom 15; 2 Tim; and the speech at Ephesus (Acts 20:17–28). The "testament" makes sense as a thing before the imminent death even if one is not on a death bed.

expectation. Peter therefore reasonably entertains the possibility of a future time, when he and the other "fathers" will have died, at which "scoffers" will come and cast mocking judgments on the remaining Christians, whose ties with the earthly Jesus will have been irrevocably severed by Peter's death. But that death will be "past" only on the lips of the coming scoffers; it is still in the future for Peter and his readers.

Other objections, e.g., about the difference in theology between 1 and 2 Peter seem question-begging due to the small sample size.[75] To be sure, certain ideas do seem to recur in Pauline literature. But these recurrences are not comprehensive; the comparison of 2 Cor 10–13 to 1 Thessalonians might motivate a similar judgment.

Finally, as damaging as the problem of attestation and reception seems to be, a bad judgment on Bauckham's part blinds him to an attestation that speaks more loudly than all the late first century silence. Bauckham notes the relationship between Jude and 2 Peter, arguing that 2 Peter is dependent upon Jude. Motivating this judgment is his analysis of Jude 4–18, a section of Jude that has several points of connection with 2 Peter. Bauckham's investigation of vv. 4–18 reveals a tightly woven, careful Jewish midrashic performance, containing "many allusions to the OT and to *1 Enoch*, and the technique of catchword connections."[76] By contrast, the parallel section in 2 Pet 2:3–10 is fairly formless, containing only a few biblical citations.

At first glance, this argument is compelling, but it fails to note that one of the connections between the two letters, in Jude's version, is preceded by an attribution that is tellingly divergent from its parallel in 2 Peter. Jude exhorts his readers, "but you must remember, beloved, the predictions of the apostles (*hypo tōn apostolōn*) of our Lord Jesus Christ" (Jude 17). But the parallel occurrence in 2 Pet 3:2 attributes no prediction to the apostles, only to the prophets: "*hypo tōn hagiōn prophetōn.*" What comes through the apostles is instead the commandment of the Lord ("*tēs tōn apostolōn humōn entolēs tou kyriou kai sōtēros.*" This is because, in the structure of 2 Peter, the fulfilled promise of the Lord's *first* coming,

---

75. Bauckham, *Jude, 2 Peter*, 143–47.

76. Bauckham, *Jude, 2 Peter*, 142. It is worth nothing that Ehrman also agrees with Bauckham's judgment on the direction of dependence. For him, "there is little doubt that [2 Peter] borrowed a good deal from [Jude]. . . . But the source of the argument is a forgery, as is the text that uses the source" (Ehrman, *Forgery and Counterforgery*, 55). Second Peter's dependence upon the (pseudonymous) Jude, that is, shows conclusively that 2 Peter must have been written in the post-apostolic generation.

spoken through the prophets ("*ton prophetikon logon*" [1:19]), is meant to resource obedience to the commandment (presumably that found in 1:5–7 to "make every effort to supplement your faith with virtue, and virtue with knowledge, and knowledge with self-control, and self-control with steadfastness, and steadfastness with godliness, and godliness with brotherly affection, and brotherly affection with love" [RSV]), this in hope of that the Lord truly will come in the end. The prophetic word, which seemed in doubt due to the presence of *pseudoprophētai* in 2:1, has as its analogue the "holy commandment," the *hagias entolēs* (2:21; cf. 3:2), which is being perverted by the false teachers, the *pseudodidaskaloi* (2:1), and their twisted libertine ethic.

This is crucial to note because the presence of "words spoken beforehand" in Jude has caused many to misunderstand what is actually happening in the letter. The apparent echo of between Jude and 2 Peter has caused many to overlook a crucial fact: clear literary dependence makes differences striking. And in 2 Peter, the hearers will find motivation to obey the command of the Lord when they remember that the *logon prophetikon* was fulfilled by the coming of Jesus to which 2 Peter witnesses (1:16–18, clearly named as fulfilled prophetic word in 1:19). All of this means that what follows in 3:3, "first of all you must understand this, that scoffers will come in the last days with scoffing, following their own passions," is the prediction not of the prophets or the apostles *but of the writer himself!* This judgment is confirmed by the fact that no OT or LXX manuscript preserves any witness to the prediction found in 2 Pet 3:3[77] as well as by the fact that the participle *ginōntes hoti* in 3:3 agrees with the command "to remember," suggesting that what follows comes in the author's own voice ("remember *x*, knowing that *y*"). The hearers are to remember the words of the prophets, fulfilled in the coming of Jesus, as a bastion to hope in his second coming, "knowing," as 2 Peter predicts, "that scoffers will come scoffing."[78] It is significant, then, that in its own version of 2 Pet 3:2–3, Jude rightly attributes these words to the (for Jude) *apostolic* writer of 2 Peter, echoing the phraseology by which

---

77. That fact that the author's prediction here, "in the last days . . . ," is attributed to the apostles here becomes impossibly problematic if dependence is held to run the other way, since the author of 2 Peter would have to (erroneously!) attribute to the prophets what Jude attributes to the apostles.

78. The nominal dative followed by the verb, here, ἐμπαιγμονῇ ἐμπαῖκται, seems to make the best sense as a translated Hebrew infinitive absolute, also corroborates the judgment that Peter's is the voice behind this letter, even if it is written with help of better Greek speakers than Peter himself may have been.

In Memoriam 175

2 Peter's author rehearses the prophets promise of the coming of Jesus (2 Pet 1:16-19) to which 2 Peter claims to be an eyewitness.[79]

And Jude's reception of 2 Peter as apostolic explains what Bauckham finds to be the clinching argument for the former's dependence upon the latter. The apostolic message was known fairly early as a message from God (1 Cor 14:36; 2 Cor 2:17; Heb 13:7; esp. 2 Pet 3:2!). It therefore makes perfect sense for a capable Jewish exegete to interlace themes and motifs from a letter written by the leader of the apostles with OT and Jewish apocryphal writings as if they belonged together. Thus, the best explanation for the literary relationship between the two letters is that Jude constitutes a first-century[80] recognition of 2 Peter as the work of an apostle.[81] And that the letter Jude recognizes as apostolic (likely) claims as its successor the first letter of Peter suggests that Peter kept in his company assistants through whom (1 Pet 5:12) he maintained an epistolary relationship, like that of Paul, to churches in the gentile world.

(b) Hearing Peter Speak[82]

This is crucial to note because, if I'm right, the New Testament canon preserves the voice of Peter as the first witness to the canonicity of Paul's writings (2 Pet 3:15): "so also our beloved brother Paul wrote to you according to the wisdom given him, speaking of this as he does in all his

---

79. This being, of course, characteristic of the midrashic, catchword-style rehearsal of Scripture and tradition Jude performs.

80. Bauckham, who has a decent claim to be the most knowledgeable person on earth concerning Jewish Apocalyptic Christianity, dates the letter to the second half of the first century on the strength of its obvious attachments to Jewish apocalyptic traditions (e.g., 1 Enoch), an attachment that would be far less likely in the second century CE. See Bauckham, *Jude, 2 Peter*, 13-16.

81. In a rare miss, Bauckham sees no difficulties created for his thesis that 2 Peter post-dates Jude in these citation formulae. In the sentence directly following his translation of the citation formula (Bauckham, *Jude, 2 Peter*, 287), Bauckham claims that the author of 2 Peter "appeals to the same two authorities, prophets and apostles, whose testimony was invoked to validate the preaching of the Parousia." Painfully obvious, however, is that the author attributes a prediction *only* to the prophets. Nor does Bauckham properly register the fact that the prediction actually given in 2 Pet 3:1 is in fact a prediction of the author of 2 Peter himself. Likewise, the commandment of the Lord, through the apostles, originally found in 1:5-7, is reiterated, again in the author's own voice (3:11-18).

82. I will analyze 1 and 2 Peter in reverse, since 2 Peter, I will argue, explains decisions made in 1 Peter.

letters." Peter recognizes both Paul's wisdom and his epistolary activity and receives Paul's letters as belonging with "the other Scriptures (v. 16). Even so, Peter characterizes Paul in a way that makes clear the difficulty of interpreting him (as opposed, arguably, to Peter). One can almost hear Tertullian's verdict on Paul as *apostolus haereticorum*[83] in the background of Peter's description of Paul's difficult letters. Paul is not Peter, and Peter does not hide that. Nonetheless, over against conflict-driven readings of his relationship with Paul, Peter receives him as part of the Christian family and holds his writings as coequal with the Scriptures. Bockmuehl's observation that in 1 Peter, we find Pauline tradition standing in for genuine memory of the Lord thus makes a great deal of sense; that tradition was recognized as Scripture. It can be concluded, then, that although we have much less of a testimony in the case of Peter, we do have Peter in his own words portraying himself as though in skillful concert with Paul. Some critics, like Bauckham, might argue that behind perceived similarities between Paul's letters and the Petrine epistles is some common tradition, their common reception of which minimizes the importance of their apparent similarity. But since (a) we know we have authentic Pauline letters, and (b) we have good reason to think our letters here are of Petrine origin, at some point we must reckon with the possibility that these are *authors* of common tradition spinning the broad conceptual and linguistic web that bound early Christian thinkers more closely to each other than to any of their respective backgrounds.[84] We have less Petrine literature, but what we do have justifies the claim that any accusation of whitewashing in Acts must place Peter alongside Paul in the dock.

And Peter's repeated allusions to Paul's letters makes great sense if we hold (as above) Peter to have received Paul's letters as Scripture. Peter's exhortation to his hearers to be united in thought, *homophrones* (1 Pet

---

83. Tertullian, *Adv. Marc.* 3, 6, 4.

84. See Johnson's comments on the cohesiveness of early Christian thought and the way that cohesiveness complicates facile judgments about literary dependence, denunciation, or independence. "The author of this remarkable letter identifies himself as an "apostle of Jesus Christ" (1:1) and as a "witness to the sufferings of Christ" (5:1). There is no compelling reason to deny the possibility that Peter the disciple of Jesus was that author, even as there is no decisive way to demonstrate that he was. Authorship, in any case, is of little importance except as it pertains to the question of diversity and unity in the early church. Many scholars have remarked on the striking similarity in outlook between 1 Peter and many of the Pauline letters. This similarity is less likely to be due to a later Paulinist writing in the name of Peter than it is to be due to a certain range of shared convictions even within the diversity of expressions in early Christianity" (Johnson, *Living Jesus*, 91).

3:8), is a *hapax legomenon*, but agrees elegantly with Paul's similar exhortations to the Corinthians to be united in the same mind and in the same judgment (1 Cor 1:10) and to the Philippians to be of one mind (*to auto phronēte* [Phil 2:2], probably written at Corinth).[85] Peter Davids, resisting a scholarly tendency to see connections between 1 Peter and the Pauline epistles, argues that "while we are unable to assert that our author never read Romans or other Pauline literature, there is no significant evidence that he did. Is there anything more to the Paulinism of 1 Peter than that he used phrases that were, so to speak, 'in the air?'"[86] But while many of those themes are in fact "in the air," the injunction that congregations must be "of one mind" is a strong Pauline image that is not found outside of Paul's own letters and later literature alluding to him. This motif's presence in 1 Peter provides an extremely likely instance of dependence upon Paul, which adds a measure of plausibility to the apparent presence of Pauline language and thought elsewhere in the letter. For example, while it is not possible to rule out that Paul's blend of Isa 8:14 and 28:16 in Rom 9:33 comes to him from other tradition, it is still the case that Paul's use is the earliest extant version of it, whose only parallel use is in 1 Pet 2:6–8. Additionally, the self-offering of believers as acceptable sacrifices to God (1 Pet 2:5; Rom 12:1), and the injunction against "conformity" to their former way of life (1 Pet 1:14; Rom 12:2) both seem to echo Pauline tradition. Finally (and oddly), 1 Peter seems to be aware of Colossians as well (1 Pet 1:4; Col 1:5—"hope laid up in heaven").

It is worth saying, however, that insofar as Paul is present in 1 Peter, he seems to be only faintly so. Although, as we argued, at least one of Paul's "signature" themes was present in 1 Peter, few of the concerns scholars typically associate with Paul are present within 1 Peter. There is no discussion of justification, the role of Torah, or the relation of Jewish and gentile Christians. What there *is* in common with Paul is a sense of the crucial centrality of the church as temple of God, into which the various members are built up (1 Pet 2:4–5; 1 Cor 3:9, 6:19–20). And on the reading of the two apostles pursued here, it is at just this point where we would expect them to be in agreement. Paul and Peter, as cooperative agents in the unity of the early church, have a vision of the church as the gathered house of God, joined of living parts who live with each other by a difficult act of self-sacrifice to God and one another. Peter's vision

---

85. Campbell, *Framing*, 147–51.
86. Davids, *First Epistle of Peter*, 6.

of the Church, reflected here, explains his use of Paul alongside another significant early Christian writing—the epistle of James.

The address to the Dispersion (1 Pet 1:1; Jas 1:1), the exhortation to endure the testing of faith (1 Pet 1:6; Jas 1:2), the weaving of the motif of birth through the "seed" of the word, so that we might becoming his fruits (1 Pet 1:23; Jas 1:18), and the contrast between that new birth and the flesh of self-interested mortals, which fades like grass (1 Pet 1:24; Jas 1:10) are just a few of the many overlaps between 1 Peter and James. Like Paul, the voice of James appears in 1 Peter but without controlling the letter itself. James' overwhelming concern for the poor (investigated in one of this book's earlier chapters) has little to do with 1 Peter's summons to hope and encouragement to endure suffering. The interest for our purposes is not so much what the letter is *about* as how it accomplishes its goal. Here, Paul and James are woven into Peter's own message without ranking their relative importance. There are obvious reasons why this might be so; James was, by wide attestation, an early martyr of the church, and Paul had a reputation for radical suffering on behalf of the gospel before he too suffered a martyr's death (Acts 20–28; 2 Cor 11:23–27). Peter's reception of both men's ministries in his counsel to endure suffering shapes itself literally as (perhaps) an ecumenical canon-consciousness, in which the writings of Paul and James are woven together in ways that mirror the early Christian use of the Old Testament and canonized writings.[87]

V. In Memoriam Apostolorum: Peter and Paul at Rome

Another tradition that has come under increasing critical scrutiny in the past generation of scholarship is the tradition that Peter and Paul were both executed in Rome. Otto Zwierlein famously summarized a 2009 study with the statement that "there is not a single piece of reliable literary evidence (and no archaeological evidence either) that Peter ever was in Rome."[88] But several considerations seem to militate against this conclusion, to such an extent that one wonders what Zwierlein would count as reliable evidence short of a photograph. Some of this evidence is well-known. Ignatius, for example, demurs from absolute episcopal authority over the Romans (despite his position as a bishop), asserting

---

87. This judgment is corroborated, of course, by Peter's explicit testimony to this effect regarding the letters of Paul, as observed above.

88. Zwierlein, *Petrus in Rom*.

the acquaintance of the Romans with both apostles: "I do not give *you* orders like Peter and Paul" (*Ig. Rom.* 4:3).[89] Irenaeus also, as was noted above, testifies to the powerful cooperation of Paul and Peter in founding and building up the Roman church.[90] Additionally, sometime in the last two decades of the first century, Clement advises the Corinthians from his See at Rome to imitate the faithfulness of Paul and Peter, saying "we write these things, dear friends, not only to admonish you but also to remind ourselves. For we are in the same arena (*skammati*), and the same contest (*agōn*) awaits us" (1 Clem 7:1). The gladiatorial language here may function as a metaphor, given that Clement already knows of their martyrdom (5:4–7). But Clement's insistence that he is (*esmen*—present tense) in the same arena suggests that they were once where he is and that they were there close together. This tradition has another corroboration in Eusebius' multiple independent attestations, by Caius and by Dionysius of Corinth,[91] with Dionysius attesting that they suffered martyrdom at the same time. Finally, it is significant that despite the eagerness and rigor with which Christians gathered information about their leaders, the multitude of testimonies to the martyrdoms of Peter and Paul reveal no hint of a contrary witness. Since the New Testament does attest to Peter's wide travel in the earliest church (at least to Antioch and, possibly, to Corinth), the unanimity and independence of various early witnesses leaves little room for reasonable doubt about the fates of Paul and Peter. Whether they were executed on the same day may be up for doubt, but that they were executed in the same arena (Rome) in some temporal proximity can scarcely be contested.

The testimony to the death of Paul and Peter in the same place and time causes a historical difficulty. That difficulty arises because Paul is generally held to have been executed under Nero before the fires unleashed a wave of mass persecution in 64 CE. On Douglas Campbell's account, Paul could have been executed anytime following 55 or so, the most likely candidate being 58 or after, when Poppea Sabina was on the rise as Nero's mistress. Josephus knows her to be a Jewish proselyte, who lobbied Nero on behalf of the Jews. A charge like that leveled against Paul in Acts 21:28 ("This is the man who is teaching men everywhere against the people and the law and this place; moreover he also brought Greeks

---

89. It is worth nothing that Ignatius does not call Peter and Paul together by name at any other church.

90. Irenaeus, *Adv. Haer.* 3.3.2.

91. Eusebius, *Eccl. Hist.* II.25.

into the temple, and he has defiled this holy place.") would quite likely draw the ire of Roman Jews, who had access to her and an advocate in her before Nero.

J. B. Lightfoot corroborates a situation that lends plausibility to this hypothesis, as we noted in a previous chapter, arguing that the Jews had a powerful advocate at Rome:

> If Nero ruled the world, Poppœa ruled Nero. Her power with the emperor was never so great as it was about the time when these incidents occurred . . . she would certainly have cared to save the Jews. She herself was a proselytess. She had intimate relations with Jews resident in Rome. Through one of these, an actor Aliturus by name, the historian Josephus obtained access to her, apparently in the very year of the fire; and through her intercession with the emperor he secured the release of certain Jewish priests on whose behalf he had undertaken his journey to Rome, while the empress herself loaded him with presents.[92]

Nero strictly regulated assemblies as risks to Imperial security. And while Jews had an exemption as a *religio licita*, those exemptions were subject to inconsistent protection. Local leadership under Julius, for example, had forbidden Jews the right to assemble. A praetor wrote the letter to the magistrates of the Parians, reminding them that "*even in Rome*" [i.e., where one might expect security to be tightest and assembly to be most highly regulated], Jews were not prevented from assembling.[93] There is, then, a plausible account of the kind of persecution that occurred in the period before the fires—the kind of persecution that could have taken Paul's life.

After the fires, Christians would almost certainly have been identified by their recognizability in relation to Paul, who would probably have been identified as "not Jewish" by Poppea. But what about Peter, on Baur's portrayal of him, could possibly have gotten him mixed up in this crowd such that he would be recognizably seen as "Christian" in that identifiable sense? How could Peter, Baur's lifelong champion of Jewish Christianity, get caught up in the antipathies of Poppea Sabina? Lightfoot is correct; Poppea would have wanted to protect the interests of Jews. How is it that Peter did not come under her protection, if Baur's understanding of him is correct? Perhaps Paul's rebuke in Gal 2:14 was not hyperbolic. Perhaps

---

92. Lightfoot, *The Apostolic Fathers* 2.11.
93. Josephus, *Ant.* 14.10.8 § 213–16.

instead, like Paul's, Peter's way of life differed from that of the Jews sufficiently to merit him the name "Christian" (Acts 11:26 and especially 1 Pet 4:16!) and earn him a spot on one of Nero's crosses as an enemy of the state. And it is here that the early patristic tradition that expresses the unity of the church by narrating the martyrdoms of Paul and Peter makes sense. If Paul died as someone who had been delivered up as a blasphemer against Jewish things and an enemy to Roman security, Peter's death likely testifies to a similar perspective on him. The prince of the apostles had both credibility among the Jewish Christians, having walked with the historical Jesus, and also the charismatic revelation of the Spirit (Matt 16:17; cp. Gal 1:16). But when in Rome, Peter's way of life would have to have differed from that of the Jews sufficiently to get him mixed up with a persecution that was likely aimed more at people like Paul than people like James. But Peter's death as someone recognizably similar to Paul testifies to a unity for the church purchased by blood of those who followed a crucified Lord and preached his suffering love as the cure for human factiousness.

Conclusion

The act of remembering the unity between Paul and Peter served for the earliest Christians as a mode of preserving their own fragile unity. As those acts of memory built up in the time and space of the church's traditions, they made it all but inevitable that schism in the church would render the NT picture of Peter and Paul incoherent and contradictory. I have argued that such incoherence is visible in the tradition of scholarship that began with Baur (though of course Baur had predecessors throughout the Reformation traditions). I contended that reading subsequent ecclesial conflicts into the NT texts has actually made the data opaque, such that (a) conclusions drastically overdetermine the textual evidence, and (b) NT study and Early Christian studies separate from one another and proceed (often) without reference to each other. After concluding that modern scholarship is unhelpfully wed to post-Reformation traditions, I attempted a reading of the post-NT tradition regarding the relation of Peter to Paul. Those traditions, I claimed, put pressure on facile assertions that the two apostles lived in bitter and permanent contest. On the strength of those traditions, I formulated a hypothesis that the "whitewash" Baur saw in Acts had a historical basis in the lives of the two apostles, and I read the New Testament for evidence to corroborate that hypothesis. I concluded that a hypothesis of Paul and Peter as collaborators in the trans-local unity of the church made better sense of the NT evidence than conflict-driven interpretations. Finally, I explored the early tradition of Paul's and Peter's death together in Rome. Certainly, the memory of their execution under Nero was an important resource for their successors' struggle to remain a unified testimony to the one risen body of the Lord (1 Clem 5:1–7). But the power of that memory, I suspect, lies not in some magical property of remembering, but rather in the apostles actually giving their lives for their friends and placing a mark of hermeneutical significance upon the texts that bear their name. Their legacy and the legacy of modern scholarship's confusion together press the question: can the NT be understood by those who will not do the same?

Conclusion

Prolegomena to Any Future New Testament Theology

"A picture held us captive. And we could not get outside it, for it lay in our language and language seemed to repeat it to us inexorably."
—LUDWIG WITTGENSTEIN, *Philosophical Investigations* §115.

WHAT HAVE WE ACHIEVED in this sprawling collection of essays? We hope that each chapter can stand on its own, as a contribution to the various New Testament sub-disciplines (the study of the Epistle of James or Hebrews, the formation of the Synoptic tradition, and so on). But collectively, they also carry some important lessons for New Testament studies as a whole, lessons which, if properly digested, could also provide the basis for a renewed approach to New Testament theology.

The Hermeneutic of Rupture

Least of the Apostles is aimed in particular at undermining the "hermeneutic of discontinuity and rupture" which still dominates much of NT studies, an approach which treats New Testament texts as, in the first instance, the products of isolation and conflict, and only secondarily as reflecting an underlying sociological or theological unity. This hermeneutic of rupture pervasively shapes—and arguably distorts—both contemporary historical-critical readings of the New Testament, and also efforts to reflect theologically upon it.[1]

Consider C. Kavin Rowe's discussion of New Testament Theology (NTT) as structured by a search for some unity implicit within the canon's fundamental diversity:

> There is complete consensus in terms of the scholarly necessity to respect the diversity and individuality of the NT compositions. It would also not be an overstatement, however, to say that there is an emerging consensus that for a work to count as an actual NTT it must address the problem of the NT's unity. Just how much unity is needed to retain the NT as one book, however, is unresolved.[2]

As Rowe rightly notes, this attitude is entirely typical of the field. Strecker opens his NTT as follows:

> The adopting of the customary designation for this presentation [i.e., "New Testament Theology"] does not mean that its goal is to delineate 'the' theology of the New Testament, since the theological unity of the New Testament documents suggested by this term cannot be presupposed. It is rather the case that in the writings of the New Testament we are met with a multiplicity of theological conceptions. These are to be investigated and

---

1. We are drawing here on Pope Benedict XVI's reflection on Vatican II: "On the one hand, there is an interpretation [of the Council] that I would call 'a hermeneutic of discontinuity and rupture'; it has frequently availed itself of the sympathies of the mass media, and also one trend of modern theology. On the other, there is the 'hermeneutic of reform', of renewal in the continuity of the one subject-Church which the Lord has given to us. She is a subject which increases in time and develops, yet always remaining the same, the one subject of the journeying People of God" (Benedict XVI, "Address to the Roman Curia").

2. Rowe, "NT Theology."

presented according to their own structures of thought, in relation to their own historical and literary contexts.³

NTT, and with it virtually all contemporary theological engagement with the Bible, is marked by a privileging of discord, a tendency, however grudging, to begin with catalogues of canonical diversity, and only afterwards to attempt to shoehorn them into some theological synthesis or to stitch them together with the thread of a minimalist dogmatics.⁴

For one relatively innocuous example of how the hermeneutic of rupture distorts theological exegesis, consider the frequent references in interpretations of 1 Peter to "the Petrine community."⁵ Exegetes invariably use this phrase as though it needs no explanation, but it is important to note that nothing in 1 Peter warrants such usage—the letter is addressed, not to a local community, but to Christians scattered across a huge swath of Asia Minor (1 Pet 1:1), and nothing in it indicates that these churches were founded by or are even under the sole jurisdiction of Peter. References to the "Petrine community" are a function of the picture that holds biblical studies captive, a picture in which a New Testament text must belong neatly to a distinct early Christian community, identified with one of many competing early Christian factions. This picture has so penetrated the language in which we discuss the Bible that even seemingly innocuous turns of phrase repeat it back to us, reinforcing its hold on us.

However obvious or natural this fixation on the theological diversity of the New Testament might now seem, it has a history, having arisen within the enlightened project of seeking "to read Scripture like any other book,"⁶ a history that perhaps opens with the likes of Erasmus and Spinoza, and unfolds as equal triumph and tragedy. On the one hand, the historical-critical project focused the reader's attention in an unprecedented way on the humanity of Scripture. Profound though Aquinas's reflections on the Pauline epistles might have been, specific occasions and controversies scarcely enter into his commentaries; he reads Paul as a theologian, serializing his system as the opportunity arises.⁷ It is Locke,

---

3. Strecker, *Theology of the New Testament*, 2–3.

4. Cf. Matera, *New Testament Theology*; Marshall, *New Testament Theology*; cf. also Schnelle, *Theology of the New Testament*, 49–54.

5. Cf. Volf, "Soft Difference," 16, 20–22, 27; Mbuvi, *Temple, Exile, and Identity in 1 Peter*, vi, ix, 7, 24–25, 41–42, 47, 74. The phrase also appears frequently in Elliott, *Conflict, Community, and Honor*; Williams, *Good Works in 1 Peter*.

6. Jowett, "The Interpretation of Scripture," §1.

7. This view of Paul as "serially systematic" is evident in the preface to his

by contrast, who reminded students of Scripture that to read a Pauline epistle is to read a piece of mail.[8]

From its first stirrings with J. P. Gabler in the eighteenth century, "biblical theology" was in fact conceived as a strategy for retrieving some unity from the increasingly evident diversity of the canonical texts.[9] Persuaded that Scripture itself was a welter of conflicting and contingent theologies, much of which was irrelevant for contemporary Christian life and practice, Gabler proposed a set of techniques for mediating the two; the middle term of this equation is "biblical theology," which derives a set of universally and timelessly true propositions revealed by the Bible as a whole, and which can then serve as the raw material for Christian theological reflection.[10]

Many of the nineteenth century's greatest exegetes were not only convinced that the New Testament as a whole betrayed far greater diversity than its readers had traditionally acknowledged, but indeed that it largely consisted in a sustained effort to conceal that diversity. For F. C. Baur, for instance, the picture of church unity found in Acts concealed the monumental conflict between the Pauline and Petrine factions over the schizophrenic divisions reflected in Jesus' own aims and ambitions, a conflict that was only superseded by the second-century rise of "early catholicism."[11]

Later, the history-of-religions school, notably Ernst Troeltsch and William Wrede, would reinforce this fundamental sense of the divide

---

commentary on Romans: "For this teaching is handed down by means of epistles. . . . For this doctrine is all about the grace of Christ, which certainly can be considered in three ways. . . . In one way, in relation to itself, and it is commended in this way in the epistle to the Romans; in another manner insofar as it is in commended in two epistles to the Corinthians, in the first of which he treats of the sacraments themselves, in the second about the dignity of the ministers, and in the epistle to the Galatians, in which are excluded superfluous sacraments, against those who wanted to add the old sacraments to the new; third, the grace of Christ is considered in relation to the effect of unity which it makes in the church" (Aquinas, *Romans*, Proemium).

8. "The Nature of Epistolary Writings in general, disposes the Writer to pass by the mentioning of many Things, as well known to him to whom his Letter is address'd, which are necessary to be laid open to a Stranger, to make him comprehend what is said: And it not seldom falls out, that a well Penn'd Letter which is very easy and intelligible to the Receiver, is very obscure to a Stranger" (Locke, "An Essay for the Understanding of St. Paul's Epistles," 103).

9. Gabler, "*De justo discrimine theologiae biblicae*," 133–58.

10. Gabler, "*De justo discrimine theologiae biblicae*," 139, 142–43.

11. Cf. Baur, *Church History*; Baur, *Paul*. For helpful background discussion, cf. Adams and Horrell, *Christianity at Corinth*, 13–16, 51–59.

between Paul and the Jerusalem church by calling into question even Baur's confidence in the Gospels' portrait of Jesus. Wrede argued instead that the "authentic" personality of Jesus lies hidden in the Gospels under the "top coats" of interpretive gloss,[12] such as the literary device of Jesus' "Messianic secret," by which Mark smuggled later Christology into Jesus' ministry.[13] Rather than a genuine inheritor of part of Jesus' aspirations, Paul was truly the church's "second founder."[14]

Moreover, the acids of their suspicion dissolved the very boundaries of the canon itself; Troeltsch's "principle of correlation" entailed reading the New Testament documents as a haphazard and disjointed collection of early Jewish or Greco-Roman texts, with equal interest in their entanglement with extra-canonical texts as in their relation to works within the canon.[15] Wrede put the point bluntly: "There can be no middle position between inspired writings and historical documents"; the latter are intelligible in light of their historically-conditioned surroundings, while the former prescind from history altogether. Accepting the canon, in Wrede's judgment, amounts to arbitrary submission to dogmatic decisions made by "bishops and theologians" long after Christ.[16]

Later yet, the form-criticism of the Gospels associated particularly with Rudolf Bultmann traded heavily on the presuppositions of the hermeneutic of rupture.[17] The form-critics read the Gospels as sedimented traditions layered impersonally by generations of communal use, and so consisting of texts essentially written by, about, and for their communities of origin. A generation later, redaction criticism attempted to sharpen the picture, by situating this community-centered hermeneutic within a picture of the earliest church as a collection of isolated and antagonistic communities, each of which of could lay claim to some portion of the NT (so, there were "Markan," "Matthean," and "Pauline" communities, i.a.).[18] Apart from Paul's mortal combat with the intractable Jewishness

12. Wrede, "The Tasks and Methods of 'New Testament Theology,'" 104.
13. Wrede, *Das Messiasgeheimnis in den Evangelien*.
14. Wrede, *Paul*, 179.
15. Troeltsch, "On the Historical and Dogmatic Method in Theology."
16. Wrede, "The Tasks and Methods of 'New Testament Theology,'" 69, 71.
17. See esp. Bultmann, *The History of the Synoptic Tradition*.
18. See the excellent bibliographic survey of the history and development of "Gospel communities" research in Bauckham, "For Whom Were the Gospels Written?," in *The Gospels for All Christians*, 9–48. Regarding the "Matthean community," see, Grimshaw, *The Matthean Community and the World*; Sim, *The Gospel of Matthew and*

of the Jerusalem Apostles, there were whole worlds of fascinating early Christian diversity (exemplified in, if not fetishized as, the "Johannine community") which were entirely removed from the orbit of the Apostles' struggles over the mission to the gentiles.[19]

In short, even in circles where Baur's or Wrede's or Bultmann's star has waned, their influence endures in the form of a reflexive methodological commitment to privileging the NT's diversity. On this view, the NT's texts are the products of conflict or of isolation, and so their differences from one another stand out to the reader more so than any unity they might betray.

The Hermeneutic of Continuity

But is that picture adequate to the history it frames? What if the dialectics between canonical unity and diversity have proven so irresoluble principally because they have been situated within a false picture of the NT church, as a fragmented community producing isolated or fundamentally antagonistic reflections, which must then be fitted together after the fact? What if the hermeneutic of rupture were not the product of hard-nosed historical inquiry, but of a false premise distorting it?

Regarding the Gospels especially, this reconstructed church of relatively isolated communities (the "watertight bulkheads" theory of early church history, as Michael Goulder appropriately called it)[20] is a mistake, arising not least from the redaction-critics' insistence on reading the Gospels as allegories of the histories of particular churches, whether "Johannine," "Matthean," or whatever. Richard Burridge, Richard Bauckham, and others have provided good reasons for doubting this the fixation on "Gospel communities": (1) the Gospels belong to the ancient genre of

---

Christian Judaism. Cf. Luz: "*Experiences of the Matthean community are reflected in the Matthean Jesus story*" (Luz, *Matthew 1–7*, 11).

19. The epitome of this approach (and perhaps its *reductio ad absurdum*) is the interpretive *tour-de-force* of J. L. Martyn's *History and Theology in the Fourth Gospel*, which found in John 9 and 16 an allegory of the Johannine community's agonizing separation from the synagogue. See also Brown, *The Community of the Beloved Disciple*.

20. Redaction critical "orthodoxy would have us believe that in the 70s and 80s the Church of God was like the battleship *Bismarck*, subdivided by watertight bulkheads, so that those who would pass from one to the next cannot, with the treasures of Pauline theology, or the L, M, and Q logia" (Goulder, *Midrash and Lection in Matthew*, 155).

"*bioi*," or "Lives" of significant persons;[21] (2) the Jesus traditions collected in the Gospels circulated in relative freedom from the paraenetic use to which they were put in the lives of churches;[22] (3) the Gospels were intended from the beginning to circulate widely, however they might have been shaped by concerns of local communities;[23] and (4) the Gospels offer clear internal indications of their dependence on eyewitness testimony, rather than on the repeated transformations of anonymous oral tradition.[24] In brief, the Gospels are, as Justin Martyr appropriately called them, "the memoirs of the apostles."[25]

A significant source of distortion in interpreting NT texts is the tendency to assimilate them to Pauline epistles (cf. the references to the "Petrine community" discussed above), which are ordinarily sent to local communities he founded to address some particular problem. But that only raises a further question about the place of Paul in this picture, since his letters offer many *prima facie* textual strongholds for the view that the NT church was fundamentally and irreconcilably divided over the mission to the gentiles—it is no accident that Walter Bauer based his thesis

21. Cf. Burridge, *What Are the Gospels?*

22. Bauckham, "The Study of Gospel Traditions Outside the Canonical Gospels," 375-76. He offers an illuminating example: "From 2 Pet 2:20 and Hermas, Sim. 9:17:5 . . . we know that the Q saying [sic] Matt 12:43-45 [about the exorcised man whose "end was worse than his beginning"] . . . was applied to the moral apostasy of Christians, whose post-Christian condition was considered worse than their condition before conversion. But this application has left no trace in the form of the saying in the Gospels" (p. 376). John's discussion of "*aposunagōgos*" (9:22) might indeed constitute a rare instance of anachronism in a Gospel that, as Bauckham extensively argued, shows a profound historical awareness of life in first century Palestine (cf. Bauckham, *The Testimony of the Beloved Disciple*, 137-90, 207-38). But even if John 9 were allegorical, it would, on Martyn's own reconstruction of the "Council of Jamnia," reflect a situation current all across the Mediterranean world, not one isolated to the "Johannine community" (cf. Bauckham, "For Whom Were the Gospels Written?," 23).

23. Cf. Burridge, "About People, by People, for People," 113-46. Cf. also Bauckham, "John for Readers of Mark." In our view, however, Joel Marcus is right to stress that the presumption that the Gospels would circulate widely is compatible with the view that they "were directed *in the first instance* to individual communities." For instance, Mark's reference to Simon of Cyrene as "the father of Rufus" (Mark 15:21) suggest that at least the Second Gospel had a relatively parochial initial orientation. Marcus is also right to stress the significance of the fact that "the existence of local manuscript types (Alexandrian, Western, Caesarean, Byzantine) is testimony to the strength and relative independence of the churches in which those manuscripts were preserved" (Marcus, *Mark 1-8*, 26-27).

24. Bauckham, *Jesus and the Eyewitnesses*.

25. Justin Martyr, *Dial. Try.* 106.1.

that the church in Antioch during Ignatius's day was wracked by division principally on an appeal to Gal 2:14![26]

Least of the Apostles aims to situate Paul's letters firmly within the historical framework developed by Bauckham and Burridge, and ultimately by the Books of Acts itself, which depicts the rapid post-Easter emergence of a common culture of worship, mission, and reflection—not isolated ecclesial communities, but rather an integrated field of reflection and argument. This church formed a single, intimately-united international community, with early centers along an axis running from Syrian Antioch through Asia Minor to Rome.

But despite—or perhaps, because of—its unity, this church was rarely at peace; it was wracked by controversy especially over the place of the Law in the mission to gentiles, a conflict that generated fierce polemic on all sides, and required much agonizing argument and patient discernment for its eventual resolution. These essays explore various aspects of Paul's often tense, but always committed communion with Peter, James, and the rest of the early church. As a partial record of those relations, the NT dramatizes its own unity, which was not mere theological uniformity, but a truly visible communion enacted through apostolic dialogue and mutual recognition. It is that dual impulse that gave this book its title: Paul's self-effacing insistence that he was no less an apostle for being the least among them (1 Cor 15:9) epitomizes the ecumenical disposition that constitutes the unity of the NT.

Paul's commitment comes to clearest expression in chapter two, on the place of the Apostolic Decree in structuring Paul's exhortations regarding fornication, along with idol-meat, in 1 Corinthians. But chapter 1 on the relation of James to Paul illuminates these questions as well—where generations of scholars have found, if not bitter polemic, at least ships passing in the night, we discerned a tight lineal connection between James and Paul, exactly along the lines suggested by Acts and Galatians, and offered an account of their relation that both took seriously the fact of wracking disagreement within the earliest church over the question of gentile inclusion, and also found no need to read James as in opposition to Paul. And chapter 3, on Paul's use of Synoptic dominical traditions, highlights both Paul's surprisingly deep interest in the life and teachings of Christ, and the apparently early crystallizing of a Gospel tradition that many now take to have been a late development. Chapter 6, on Peter's

---

26. Bauer, *Orthodoxy and Heresy*, 62.

relation to Paul, discerned between them another relationship that, while by no means untroubled, rested fundamentally on the two apostles' commitments to proclaiming a shared gospel within a united church. The total picture that emerges from these essays is of a church whose unity is, at the theological level, symphonic rather than monotone, and at the ecclesial level, the hard-won fruit of personal sacrifice, patient discernment, and painful disagreement.

If the authors of the NT worked in a tightly-knit international community, we should expect their various writings to be interested in and to engage one another; texts that emerged from such a milieu should be expected to display literary dependence on and intimacy with other NT texts. Again and again in these essays, we found seemingly disparate NT texts united by a shared—if by no means demure—engagement with Paul. Both Hebrews and the Gospel of John creatively develop Paul's thought in ways that would perhaps have been surprising to the Apostle, while Paul's own disciple, the good physician Luke, ventures a subtle correction of his teacher's account of the resurrection. In the case of Peter's letters, we found Paul's equal reflecting seriously and charitably on his relations with "the Apostle," and so producing the literary equivalent of the missional and ecclesial handshake that concluded the Jerusalem Conference.

Heirs of the Apostles

The hermeneutic of continuity equally suggests casting one's gaze beyond the NT itself, to challenge the declension narrative, long traded upon by NT scholars, about a supposed aboriginal defection that took place sometime early in the post-apostolic church, in which early Christianity's hothouse diversity and equality was stifled and replaced with the monoculture of an aggressively hierarchical and dogmatic Catholicism. This narrative is in many ways the direct heir of Reformation-era Protestant polemic, which privileged a hermeneutic of suspicion and of discontinuity in its interpretation of church history: Luther's narrative of early medieval decline became Conrad Grebel's stark contrast between the New Testament church and the manifold corruptions instituted in the immediate post-apostolic period, which itself slid easily into the familiar Enlightenment opposition of Protestant dogma to the pure "natural religion" of Jesus, a story told variously by Rousseau and Kant, and diversely developed in the study of the New Testament by Schleiermacher, Adolf von Harnack, and many others.[27]

We are convinced that there is an historically and theologically more adequate way of construing the movement from Jesus of Nazareth, to the church of Paul and Peter, to the episcopacies of Ignatius and Polycarp and beyond. That approach takes seriously the post-apostolic church's claim to inherit—by means of episcopal "apostolic succession"—and to creatively and faithfully develop the teaching and mission of Peter, Paul, and the rest of Jesus' apostles. After all, these were men who were acknowledged even by their enemies to have sat at those apostles' feet, or at the feet of their disciples,[28] and who acted as their immediate successors in the churches of the apostles.

This means that, rather than dreaming up a world of rabid internecine strife, in which isolated Christian communities disguised their own histories as stories about Jesus, we ought to begin our reconstruction of the shape of early Christianity with the memory of it reported by its first heirs. And that memory is one in which witnesses to the life of Jesus and the progress of his gospel circulated under apostolic authority within a single international community, whose leaders never stopped working to maintain fellowship even through their darkest disagreements. This hermeneutic of continuity, that is, entails taking seriously Acts' canonical function in providing the (primary) narrative frame within which the NT's epistles and other apostolic writings are to be situated. Interpretations of the epistolary data that are consonant with the data of Acts are to be privileged, not simply "theologically," in the sense of best serving the dogmatic or political interests of the bishops, but also historically, precisely because such interpretations do fuller justice to the fact that the earliest heirs to the NT epistles received them as paired to Acts.

Emphasizing the fundamental unity of the apostolic church and its post-apostolic heirs does not, however, commit us to describing the rise of "heresies" as in every case secondary to and parasitic upon pre-existing "Catholic" congregations. Here, it will be helpful to briefly engage Walter Bauer's classic, *Orthodoxy and Heresy in Earliest Christianity*.[29]

---

27. Cf. Luther, "Of the Babylonian Captivity of the Church"; Grebel et al., "Letter to Thomas Müntzer," 163–71; Rousseau, "Profession of Faith of a Savoyard Vicar"; Kant, *Religion within the Bounds of Mere Reason*; Schleiermacher, *Der christliche Glaube*, §§93–94; Harnack, *Das Wesen des Christentums*.

28. Cf. Irenaeus, *Adv. Haer.* 3.2.2.

29. Bauer, *Orthodoxy and Heresy*.

Bauer famously argued that early Christianity was a blooming, buzzing confusion, a welter in which especially docetic and gnostic groups mostly predominated, and were only crushed with great effort by Catholic bishops as late as the third and fourth centuries. In many cases—especially as regards Christianity in Syria and Asia Minor—Bauer's thesis depends on a dogmatic skepticism of the available evidence (from Ignatius, Polycarp, Irenaeus, and the fragments preserved by Eusebius), with little more to commend it than innuendo, silence, and sheer speculation.[30] There can be no doubt that a great variety of "gnostics" and docetists were active in these regions in the second century, but there can equally be no doubt that they always appear in the available sources as latecomers who defect from or invade recognizably Catholic churches.[31]

The situation is somewhat different, however, when we venture outside the realms of Paul's and Peter's and John's immediate influence. For instance, Bauer's account of the development of Christianity in places such as Egypt is plausible, and perhaps even probable. Our evidence for a second (much less first) century catholic presence there is weak indeed; Eusebius seems to know about little more than a succession of bishops until Clement in the late second century.[32] Likewise, the first catholic

---

30. "What is concealed behind this title [of bishop] for Ignatius is, corresponding to the situation of Palût in Edessa, the leadership of a group that is engaged in a life and death struggle against an almost overwhelming adversary. Certainly this title itself implies the claim to be the authoritative interpreter of the faith for all Christians of Syria, or at least of Antioch. But the question remains to what extent this self-evaluation was acknowledged by others. It appears to me that large segments of Antiochian Christianity flatly rejected it, in view of the almost frantic efforts of Ignatius to push his home church in the direction he desired by dispatching to Antioch delegations of eminent coreligionists from every congregation accessible to him (cf. *Philad.* 10—bishops, presbyters, deacons) or at least by sending written messages" (Bauer, *Orthodoxy and Heresy*, 64). This strikes me as an extraordinarily imaginative skepticism masquerading as historical judgment. Our best source for Christianity in Antioch in this period is Ignatius, but for no plausible reason that I can discern, Bauer chooses to stand Ignatius on his head. His principal motivation for this seems to come from tracing the trajectory of the Paul-Peter controversy in Gal 2 (cf. Bauer, *Orthodoxy and Heresy*, 62)! Bauer's sole argument for the dominance of gnostic-docetic groups in Syria is the vociferousness of Ignatius's response to them (Bauer, *Orthodoxy and Heresy*, 66–67).

31. Cf. 1 John 2:19; 2 John 1:7; Ignatius, *Eph.* 9:1; Ignatius, *Mag.* 4; Ignatius, *Trall.* 6–7; Ignatius, *Philad.* 3; Ignatius, *Smyr.* 3; Irenaeus, *Adv. Haer.* 3.4.3. Third John 1:9–10 might reflect the takeover of a local congregation by someone the Elder considers unworthy, but this is not connected in any way to the docetic heresy that is otherwise so prominent in the Johannine epistles.

32. Eusebius, *Hist. Eccl.* 2.16, 24, 4.14, 21.

Christian whom we can identify with Alexandria with real confidence is Clement, in the second half of the second century. But prior to Clement, we know that figures such as Valentinus and Basilides were active there, and that a document called *The Gospel of the Egyptians* was in circulation.[33] Bauer does not deny that a Catholic presence in Alexandria long preceded Clement, but he presses the point that the "gnostics" and Encratites seemed to be dominant at least until the third century episcopacy of Demerius.[34]

But does this challenge our primary thesis that a "hermeneutic of continuity" is the most credible means of tracing the movement from Pentecost to Polycarp? We see no reason to think so. We know that gnostics and docetists of one stripe or another were recognized by second-century Catholics as a grave threat; we equally know that those same Catholics understood themselves to belong to a tight-knit community that originated with the Apostles. None of these claims, however, is incompatible with Bauer's further contention that the Catholic Church's opponents achieved an early dominance in some regions (such as Egypt) that later became Catholic strongholds.

The Problem of Canon

We have already encountered William Wrede's declaration that accepting the canon amounts to arbitrary submission to dogmatic decisions made by "bishops and theologians."[35] By contrast, a hermeneutic of continuity encourages us to hold together the apostolic witness embodied in the New Testament with the canonizing act by which the post-apostolic church received that witness as authoritative for worship, belief, and practice. In brief, it reflects a commitment not to oppose Scripture and Tradition, but to see them as inseparably bound one to another, indeed as interpenetrating one another at every level.

This is not initially a theological commitment, but rather an historical one: the New Testament texts constantly betray their character as epitomizing, crystallizing, and reinforcing the apostolic witness that had

---

33. Bauer, *Orthodoxy and Heresy*, 48–49, 57.

34. Bauer, *Orthodoxy and Heresy*, 57. Whether by necessity or out of a measured sympathy with them, Clement even adopted the term "gnostic" as his label for the true Christian (cf. Brown, *Body and Society*, 125).

35. Bauer, *Orthodoxy and Heresy*, 71.

already been handed on as authoritative (cf. Rom 1:8, 12, 16:25; 1 Cor 15:3–8; Gal 1:8).³⁶ Tradition is therefore not a "second century" phenomenon, but the foundation for the earliest Christian preaching and teaching, a stream of authoritative testimony that flowed unbroken from Jesus to John the Elder to Polycarp to Irenaeus, who insists, "We have learned from none others the plan of our salvation, than from those through whom the Gospel has come down to us, which they did at one time proclaim in public, and, at a later period, by the will of God, handed down to us in the Scriptures."³⁷ Tradition as reverence for unwritten apostolic testimony is both temporally and logically prior to the New Testament itself; the few documents collected therein float upon a sea of ecclesial witness, reflection, and argument, much of which was never or only much later captured in written form.³⁸

But that does not mean that the "canon-consciousness" so clearly evident by the second-century was the purely theological, *ex post facto* construction of a churchly book, compiled by arbitrary selection from among a vast array of possible candidates. No, the ecclesial reception of the NT as canon was responsive to and intimate with the recognition, already evident in the NT, that apostolic writings bore a unique authority in the life of the church. As Adolf Schlatter stressed, the "distinction" between canonical and non-canonical texts "is not based upon an arbitrary fiat."³⁹ Rather, the early church, in its reception of the soon-to-be canonical writings, demonstrated its concern for stewarding authoritative, apostolic testimony to Christ: "The exhortation of a bishop never possessed the same weight as that of an apostle."⁴⁰ Brevard Childs rightly observes, "Canon-consciousness lay deep within the formation of the literature."⁴¹ Even as (or perhaps, precisely because) he struggles with them, Peter finds himself compelled to fold Paul's letters within "the Scriptures" (2 Pet 3:16).

36. Cf. Wainwright, *Doxology*, 156–58, 164, 196.

37. Irenaeus, *Adv. Haer.* 3.3.1–4.

38. While I would quibble with his assignment of the relevant time spans, Robert Jenson puts the general point clearly: "The textual collection we call the New Testament is necessary for the perdurance of the church only at one remove: it provides a norm for the message on the authenticity of which the perdurance of the church does indeed depend—'the gospel'—a message that is itself primarily verbal and linguistically fluid. Indeed, the church perdured without a New Testament for more than a century" (Jenson, *Canon and Creed*, 14).

39. Schlatter, "The Theology of the New Testament and Dogmatics," 146.

40. Schlatter, "The Theology of the New Testament and Dogmatics," 146.

41. Childs, *Biblical Theology*, 70.

"Canon-consciousness," far from being a theological top-coat obscuring these text's historical meaning, is a mode of fidelity to the mutual recognition enacted within and by the NT itself. In that light, then, there is no *prima facie* reason to drive a wedge between the original significance and aims of (say) Luke, and its reception in the second-century "Great Church." *Dei verbum*, the Second Vatican Council's Dogmatic Constitution on Scripture, puts the point beautifully: "This sacred tradition, therefore, and Sacred Scripture of both the Old and New Testaments are like a mirror in which the pilgrim Church on earth looks at God."[42]

Rediscovering Our Homeland

These essays began, some years ago, as a set of modest extrapolations from the work of our teacher Douglas Campbell on the chronology of Paul's mission, a project come to partial fruition in his *Framing Paul*. Our conversations on the role of the Jerusalem Conference, the Apostolic Decree, and "the Teachers" in illuminating the Epistle of James and 1 Corinthians, however, soon began to absorb seemingly more disparate writings—before we knew it, Hebrews was in play, then the Gospels, the Petrine Epistles and Jude. Our haphazard reflections had unwittingly incorporated most of the NT, which now seemed to constitute a single, albeit fractious and difficult, conversation within a tightly knit group of church leaders, all of whom were named in the Gospels or in Acts. Our mingled shock and delight is best captured by Chesterton's story "about an English yachtsman who slightly miscalculated his course and discovered England under the impression that it was a new island in the South Seas." We too "tried to be some ten minutes in advance of the truth," and "found that [we were] eighteen hundred years behind it."[43] We had set out to canvass Paul's place in the New Testament church, and found, to our amusement, that most of our discoveries had been waiting for us in Papias, Irenaeus, and Clement—not to mention Acts!—had we only allowed ourselves to see it.

The direct aim of these essays (their attempted illocutionary act) is to speak truly, for a failure in that regard outweighs success in any other respect. But there are many (perlocutionary) actions which one might

---

42. Second Vatican Council, *Dei verbum*, II.7.
43. Chesterton, *Orthodoxy*, 9.

perform by speaking the truth,⁴⁴ and the one nearest our hearts is to free theological readers to venture fearlessly into the "strange new world" opened up by Scripture.⁴⁵ These essays gesture toward the possibility of a second naiveté of trust in the story depicted in and through the New Testament's epistles and narratives, a trust won precisely by its having abided unconsumed in the furnace of post-Enlightenment skepticism. The far side of historicist suspicion is not a simple return to "pre-critical theology," but rather a theologically-attuned historical criticism that "out-historicizes" Baur and Wrede and their epigones. That, of course, remains an aspiration rather than an achievement; at most, these essays are markers along the way towards a "city ... that is to come" (Heb 13:14).

---

44. The distinction of "illocutionary" from "perlocutionary" acts comes, of course, from Austin, *How To Do Things with Words*.

45. Cf. Barth, "The New World in the Bible."

Bibliography

Adams, Edward, and David Horrell, eds. *Christianity at Corinth: The Quest for the Pauline Church*. Louisville: Westminster John Knox, 2004.
Allen, David L. *Hebrews: An Exegetical and Theological Explanation of Holy Scripture*. New American Commentary 35. Nashville: B&H, 2010.
———. *Lukan Authorship of Hebrews*. Nashville: B&H, 2010.
Allison, Dale C., Jr. *A Critical and Exegetical Commentary on the Epistle of James*. International Critical Commentary. London: Bloomsbury, 2013.
———. *The New Moses: A Matthean Typology*. Minneapolis: Augsburg Fortress, 1993.
———. "The Pauline Epistles and the Synoptic Gospels: The Pattern of the Parallels." *New Testament Studies* 28.1 (1982) 1–32.
Aquinas, Thomas. *Commentary on the Epistle to the Romans*. http://www.corpusthomisticum.org/cro00.html.
Attridge, Harold W. *Hebrews*. Hermeneia. Minneapolis: Fortress, 1989.
Augustine. *Confessions*. http://www.newadvent.org/fathers/110101.htm.
———. *On the Spirit and the Letter*. In *Selected Writings on Grace and Pelagianism*, translated by Roland Teske, 217–84. Hyde Park, NY: New City, 2011.
Austin, J. L. *How To Do Things with Words*. New York: Oxford University Press, 1975.
Baldwin, Barry. "Greek in Cicero's Letters." *Acta Classica* 35 (1992) 1–17.
Barbaglio, Giuseppe. *Antipaolinismo: reazioni a Paolo tra il I e il II secolo*. Edited by Romano Penna. Ricerche Storico-Bibliche 2. Bologna: Dehoniane, 1989.
Barclay, John. "Mirror-Reading a Polemical Letter: Galatians as a Test Case." *Journal for the Study of the New Testament* 31 (1987) 73–93.
———. "Paul and Jesus." In *The Dictionary of Paul and His Letters*, edited by Gerald Hawthorne and Ralph Martin, 492–503. Downers Grove, IL: InterVarsity, 1993.
Barrett, C. K. *The Acts of the Apostles*. Vol. 1. International Critical Commentary. Edinburgh: T. & T. Clark, 1994.
———. "Things Sacrificed to Idols." In *Essays on Paul*, 40–59. Philadelphia: Westminster, 1982.

Bibliography

Barth, Karl. "The New World in the Bible." In *The Word of God and Theology*, translated by Amy Marga, 15–30. London: T. & T. Clark, 2011.
Bauckham, Richard, ed. *The Gospels for All Christians: Rethinking the Gospel Audiences*. Grand Rapids: Eerdmans, 1998.
———. *James: Wisdom of James, Disciple of Jesus the Sage*. New York: Routledge, 1999.
———. *Jesus and the Eyewitnesses*. Grand Rapids: Eerdmans, 2006.
———. *Jude, 2 Peter*. Word Biblical Commentary 50. Waco, TX: Word, 1983.
———. "The Study of Gospel Traditions outside the Canonical Gospels." In *Gospel Perspectives*. Vol. 5, *The Jesus Tradition outside the Gospels*, edited by David Wenham, 369–404. Sheffield: JSOT, 1984.
———. *The Testimony of the Beloved Disciple*. Grand Rapids: Baker Academic, 2007.
Baur, Ferdinand Christian. *The Church History of the First Three Centuries*. 2 vols. London: Williams and Norgate, 1878.
———. *Kritische Untersuchungen über die kanonischen Evangelien, ihr Verhältniss zu einander, ihren Charakter und Ursprung*. https://books.google.com/books?id=G25AAAAAcAAJ&printsec=frontcover&hl=de#v=onepage&q&f=false).
———. *Paul: The Apostle of Jesus Christ*. 2 vols. London: Williams and Norgate, 1875.
Baur, Walter, et al. *Greek-English Lexicon of the New Testament and Other Early Christian Literature*. 3rd ed. Chicago: University of Chicago Press, 2000.
———. *Orthodoxy and Heresy in Earliest Christianity*. Translated by Robert Kraft. Minneapolis: Fortress, 1979.
Benedict of Nursia. *The Rule of St. Benedict*. Translated by Anthony Meisel and M. L. de Mastro. New York: Image, 2010.
Benedict XVI, Pope. "Address to the Roman Curia." http://www.vatican.va/holy_father/benedict_xvi/speeches/2005/december/documents/hf_ben_xvi_spe_20051222_roman-curia_en.html.
Blight, David W. *Frederick Douglass: Prophet of Freedom*. New York: Simon & Schuster, 2020.
Bockmuehl, Markus. *Seeing the Word: Refocusing New Testament Study*. Grand Rapids: Baker Academic, 2006.
———. *Simon Peter in Scripture and Memory: The New Testament Apostle in the Early Church*. Grand Rapids: Baker Academic, 2012.
Book of Common Prayer. https://www.bcponline.org/.
Borg, Marcus. *Conflict, Holiness, and Politics in the Teaching of Jesus*. New York: Continuum, 1998.
Boyarin, David. "Gospel of the *Memra*: Jewish Binitarianism and the Prologue to John." *Harvard Theological Review* 94.3 (2001) 243–84.
Brown, Alexandra. "The Gospel Takes Place: Paul's Theology of Power-in-Weakness in 2 Corinthians." *Interpretation* 52.3 (1998) 271–86.
Brown, Peter. *Body and Society: Men, Women, and Sexual Renunciation in Early Christianity*. New York: Columbia University Press, 1998.
Brown, Raymond E. *The Community of the Beloved Disciple*. Mahwah, NJ: Paulist, 1979.
———. *The Gospel according to John*. 2 vols. Anchor Bible 29–29A. Garden City, NY: Doubleday, 1966–70.
Bruce, Frederick Fyvie. *The Book of the Acts*. New International Commentary on the New Testament Grand Rapids: Eerdmans, 1988.
Bultmann, Rudolf. *The History of the Synoptic Tradition*. Translated by John Marsh. New York: Oxford University Press, 1963.

———. *Theology of the New Testament*. Translated by Kendrick Grobel. Waco, TX: Baylor University Press: 2007.

Burridge, Richard. "About People, by People, for People: Gospel Genre and Audiences." In *The Gospels for All Christians: Rethinking the Gospel Audiences*, edited by Richard Bauckham, 113–46. Grand Rapids: Eerdmans, 1998.

———. *What Are the Gospels?* 2nd ed. Grand Rapids: Eerdmans, 2004.

Butler, B. C. *The Originality of St. Matthew: A Critique of the Two-Document Hypothesis*. New York: Cambridge University Press, 2011.

Campbell, Douglas. "An Anchor for Pauline Chronology: Paul's Flight from 'the Ethnarch of King Aretas' (2 Corinthians 11:32–33)." *Journal of Biblical Literature* 121.2 (2002) 279–302.

———. "Beyond the Torah at Antioch." *Journal for the Study of Paul and His Letters* 4.2 (2014) 187–214.

———. *The Deliverance of God*. Grand Rapids: Eerdmans, 2009.

———. *Framing Paul*. Grand Rapids: Eerdmans, 2014.

———. "Galatians 5.11: Evidence of an Early Law-Observant Mission by Paul?" *New Testament Studies* 57 (2011) 325–47.

———. *The Quest for Paul's Gospel*. New York: Bloomsbury Academic, 2005.

Campenhausen, Hans von. *Ecclesiastical Authority and Spiritual Power in the Church of the First Three Centuries*. Translated by J. A. Baker. Stanford: Stanford University Press, 1969.

Carlson, Stephen. "Clement of Alexandria on the 'Order' of the Gospels." *New Testament Studies* 47.1 (2001) 118–25.

Case, Brendan. *The Accountable Animal: Justice, Justification, and Judgment*. London: T. & T. Clark, 2021.

Chance, J. Bradley. *Acts*. Macon, GA: Smith & Helwys, 2007.

Chesterton, G. K. *Orthodoxy*. http://www.gutenberg.org/cache/epub/130/pg130.html.

Cheung, Alex. *Idol Food in Corinth: Jewish Background and Pauline Legacy*. Journal for the Study of the New Testament Supplement Series 176. Sheffield: Sheffield Academic, 1999.

Childs, Brevard. *Biblical Theology of the Old and New Testaments: Theological Reflection on the Christian Bible*. Minneapolis: Fortress, 1993.

Cicero. *De Natura Deorum*. Translated by H. Rackham. Loeb Classical Library 268. Cambridge: Harvard University Press, 1951.

Clark, Alexander. *Supersizing the Mind: Embodiment, Action, and Cognitive Extension*. New York: Oxford University Press, 2011.

Clavier, H. "Brèves remarques sur la notion de *sōma pneumatikon*." In *Background of the New Testament and Its Eschatology: Studies in Honor of C. H. Dodd*, edited by W. D. Davies and D. Daube, 342–62. Cambridge: Cambridge University Press, 1956.

Clement of Alexandria. *Stromateis*. In vol. 2 of *Ante-Nicene Fathers*, edited by Alexander Roberts et al., translated by William Wilson. Buffalo, NY: Christian Literature, 1885.

Cohn, Leopold, and Paul Wendland. *Philonis Alexandrini Opera Quae Supersunt*. 6 vols. Berlin: de Gruyter, 1896–1930.

Collins, Raymond. *First Corinthians*. Collegeville, MN: Liturgical, 1999.

Conzelmann, Hans. *1 Corinthians: A Commentary*. Philadelphia: Fortress, 1975.

Cranfield, C. E. B. *The Epistle to the Romans*. Vol. 2. International Critical Commentary. Edinburgh: T. & T. Clark, 1979.

Crossan, John D. *The Historical Jesus: The Life of a Mediterranean Peasant*. San Francisco: HarperSanFrancisco, 1991.
Davids, Peter. *The First Epistle of Peter*. New International Commentary on the New Testament. Grand Rapids: Eerdmans, 1990.
Davies, W. D. *Paul and Rabbinic Judaism: Some Rabbinic Elements in Pauline Theology*. 3rd ed. London: SPCK, 1977.
Dibelius, Martin. *James*. Translated by Heinrich Greeven. Minneapolis: Fortress, 1976.
Dodd, C. H. *The Apostolic Preaching and Its Developments*. New York: Harper & Row, 1964.
Dungan, David. *The Sayings of Jesus in the Churches of Paul: The Use of the Synoptic Tradition in the Regulation of Early Church Life*. Minneapolis: Fortress, 1971.
Dunn, James. *1 Corinthians*. London: T. & T. Clark, 1999.
———. "Jesus and Purity: An Ongoing Debate." *New Testament Studies* 48.4 (2002) 449–67.
———. *Jesus according to the New Testament*. Grand Rapids: Eerdmans, 2019.
———. *Jesus Remembered*. Christianity in the Making 1. Grand Rapids: Eerdmans, 2003.
———. *Jesus, Paul, and the Gospels*. Grand Rapids: Eerdmans, 2011.
———. *Jesus, Paul, and the Law: Studies in Mark and Galatians*. London: SPCK, 1990.
———. *The Theology of Paul the Apostle*. Grand Rapids: Eerdmans, 1998.
Edwards, James R. *The Hebrew Gospel and the Development of the Synoptic Tradition*. Grand Rapids: Eerdmans, 2009.
Ehrman, Bart. *Did Jesus Exist: The Historical Argument for Jesus of Nazareth*. New York: HarperOne, 2013.
———. *Forgery and Counterforgery: The Use of Literary Deceit in Early Christian Polemics*. New York: Oxford University Press, 2013.
Ellingworth, Paul. *The Epistle to the Hebrews*. New International Greek Testament Commentary. Grand Rapids: Eerdmans, 1993.
Elliott, John. *Conflict, Community, and Honor: 1 Peter in Social-Scientific Perspective*. Eugene, OR: Cascade, 2007.
Engberg-Pedersen, Troels. *Cosmology and Self in the Apostle Paul: The Material Spirit*. New York: Oxford University Press, 2010.
———. *John and Philosophy: A New Reading of the Fourth Gospel*. Oxford: Oxford University Press, 2017.
———. *Paul and the Stoics*. Louisville: Westminster John Knox, 2000.
Eusebius. *Ecclesiastical History, Books 1–5*. Translated by Lake Kirsopp. Loeb Classical Library 153. Cambridge: Harvard University Press, 1926.
———. *Ecclesiastical History, Books 6–10*. Translated by J. E. L. Oulton. Loeb Classical Library 265. Cambridge: Harvard University Press, 1926.
Fee, Gordon. *The First Epistle to the Corinthians*. Grand Rapids: Eerdmans, 1987.
———. *God's Empowering Presence: The Holy Spirit in the Letters of Paul*. Peabody, MA: Hendrickson, 2009.
Fitzmeyer, Joseph. *Romans*. Anchor Bible 33. New York: Doubleday, 1993.
France, R. T. *The Gospel of Matthew*. Grand Rapids: Eerdmans, 2007.
Fredriksen, Paula. *Paul: The Pagans' Apostle*. New Haven: Yale University Press, 2017.
———. *When Christians Were Jews: The First Generation*. New Haven: Yale University Press, 2018.
Funk, Robert. *The Five Gospels: The Search for the Authentic Words of Jesus*. San Francisco: HarperSanFrancisco, 1993.

Bibliography

Furnish, Victor Paul. *II Corinthians*. Anchor Bible 32A. Garden City, NY: Doubleday, 1984.

Gabler, J. P. *"De justo discrimine theologiae biblicae et dogmaticae regundisque recte utriusque finibus."* In "J. P. Gabler and the Distinction between Biblical and Dogmatic Theology: Translation, Commentary, and Discussion of His Originality," by John Sandys-Wunsch and Laurence Eldredge. *Scottish Journal of Theology* 33.2 (1980) 133–58.

Gaston, Lloyd. *Paul and the Torah*. Eugene, OR: Wipf & Stock, 2006.

Gonazlez, Justo. *The Story of Christianity*. Vol. 1, *The Early Church to the Dawn of the Reformation*. San Francisco: Harper & Row, 1984.

Goulder, Michael. "Did Luke Know Any of the Pauline Letters?" *Perspectives in Religious Studies* 13.2 (1986) 97–112.

———. *Midrash and Lection in Matthew: The Speaker's Lectures in Biblical Studies, 1969-71*. London: SPCK, 1974.

———. *Paul and the Competing Mission at Corinth*. Library of Pauline Studies. Peabody, MA: Hendrickson, 2001.

Grebel, Conrad, et al. "Letter to Thomas Müntzer." In *The Protestant Reformation*, edited by Hans J. Hillerbrand, 163–71. New York: Harper Perennial, 2009.

Green, Gene. *The Letters to the Thessalonians*. Pillar New Testament Commentary. Grand Rapids: Eerdmans, 2002.

Greene, Gene L. *Vox Petri: A Theology of Peter*. Eugene, OR: Cascade, 2020.

Greenfield, Guy. Review of *The Origin of I Corinthians*, by John C. Hurd. *Southwestern Journal of Theology* 27.1 (1984) 63.

Gregory, Andrew. "1 Clement and the Writings That Later Formed the New Testament." In *The Reception of the New Testament in the Apostolic Father*, edited by Andrew Gregory and Christopher Tuckett, 129–57. Oxford: Oxford University Press, 2005.

Griesbach, J. J. *Synoptic and Text Critical Studies*. Edited and translated by Thomas Longstaff and Bernard Orchard. New York: Cambridge University Press, 2011.

Grimshaw, James. *The Matthean Community and the World*. Studies in Biblical Literature 111. New York: Lang, 2008.

Gutwenger, Engelbert. "The Anti-Marcionite Prologues." *Theological Studies* 7.2 (1946) 393–409.

Hainz, Josef. *Ekklesia: Strukturen paulinischer Gemeinde-Theologie und Gemeinde-Ordnung*. Biblische Untersuchungen 9. Regensburg: Puster, 1972.

Harnack, Adolf von. "Lightfoot on the Ignatian Epistles: II. Genuineness and Date of the Epistles." *The Expositor* 3.1 (1886) 9–22.

———. *Das Wesen des Christentums*. Leipzig: Hinrichs, 1902.

———. *Die Zeit des Ignatius und die Chronologie der antioschentschen Bischöfe bis Tyrannus nach Julius Africanus und den späteren Historikern*. Leipzig: Hinrichs, 1876.

Harris, Murray. *2 Corinthians*. New International Greek Testament Commentary. Grand Rapids: Eerdmans, 2005.

Hart, David Bentley. *The New Testament: A Translation*. New Haven: Yale University Press, 2017.

Hartman, Lars. *Prophecy Interpreted: The Formation of Some Jewish Apocalyptic Texts and of the Eschatological Discourse (Mark 13 Par.)*. Coniectanea Biblica NT Series 1. Lund: CWK Gleerup, 1966.

Hartwig, Charlotte, and Gerd Thiessen. "*Die Korinthische Gemeinde als Nebenadressat des Römerbriefs. Eigentextreferenzen des Paulus und Kommunikativer Kontext des Längsten Paulusbriefes.*" Novum Testamentum 46.3 (2004) 229–52.

Hays, Richard B. *Echoes of Scripture in the Letters of Paul*. New Haven: Yale University Press, 1989.

———. *First Corinthians*. Interpretation. Louisville: Westminster John Knox, 1997.

———. *The Moral Vision of the New Testament: Community, Cross, New Creation*. San Francisco: HarperSanFrancisco, 1996.

Hengel, Martin. *The "Hellenization" of Judea in the First Century after Christ*. Translated by John Bowden. Philadelphia: Trinity Press International, 1989.

———. *Judaism and Hellenism*. Translated by J. Bowden. Eugene, OR: Wipf & Stock, 2003.

———. *Paulus und Jakobus*. Wissenschaftliche Untersuchungen zum Neuen Testament 141. Tübingen: Mohr, 2002.

———. "The Stance of the Apostle Paul toward the Law in the Unknown Years between Damascus and Antioch." In *Justification and Variegated Nomism*. Vol. 2, *The Paradoxes of Paul*, edited by D. A. Carson et al., 75–104. Grand Rapids: Baker Academic, 2004.

Hoegen-Rohls, Christina. "Johanneische Theologie im Kontext paulinischen Denkens?" In *Kontexte des Johannesevangeliums*, edited by Jörg Frey and Udo Schnell, 593–612. Wissenschaftliche Untersuchungen zum Neuen Testament 175. Tübingen: Mohr Siebeck, 2004.

Holmes, Michael, ed. *The Apostolic Fathers: Greek Texts and English Translations*. 3rd ed. Grand Rapids: Baker Academic, 2007.

Hoppe, Rudolf. *Der Erste Thessalonikerbrief*. Freiburg im Breisgau: Herder, 2016.

Hoppin, Ruth. "The Epistle to the Hebrews Is Priscilla's Letter." In *Feminist Companion to the Catholic Epistles and Hebrews*, edited by Amy-Jill Levine, 147–70. London: T. & T. Clark International, 2004.

———. *Priscilla: Author of the Epistle to the Hebrews, and Other Essays*. New York: Exposition, 1969.

Horsley, Richard, ed. *Paul and Empire: Religion and Power in Roman Imperial Society*. Harrisburg, PA: Trinity, 1998.

Hurd, John C. *The Origin of I Corinthians*. Macon, GA: Mercer University Press, 1983.

Hurst, L. D. *Hebrews: Its Background of Thought*. Cambridge: Cambridge University Press, 1990.

Irenaeus of Lyons. *Against the Heresies*. Vol. 1. Translated by Dominic J. Unger. Ancient Christian Writers 55. Mahwah, NJ: Paulist, 1992.

Jacobi, Christine. *Jesusüberlieferung bei Paulus? Analogien zwischen den echten Paulusbriefen und den synoptischen Evangelien*. Beihefte zur Zeitschrift für die neutestamentliche Wissenschaft 213. Berlin: de Gruyter, 2015.

Jenson, Robert. *Canon and Creed*. Louisville: Westminster John Knox, 2010.

———. *Systematic Theology*. Vol. 2. New York: Oxford University Press, 1999.

Jewett, Robert. *A Chronology of Paul's Life*. London: SCM, 1979.

———. *Dating Paul's Life*. London: SCM, 1979.

———. *Romans*. Hermeneia. Minneapolis: Fortress, 2007.

Johnson, Luke Timothy. *The First and Second Letters to Timothy*. Anchor Bible 35A. New York: Doubleday, 2001.

———. *Hebrews: A Commentary*. New Testament Library. Louisville: Westminster John Knox, 2012.

———. *The Letters to Timothy and Titus*. Grand Rapids: Eerdmans, 2006.

———. *Living Jesus: Learning the Heart of the Gospel*. San Francisco: HarperSanFrancisco, 1998.

Josephus. *Against Apion*. Translated by H. St. J. Thackerary. Loeb Classical Library 186. Cambridge: Harvard University Press, 1926.

———. *Jewish Antiquities*. Translated by H. St. J. Thackerary. Loeb Classical Library 242. Cambridge: Harvard University Press, 1930.

———. *The Jewish War*. Translated by H. St. J. Thackerary. Loeb Classical Library 203. Cambridge: Harvard University Press, 1927.

Jowett, Benjamin. "The Interpretation of Scripture." In *Essays and Reviews*, edited by John Williams Parker, 330–443. London: Parker and Son, 1860.

Jüngel, Eberhard. *Justification: The Heart of the Church's Faith*. New York: Continuum, 2006.

Justin Martyr. *Dialogue with Trypho*. http://www.newadvent.org/fathers/0128.htm.

———. *First and Second Apologies*. Translated by Leslie William Barnard. Ancient Christian Writers 56. New York: Paulist, 1997.

Kant, Immanuel. *Religion within the Bounds of Mere Reason, and Other Writings*. Edited and translated by Allen Wood and George D. Giovanni. New York: Cambridge University Press, 1998.

Käsemann, Ernst. *Perspectives on Paul*. Philadelphia: Fortress, 1971.

Keith, Chris. *Jesus' Literacy: Scribal Culture and the Teacher from Galilee*. Library of Historical Jesus Studies 8. Library of New Testament Studies 413. London: T. & T. Clark, 2011.

———. "The Kerygmatic Narratives of the Gospels and the Historical Jesus: Current Debates, Prior Debates, and the Goal of Historical Jesus Research." *Journal for the Study of the New Testament* 4 (2016) 426–55.

Kim, Seyoon. "The Jesus Tradition in 1 Thess. 4:13—5:11." *New Testament Studies* 48 (2002) 225–42.

Kistemaker, Simon. "The Authorship of Hebrews." *Faith and Mission* 18.2 (2001) 57–69.

Klijn, Albertus Frederik Johannes, and G. J. Reinik. *Patristic Evidence for Jewish Christian Heresies*. Leiden: Brill, 1973.

Kloppenborg, John. *Excavating Q: The History and Setting of the Sayings Gospel*. Minneapolis: Fortress, 2000.

Knox, John. *Chapters in a Life of Paul*. Macon, GA: Mercer University Press, 1987.

Kümmel, Werner Georg. *Introduction to the New Testament*. Translated by Howard Clark Kee. Nashville: Abingdon, 1996.

LeDonne, Anthony. *Historical Jesus: What Can We Know and How Can We Know It?* Grand Rapids: Eerdmans, 2011.

———. *The Historiographical Jesus: Memory, Typology and the Son of David*. Waco, TX: Baylor University Press, 2009.

Lee, Simon S. *Jesus' Transfiguration and the Believers' Transformation*. Wissenschaftliche Untersuchungen zum Neuen Testament 2.265. Tübingen: Mohr Siebeck, 2009.

Leithart, Peter. *Delivered from the Elements of the World: Atonement, Justification, Mission*. Downers Grove, IL: IVP Academic, 2016.

Lemaire, Andre. *Les Ministères aux Origines de l'Église: Naissance de la Triple Hierarchie— Évêques, Presbytres, Diacres*. Lectio Divina 68. Paris: Éditions du Cerf, 1971.

Lessing, Gotthold Ephraim. "On the Proof of the Spirit and of Power (1777)." *Lessing: Philosophical and Theological writings*, edited and translated by H. B. Nisbet, 37–60. Cambridge Texts in the History of Philosophy. New York: Cambridge University Press, 2005.

Lewis, C. S. *The Great Divorce: A Dream*. New York: HarperOne, 2000.
Liddell, Henry George, et al. *A Greek-English Lexicon*. 9th ed. Oxford: Clarendon, 1996.
Lightfoot, J. B. *The Apostolic Fathers, pt. 1: S. Clement of Rome*. 2 vols. London: Macmillan, 1890.
———. *The Apostolic Fathers, pt. 2: S. Ignatius, S. Polycarp*. 3 vols. London: Macmillan, 1889.
———. *Dissertations on the Apostolic Age*. London: Macmillan and Co., 1892.
Lindemann, Andreas. *Erste Korintherbrief*. Handbuch zum Neuen Testament 9/1. Tübingen: Mohr Siebeck, 2000.
List, Nicholas. "Δίψυχος: Moving beyond Intertextuality." *New Testament Studies* 67.1 (2021) 85–104.
Locke, John. "An Essay for the Understanding of St. Paul's Epistles, by Consulting St. Paul Himself." In *The Clarendon Edition of the Works of John Locke: A Paraphrase and Notes on the Epistles of St. Paul*, edited by Arthur Wainwright, 103–19. New York City: Oxford University Press, 1987.
Lohse, Eduard. "St. Peter's Apostleship in the Judgment of St. Paul, the Apostle to the Gentiles: An Exegetical Contribution to an Ecumenical Debate." *Gregorianum* 72.3 (1991) 419–35.
Longenecker, Richard. *Galatians*. Word Biblical Commentary 41. Nashville: Nelson, 1990.
Lüdemann, Gerd. *The Great Deception: And What Jesus Actually Said and Did*. London: SCM, 1998.
———. *Paul, Apostle to the Gentiles: Studies in Chronology*. Translated by F. Stanley Jones. Philadelphia: Fortress, 1984.
———. *Paul: The Founder of Christianity*. Amherst: Prometheus, 2002.
Luther, Martin. "Of the Babylonian Captivity of the Church." In *Three Treatises*, translated by A. T. W. Steinhauser. Philadelphia: Fortress, 1970.
Luz, Ulrich. *Matthew 1–7*. Translated by James E. Crouch Hermeneia. Minneapolis: Fortress, 2007.
———. *Matthew 8–20*. Translated by James E. Crouch Hermeneia. Hermeneia. Minneapolis: Fortress, 2001.
———. *Matthew 21–28*. Translated by James E. Crouch Hermeneia. Hermeneia. Minneapolis: Fortress, 2005.
MacIntyre, Alasdair. *Whose Justice, Which Rationality?* Notre Dame: University of Notre Dame Press, 1988.
Malherbe, Abraham. *The Letters to the Thessalonians*. Anchor Bible 32B. New Haven: Yale University Press, 2000.
Marcus, Joel. *Mark 1–8*. Anchor Bible 27. New Haven: Yale University Press, 1999.
———. *Mark 8–16*. Anchor Bible 27A. New Haven: Yale University Press, 2009.
———. Review of *Not by Paul Alone*, by David R. Nienhuis. *Catholic Biblical Quarterly* 70.2 (2008) 384–85.
———. "'The Twelve Tribes in the Diaspora' (James 1.1)." *New Testament Studies* 60.4 (2014) 433–47.
Marshall, I. Howard. *1 and 2 Thessalonians*. Vancouver: Regent College, 2002.
———. *The Gospel of Luke: A Commentary on the Greek Text*. New International Greek Testament Commentary. Grand Rapids: Eerdmans, 1978.
———. *New Testament Theology: Many Witnesses, One Gospel*. Downer's Grove, IL: InterVarsity, 2004.

Martin, Dale B. *The Corinthian Body*. New Haven: Yale University Press, 1995.
Martyn, J. Louis. *Galatians*. Anchor Bible 33. New Haven: Yale University Press, 1997.
———. *History and Theology in the Fourth Gospel*. 3rd ed. Louisville: Westminster John Knox, 2003.
———. *Theological Issues in the Letters of Paul*. Nashville: Abingdon, 1997.
Massaux, Edouard. *Influence de l'évangile de saint Matthieu sur la littérature chrétien avant S. Irénée*. Louvain: Universitas Catholica Lovaniensis, 1950.
Matera, Frank. *New Testament Theology: Exploring Diversity and Unity*. Louisville: Westminster John Knox, 2007.
Matson, Jason. "Anthropological Crisis and Solution in the *Hodayot* and 1 Corinthians 15." *New Testament Studies* 62.4 (2016) 533–48.
Mbuvi, Andrew Mutua. *Temple, Exile, and Identity in 1 Peter*. London: Bloomsbury, 2007.
McFadden, Kevin. *Judgment according to Works in Romans: The Meaning and Function of Divine Judgment in Paul's Most Important Letter*. Minneapolis: Fortress, 2013.
McGrath, Alister. *Iustitia Dei*. Cambridge: Cambridge University Press, 1986.
McKnight, Scott. *The Letter of James*. New International Commentary on the New Testament. Grand Rapids: Eerdmans, 2011.
Meier, John P. *A Marginal Jew*. 4 vols. New York: Doubleday, 1991.
Meisner, Balthasar. *Anthropologia Sacra*. Wittenberg: Gormannus, 1615.
Ménégoz, Eugéne. *La Theologie de l'epitre aux Hébreux*. Paris: Fischbacher, 1894.
Merkel, Helmut. "Clemens Alexandrinus uber die Reihenfolge der Evangelien." *ETL* 60 (1984) 382–85.
Metzger, Bruce. *Canon: Its Origin, Significance, and Development*. New York: Oxford University Press, 1989.
Mitchell, Allan. *Hebrews*. Sacra Pagina. Collegeville, MN: Liturgical, 2007.
Mitchell, Margaret. Review of *The Corinthian Body*, by Dale Martin. *Journal of Religion* 77.2 (1997) 290–92.
Moffatt, James. *An Introduction to the Literature of the New Testament*. New York: Scribner's Sons, 1911.
Montefiore, Hugh. *A Commentary on the Epistle to the Hebrews*. Harper's New Testament Commentaries. New York: Harper & Row, 1964.
Moo, Douglas. *James*. Pillar New Testament Commentary. Grand Rapids: Eerdmans, 2000.
———. *Romans*. New International Commentary on the New Testament. Grand Rapids: Eerdmans, 1996.
The Muratorian Canon. http://www.earlychristianwritings.com/text/muratorian.html.
Murphy-O'Connor, Jerome. *Paul: A Critical Life*. New York: Oxford University Press, 1996.
Najman, Hindy. "The Writings and Reception of Philo of Alexandria." In *Christianity in Jewish Terms*, edited by Tivka Simone Frymer-Kensky et al., 99–106. Boulder, CO: Westview, 2000.
Nanos, Mark D. *The Mystery of Romans: The Jewish Context of Paul's Letters*. Minneapolis: Fortress, 1996.
———. "The Polytheist Identity of the 'Weak' and Paul's Strategy to 'Gain' Them: A New Reading of 1 Corinthians 8:1—11:1." In *Paul: Jew, Greek, and Roman*, edited by Stanley E. Porter, 179–210. Pauline Studies 5. Leiden: Brill, 2008.
Neirynck, Frans. "Paul and the Sayings of Jesus." In *L'Apôtre Paul*, edited by Albert Vanhoye, 265–321. Leuven: Leuven University Press, 1986.

Newman, John Henry. *Lectures on the Doctrine of Justification.* https://www.newmanreader.org/works/justification/index.html.

Nienhuis, David. *Not by Paul Alone: The Formation of the Catholic Epistle Collection and the Christian Canon.* Waco, TX: Baylor, 2007.

Omanson, Roger L. Review of *The Origin of I Corinthians*, by John C. Hurd. *Review & Expositor* 80.4 (1983) 621–22.

Origen. *Contra Celsum.* http://www.newadvent.org/fathers/0412.htm.

———. *Commentary on the Epistle to the Romans, Books 1–5.* Translated by Thomas Scheck. Washington, DC: Catholic University of America Press, 2001.

———. *De Principiis.* http://www.newadvent.org/fathers/0412.htm.

———. *Homilies on Joshua.* Edited by Cynthia White. Translated by Barbara J. Bruce. The Fathers of the Church 105. Washington, DC: Catholic University of America Press, 1996.

———. *Homilies on Luke.* Translated by Joseph Lienhard. The Fathers of the Church 94. Washington, DC: Catholic University of America Press, 2002.

———. *To Africanus.* http://www.newadvent.org/fathers/0412.htm.

Overbeck, Franz. *Zur Geschichte des Kanons, 2 Abhandlungen.* Chemitz: Schmeitzer, 1880.

Owen, Paul. "The 'Works of the Law' in Romans and Galatians: A New Defense of the Subjective Genitive." *Journal of Biblical Literature* 126.3 (2007) 553–77.

Pagels, Elaine. *The Gnostic Paul: Gnostic Exegesis of the Pauline Letters.* London: Continuum International, 1992.

———. *The Johannine Gospel in Gnostic Exegesis: Heracleon's Commentary on John.* Society of Biblical Literature Monograph Series 17. Nashville: Abingdon, 1973.

Peel, Malcolm L. "The Treatise on the Resurrection: Text, Translation, and Commentary." In *Coptic Gnostic Library Online*, edited by James M. Robinson. Brill: Leiden, 2000. http://dx.doi.org.ezp-prod1.hul.harvard.edu/10.1163/9789004228900_cgl_aTTOTR.

Pervo, Richard I. *Acts.* Minneapolis: Fortress, 2009.

———. Review of *The Origin of 1 Corinthians*, by John C. Hurd. *Anglican Theological Review* 65.4 (1983) 459–60.

Philo. *Legum Allegoriae.* Translated by F. H. Colson and G. H. Whitaker. Loeb Classical Library 226. Cambridge: Harvard University Press, 1929.

———. *On the Confusion of Tongues. On the Migration of Abraham. Who Is the Heir of Divine Things? On Mating with the Preliminary Studies.* Translated by F. H. Colson and G. H. Whitaker. Loeb Classical Library 261. Cambridge: Harvard University Press, 1932.

———. *On the Decalogue. On the Special Laws, Books 1–3.* Translated by F. H. Colson. Loeb Classical Library 320. Cambridge: Harvard University Press, 1937.

Pirkei Avot. Translated by R. Travers Herford. New York: Jewish Institute of Religion, 1945.

Pitre, Brant. *Jesus and the Last Supper.* Grand Rapids: Eerdmans, 2015.

Pitre, Brant, et al. *Paul, a New Covenant Jew: Rethinking Pauline Theology.* Grand Rapids: Eerdmans, 2019. Kindle.

Porter, Stanley E. "Luke: Companion or Disciple of Paul?" In *Paul and the Gospels: Christologies, Conflicts, and Convergences*, edited by Michael Bird and Joel Willitts, 146–68. New York: T. & T. Clark, 2011.

Powell, Mark Alan. *Jesus as a Figure in History: How Modern Historians View the Man from Galilee.* 2nd ed. Louisville: Westminster John Knox, 2013.

Powers, B. Ward. *The Progressive Publication of Matthew: An Explanation of the Writing of the Synoptic Gospels*. Nashville: B&H, 2010.

Prothero, Stephen. *American Jesus: How the Son of God Became a National Icon*. New York: Farrar, Straus, and Giroux, 2003.

Ratzinger, Joseph. "Biblical Interpretation in Crisis: The 1988 Erasmus Lecture." https://www.firstthings.com/web-exclusives/2008/04/biblical-interpretation-in-crisis.

Reasoner, Mark. *The Strong and the Weak: Romans 14:1—15:13 in Context*. Society for New Testament Studies Monograph Series 103. Cambridge: Cambridge University Press, 1999.

Regul, Jürgen. *Die antimarcionitischen evangelienprologe*. Freiburg: Herder: 1969.

Reumann, John. *Philippians*. Anchor Bible 33B. New Haven: Yale University Press, 2008.

Richards, E. Randolph. *Paul and First-Century Letter Writing: Secretaries, Composition, and Collection*. Downers Grove, IL: InterVarsity, 2004.

Riesner, Rainard. "Pauline Chronology." In *A Blackwell Companion to Paul*, edited by Stephen Westerholm, 9–29. Chichester: Wiley-Blackwell, 2011.

Riley, Harold, and Bernard Orchard. *The Order of the Synoptics: Why Three Synoptic Gospels?* Macon, GA: Mercer University Press, 1987.

Robinson, James M., ed. *Coptic Gnostic Library Online*. https://scholarlyeditions.brill.com/cglo/.

———. *The Nag Hammadi Library in English*. Leiden: Brill Academic, 1977.

Robinson, James M., et al., eds. *The Critical Edition of Q*. Minneapolis: Fortress, 2000.

Robinson, John Arthur Thomas. *The Priority of John*. Eugene, OR: Wipf & Stock, 2011.

———. *Redating the New Testament*. London: SCM, 1976.

Rothschild, Clare. *Hebrews as Pseudepigraphon: The History and Significance of the Pauline Attribution of Hebrews*. Wissenschaftliche Untersuchungen zum Neuen Testament. Tübingen: Mohr-Siebeck, 2009.

Rousseau, Jean-Jacques. "Profession of Faith of a Savoyard Vicar." In *Émile, or, On Education*, translated by Alan Bloom, 425–98. New York: Basic, 1979.

Rowe, C. Kavin. "NT Theology: The Revival of a Discipline." *Journal of Biblical Literature* 125.2 (2006) 393–419.

———. *World Upside Down: Reading Acts in the Graeco-Roman Age*. New York: Oxford University Press, 2010.

Runia, David T. *Philo in Early Christian Literature: A Survey*. Compendia Rerum Iudaicarum ad Novum Testamentum 3. Minneapolis: Fortress, 1995.

Sampley, Paul. *The First Letter to the Corinthians*. In vol. 10 of *New Interpreter's Bible*, edited by Leander E. Keck, 771–1003. Nashville: Abingdon, 2002.

Sanders, E. P. *Jesus and Judaism*. Philadelphia: Fortress, 1985.

———. *Paul and Palestinian Judaism*. Philadelphia: Fortress, 1977.

———. *Paul: A Very Short Introduction*. Oxford: Oxford University Press, 2001.

Sanders, E. P., and Margaret Davies. *Studying the Synoptic Tradition*. London: SCM, 1989.

Schlatter, Adolf. "The Theology of the New Testament and Dogmatics." In *The Nature of New Testament Theology: The Contribution of William Wrede and Adolf Schlatter*, edited by Robert Morgan, 117–66. Studies in Biblical Theology 25. Norwich: SCM, 2002.

Schleiermacher, Friedrich. *Der christliche Glaube*. Band I. Berlin: de Gruyter, 1984.

Schnelle, Udo. *The Theology of the New Testament*. Translated by M. Eugene Boring. Grand Rapids: Baker Academic, 2009.

Schweitzer, Albert. *Mysticism of Paul*. Translated by William Montgomery. Baltimore: Johns Hopkins University Press, 1998.

Scroggs, Robin. "Romans VI. 7." *New Testament Studies* 10.1 (1963) 104–8.

Second Vatican Council. *Dei verbum*. https://www.vatican.va/archive/hist_councils/ii_vatican_council/documents/vat-ii_const_19651118_dei-verbum_en.html.

Shogren, Gary. *1 and 2 Thessalonians*. Zondervan Exegetical Commentary Series on the New Testament. Grand Rapids: Zondervan, 2012.

Sim, David. *The Gospel of Matthew and Christian Judaism: The History and Social Setting of the Matthean Community*. London: Bloomsbury Academic, 1998.

Sowers, Sidney. *The Hermeneutics of Philo and Hebrews: A Comparison of the Interpretation of the Old Testament in Philo Judaeus and the Epistle to the Hebrews*. Zurich: EVZ, 1965.

Spicq, Ceslas. *L'Epitre aux Hébreux*. 2 vols. Paris: Gabalda, 1977.

Stanton, Graham. *A Gospel for a New People: Studies in Matthew*. Louisville: Westminster John Knox, 1993.

Steele, R. B. "The Greek in Cicero's Epistles." *The American Journal of Philology* 21.4 (1900) 387–410.

Stowers, Stanley. *The Diatribe and Paul's Letter to the Romans*. Society of Biblical Literature Dissertation Series 57. Atlanta: Society of Biblical Literature, 1981.

Strecker, Georg. *Theology of the New Testament*. New York: de Gruyter, 2012.

Streeter, Burnett Hillman. *The Four Gospels: A Study of Origins, Treating of the Manuscript Tradition, Sources, Authorship, & Dates*. London: Macmillan & Co., 1930.

Styler, G. M. "The Priority of Mark." In *The Two-Source Hypothesis: A Critical Appraisal*, edited by Arthur Bellinzoni Jr., 63–76. Macon, GA: Mercer University Press, 1985.

Tacitus. *Annals*. Translated by William Jackson Brodribb. New York: Macmillan, 1921.

Talmud Bavli. https://www.sefaria.org/texts/Talmud/Bavli.

Tertullian. *Adversus Marcionem*. Vol. 2, *Books IV–V*. Edited and translated by Ernest Evans. Oxford: Clarendon, 1972.

Theissen, Gerd. *The Gospels in Context: Social and Political History in the Synoptic Tradition*. Translated by Linda Maloney. Minneapolis: Fortress, 1991.

Theological Dictionary of the New Testament. 10 vols. Edited by Gerhard Kittel and Gerhard Friedrich. Translated by Geoffrey W. Bromiley. Grand Rapids: Eerdmans, 1964–76.

Thiessen, Matthew. "Hebrews 12:5–13, the Wilderness Period, and Israel's Discipline." *New Testament Studies* 55 (2009) 366–79.

Thiselton, Anthony C. *The First Epistle to the Corinthians*. New International Greek Testament Commentary. Grand Rapids: Eerdmans, 2000.

Thompson, A. C. C. "Refuge of Oppression. From the Delaware Republican to the PUblic. Falsehood Refuted." http://docsouth.unc.edu/neh/douglass/support2.html.

Thompson, Michael. *Clothed with Christ: The Example and Teaching of Jesus in Romans 12.1—15.13*. Eugene, OR: Wipf & Stock, 1991.

Thrall, Margaret E. *The Second Epistle to the Corinthians*. Vol. I. International Critical Commentary. Edinburgh: T. & T. Clark, 1994.

Troeltsch, Ernst. "On the Historical and Dogmatic Method in Theology." In *Gesammelte Schriften, Volume II*, translated by Jack Forstman, 728–53. Tubingen: Mohr Siebeck, 1913.

Tuckett, Christopher. *From the Sayings to the Gospels*. Wissenschaftliche Untersuchungen zum Neuen Testament 328. Tübingen: Mohr Siebeck, 2014.
Vermes, Geza, trans. and ed. *The Complete Dead Sea Scrolls in English*. New York: Penguin, 1997.
Volf, Miroslav. "Soft Difference: Theological Reflections on the Relation between Church and Culture in 1 Peter." *Ex Auditu* 10 (1994) 15–30.
Voulgaris, Christos S. "Hebrews: Paul's Fifth Epistle from Prison." *Greek Orthodox Theological Review* 44 (1999) 199–206.
Wagner, Jochen. *Die Anfange des Amtes in der Kirche*. Tübingen: Francke, 2011.
Wainwright, Geoffrey. *Doxology: The Praise of God in Worship, Doctrine, and Life*. New York City: Oxford University Press, 1984.
Watson, Francis. *Gospel Writing: A Canonical Perspective*. Grand Rapids: Eerdmans, 2013.
Wenham, David. *Paul and Jesus: The True Story*. Grand Rapids: Eerdmans, 2002.
———. "Paul's Use of the Jesus Tradition: Three Samples." In *Gospel Perspectives*. Vol. 5, *The Jesus Tradition outside the Gospels*, edited by David Wenham, 7–38. Sheffield: JSOT, 1984.
Wenham, John. *Redating Matthew, Mark, and Luke: A Fresh Assault on the Synoptic Problem*. London: Hodder & Stoughton, 1991.
Weschler, Andreas. *Geschichtsbild und Apostelstreit: Eine forschungsgeschichtliche und exegetische Studie über den antioschenischen Zwischenfall (Gal 2,11–14)*. Beihefte zur Zeitschrift für die neutestamentliche Wissenschaft 62. Berlin: de Gruyter, 1991.
Williams, Travis. *Good Works in 1 Peter: Negotiating Social Conflict and Christian Identity in the Greco-Roman World*. Berlin: Mohr Siebeck, 2014.
Williamson, Ronald. *Philo and the Epistle to the Hebrews*. Netherlands: Leiden, 1970.
Willitts, Joel. "Paul and Matthew: A Descriptive Approach from a Post-New Perspective Interpretative Framework." In *Paul and the Gospels: Christologies, Conflicts, Convergences*, edited by Michael Bird and Joel Willitts, 62–85. New York: T. & T. Clark, 2011.
Winter, Bruce. *After Paul Left Corinth: The Influence of Secular Ethics and Social Change*. Grand Rapids: Eerdmans, 2001.
Witherington, Ben, III. *Conflict and Community in Corinth: A Socio-Rhetorical Commentary on 1–2 Corinthians*. Grand Rapids: Eerdmans, 1995.
———. *Letters and Homilies for Early Jewish Christians*. Downers Grove, IL: InterVarsity, 2007.
———. *Matthew*. Macon, GA: Smyth & Helwys, 2006.
———. Review of *Forged*, by Bart Ehrman. http://www.patheos.com/blogs/bibleandculture/2011/04/07/forged-chapter-four-alternatives-to-forgery/
Wittgenstein, Ludwig. *Philosophical Investigations*. Translated by G. E. M Anscombe et al. Hoboken, NJ: Wiley-Blackwell, 1963.
Wrede, William. *Das Messiasgeheimnis in den Evangelien; Zugleich ein Beitrag zum Verständnis des Markusevangeliums*. Göttingen: Vandenhoeck & Ruprecht, 1901.
———. *Paul*. Translated by Edward Lummis. London: Green, 1907.
———. "The Tasks and Methods of 'New Testament Theology.'" In *The Nature of New Testament Theology: The Contribution of William Wrede and Adolf Schlatter.*, edited by Robert Morgan, 68–116. Studies in Biblical Theology 25. Norwich: SCM, 2002.

Wright, N. T. *Jesus and the Victory of God*. Christian Origins and the Question of God 2. Minneapolis: Fortress, 1996.
———. *Justification: God's Plan and Paul's Vision*. Downers Grove: InterVarsity, 2009.
———. *The New Testament and the People of God*. Christian Origins and the Question of God 1. Minneapolis: Fortress, 1992.
———. *Paul and the Faithfulness of God*. Christian Origins and the Question of God 4. Minneapolis: Fortress, 2013.
———. *Paul and His Recent Interpreters: Some Contemporary Debates*. London: SPCK, 2015.
———. *The Resurrection of the Son of God*. Christian Origins and the Question of God 3. Minneapolis: Fortress, 2003.
———. *What St. Paul Really Said: Was Paul the Real Founder of Christianity?* Oxford: Lion, 1997.
Zahn, Theodor. *Ignatius von Antiochen*. Gotha: Perthes, 1873.
Ziesler, John A. *Paul's Letter to the Romans*. TPI New Testament Commentaries. Philadelphia: Trinity International, 1989.
Zwierlein, Otto. *Petrus in Rom: die literarischen Zeugnisse: mit einer kritischen Edition der Martyrien des Petrus und Paulus auf neuer handschriftlicher Grundlage*. Berlin: de Gruyter, 2009.
Zwingli, Huldrich. *Commentary on True and False Religion*. Edited by Samuel Macauley Jackson and Clarence Nevin Heller. Durham, NC: Labyrinth, 1981.

Scripture Index

OLD TESTAMENT

Genesis
1:26	139
2:7	137–39, 144
3:46	39
15:5–6	23, 39
17	39
17:13	37
22:1–18	23
28:15	97–99

Exodus
16:4	143
20:17	43
34:29–35	83–84
48	137

Leviticus
17:10	38
18	37
18:5	38
18:7–18	80
18:30	38

19	38
19:12	38
19:13	38
19:15	38
19:16	38
19:17b	38
19:18a	38
19:18	86–87

Numbers
1	25

Deuteronomy
1:6	97
6:4	23
6:5	87
8:5	98
8	98
10:30	97
22:13–24	80
27:15–26	43
28:15–68	43
30:6	39
31	98
31:6	97, 99–100

2 Kingdoms

25:1	77

1 Chronicles

12:33	21
28	101

Ezra

3:31–32	26

Psalm

12:3	21
72:12	41
96:5	26
96:10	26

Proverbs

3:11–12	98
8	138

Ecclesiastes

	193

Isaiah

8:14	177
13:10	77
27:13	72
28:16	177
58	26
58:1–8	25
65:8	77

Jeremiah

31:31–34	83–84

Ezekiel

33:3–32	25
36:22–38	40
36:22–26	136
36:27	137
37	40, 41
37:1–6	142
37:1–14	44
37:5	44
37:6	137
37:14	136–37
37:12–14	137
37:28	137

Daniel

7	74
7:13	74
7:13–14	143
11:31	77
12:2–3	74–75

Joel

2	75
2:1	75
3:15	77

NEW TESTAMENT

Matthew

1:2	89
5:31–32	77
5:32	79
8–20	81, 85
9:36–37	81
10:1–2	81
10:1–15	81
10:1–16	82
10:3	14
10:8	81
10:10	80, 81, 89
10:28	89
12:31	89
12:38–40	78
12:43–45	189
15:1–20	70
15:11	87
15:21–28	70, 81
16	85
16:13–20	70, 84
16:17–18	84–85, 160, 181
17	84
17:1–8	70
17:2	83
17:5	83, 89
17:6	83
17:20	36

19	80	**Mark**	
19:1–11	70	1:15	36
19:3	79	1:19	14
19:3–12	77	1:29	168
19:6	80	4:26–29	70
19:9	79, 80	5:39	75
19:10–12	80	6:3	16
19:16–22	70	6:6–13	81, 82
19:18–19	86–87	6:7	14
19:20	86	6:8–11	81
19:28	15	6:37	141
21:21	89	7:31–37	70
22:36–40	24, 87	7:1–23	70
22:37	89	7:18–19	87
23:3	25	7:24–30	70
23:31–32	72	8:12	78
23:37	72	8:22–26	70
24	70–77	8:27–30	84
24:2	76	9:2	83
24:4	76	9:14–27	70
24:6	76	9:33–37	70
24:12	76	10:1–10	70
24:15	77	10:2	79
24:15—31:1	72	10:2–12	78
24:16	77	10:11–12	78
24:22	77	10:17–27	86
24:24	72, 76	10:18	86
24:27	72, 76	13	71
24:29	77	13:5	76
24:30	89	13:7	76
24:30–31	72–75	13:14	76, 77
24:31	72, 76	13:20	77
24:33	89	13:22	76
24:42	76, 89	13:24	77
24:42–43	72, 75	13:35	89
24:44	75	13:37	89
24:47–49	72, 76	14:24	82
24–25	72	15:21	189
25:1–13	74	15:40	14
25:5	74	16:9–11	82
25:6	74		
25:7	75	**Luke**	
25:42–43	89	1:1–2	69
26:17–29	70	4:16–17	16
26:28	82	4:36	131
28:1–10	82	4:38	168
28:9	130	6:18	131
28:17	82	7:21	131

Luke (*cont.*)

8:2	131
9:18–22	84
9:32	84
9:35	89
10	81
10:1	81
10:2	81
10:1–16	80
10:4–12	81
10:7	80, 81
10:7–8	81
10:19	81
10:27	89
11:28	78
11:49–50	72
12	72
12:35	89
12:37	72, 76
12:39–40	72, 75
12:45	72, 76
16:18	78
17:6	36
18:18	86
18:20	86
21	71
21:20	77
21:34–36	76
22:17	141
22:19	82
22:20	82
22:24	82
23:32	152
23:47	44
24	131
24:1–11	82
24:13–27	130
24:16	131
24:31	131
24:34	82, 130
24:36	131
24:37	131
24:38–41	132
24:39	8, 127, 131
24:42	132

John

1:1–18	138
1:7	193
1:9–10	193
1:44	168
2:19	193
3	140
3:3	136, 140
3:5	140
3:6	140
3:12	140
3:13	140
3:16	36
3:23	36
6	126, 141
6:7	141
6:22–71	140
6:50a	143
6:54	142
6:62	143
6:63	142
9	188
11:25–26	73
11:11	75
12:20–21	143
12:24	135, 143
16	188
19:41	135, 144
20	144
20:1–2	82
20:11–18	82, 130
20:19	82
20:14	131
20:15	135
20:22	135, 144
20:27	127
20:31	36

Acts

1	152
1:2	94
2	152
2:5–14	19
3	152
4:13	166
6:1	19
9:26–30	151

10:9–16	88	2:1	31
10:15	88	2:6	41
11:26	181	2:11	21, 41
11:28	94	2:13	41, 43
11:29–30	19	2:15–46	43
11:30	151	2:17–25	42
12:17	14	2:25–29	25
12:25	151	2:26–29	42
15	6	2:28–29	31, 142
15:1	6, 35, 161	2:29	43
15:1–2	32, 158	3:8	31
15:1–4	32	3:10–18	43
15:1–29	19, 151	3:18	31, 38
15:2	32, 151	3:19–20	43
15:5	32	3:20	43
15:6–11	161	3:20–22	31
15:13	14	3:26–27	56
15:13–21	46	3:28–30	25
15:19	34	3:30	21
15:20	16, 38	4	13
15:22–29	52	4:1–25	31
15:29	112	4:3	154, 179
18:8	119	4:9–25	39
18:11	84	4:10–13	25
18:22	151	4:13–25	105
18:24	107	4:15	42
18:26	108	4:25	45
19:16	133	5:2	94
20:5	133	5:5	94
20:17–28	172	5:10	31
20:28	178	6:1	31, 38
21:4	94	6:2–4	45
21:17	151	6:3–4	31
21:21	25	6:5	44
21:26	133	6:7	44
21:27	133	7	43, 44
21:28	179	7:1	57, 128
23:8	133	7:2	41
26:26	3	7:2–3	79
27:1	133	7:7	38, 43
		7:7–25	43
Romans		7:9–11	31
1:8	195	7:11	41
1:13	57	7:12	43
1:17	159	7:13	43
1–2	61	7–8	33, 45
1–4	31	8	43, 137
2	29, 33	8:1	31

Romans (cont.)

8:1–13	31
8:2	43, 137
8:3	31
8:9	144
8:9–11	44
8:10	135
8:11	66
8:12	57
8:19–23	138
8:29	31
8:32	31
8:39	31
9	105
9:33	177
10:1	57
11:25	57
12	105, 195
12:1	57, 177
12:2	177
12:5	31, 111
12:9a	105
12:9–21	105
12:13	105
12:13b	105
12:10	105
12:10–21	110
13:8–9	86
13:9	86
14	58, 85
14:2	118
14:14	62, 87
14:14–15	163
14:15	57
14:20	87
15	172
15:7	113
15:14	57
15:25	59
15:25–32	33
15:26	35
15:30	57
15:30–32	161
15:33	104
16	117
16:1–16	19
16:3	108
16:7	31
16:18	31
16:20	104
16:23	117
16:25	160, 195

1 Corinthians   78–82

1:2	31, 67
1:10	57, 177
1:11	57
1:12	33, 155
1:13	119
1:22	78
1:26	57
2:1	57
2:5	36
2:6	114
2:11b–12	64
2:12	128
2:12–15	128
2:15	128
2:16	62
3	114
3:1	57
3:1–23	162
3:4	116
3:5	107
3:5–9	125
3:6	107
3:8	81
3:9	177
3:13–15	37
3:14	81
3:22	107
4	6, 107
4:15	63
5	49
5:1	6
5:2	50
5:2–5	47
5:3	64
5:5	31
5:9	52
5	11, 57
6	49
6:6	58
6:9	135
6:19–20	177

7	79	14:6	57
7:1b	55	14:20	57, 115
7: 1–7	80	14:22–25	58
7:1–16	80	14:36	175
7:10–11	78	15	7, 68, 129, 140
7:12	58	15:1	57
7:13	58	15:1–11	158
7:15	79	15:3	59, 67, 82, 131
7:20	47	15:3–8	195
7:40	66	15:4	137
7–8	162	15:5	10, 82, 130
8:1	162	15:5–7	82
8:2	65	15:6	57
8:6	78	15:8	152
8:7	58, 112	15:9	190
8:11	57	15:10	63
8–9	111	15:14	36
8–10	55	15:17	36
9	80	15:21–22	144
9:1	81, 152	15:30	57
9:2	81	15:35–50	8, 126, 137, 143
9:4–6	81	15:36–37	144
9:5	18, 34, 81	15:40	140
9:7	81	15:44	128, 139
9:11	81	15: 45	8, 45, 130
9:13	81	15:45–49	138, 144
9:14	80, 81	15:46	138
9:17–18	81	15:47	140
9:18	81	15:50	8, 45, 57, 131
9:19–23	124	15:52	72
10:27	58, 81	16	59
11:16	82	16:1	35, 54
11:23–26	82	16:1–4	33
11:24	141	16:1–9	53
11:25	82	16:11	57
11:33	57	16:12	57, 108, 162
12	125	16:15	19, 57
12:1	57	16:19	116
12:1–11	128	16:20	57
12:12	110		
12:12–27	110	**2 Corinthians**	83–84
12:13	31	1:24	36
12:21	65	2:17	31, 175
13	162	3	32, 40
13:2	36	3:1	34, 40
13:12	65	3:1–3	63
13:13	31, 36	3:1–9	83
14	125		

2 Corinthians (cont.)

3:2	40
3:3	42
3:3–6	83
3:6	31, 33, 40, 137
3:7–11	84
3:7–15	83
3:10–13	63
3:17	135
3:18	83, 84
3–4	83
4:1–6	83
4:4	83–84
4:5	83
4:6	83–84
4:13	36
5:7	36
5:10	37
5:16	89
8:7	36
8–9	33
9	53, 59
9:8	37
10:15	36
10–13	115
11:4	33, 66
11:5	33
11:14	64
11:22	33
11:23–27	178
11:32–33	201

Galatians

1	160
1:6	161
1:6–7	33
1:8	195
1:12	159
1:15–16	84, 85
1:16	152, 181
1:18	26, 36
1:18–19	71
2	48
2:1	26
2:1–10	36, 151
2:1–15	85, 159
2:2	157
2:2a	159
2:2–5	61
2:2–9	25
2:3	66
2:4	32, 61
2:6	68
2:7–8	85
2:9	14, 32, 34, 52, 85
2:9–10	68
2:10	18, 32, 34
2:11–14	85
2:11–16	8, 25, 32, 88, 158
2:12	32, 33, 35, 159
2:12–16	113
2:13	159
2:14	36, 180
2:16	25, 37, 38, 45
2:19	45
2:20	45
3	24
3:1–2	37
3:6–8	39
3:6–16	31
3:7	105
3:10	43
3:12	38
3:17–25	31
3:23	44
3:24	44
3:24–27	45
3:27–28	31
3	28, 151
4:4	31
4:10	33
4:21–30	33
4:25	33, 35
4:26	33, 34, 35
4	23, 135
4:29	135
5:6	25, 31, 46
5:11	36, 201
5:12	33, 64
5:13	31, 35, 38
5:15	24
5:16	39
5:17	31
6:12	161
6:13	33

Ephesians

2:8–9	30
2:10	37
2:11–14	151
2:11–19	30, 67
2:20	85
4:5	31
6:9	21
6:12	31

Philippians

2:2	177
2:5–11	65
2:12	37
3:2–3	25
3:2–8	31
3:3	31
3:9	30
3:18–19	31
3:19	31

Colossians

1:4–5	31
1:5	177
1:10	37
1:13	31
2:5	31
2:11–12	42
2:12	31
2:16	88
3:25	21

1 Thessalonians

1:2	36
1:3	31, 37
1:7–8	19
1:8	36
1:9	34
1:10	31
2:14–16	72
3:2	36
3:5–7	36
3:10	36
4:8	137
4:13	73, 74
4:15	72
4:15–17	73
4:16	74
4:16–17	72
4:17	74
4–5	77
5:1–11	75
5:2	72, 75
5:3	76
5:6–7	72, 76
5:8	31, 36
5:11	73
5:22	131
5:23	104

2 Thessalonians

1:3	31
1:3–4	36
2	72
2:1	72, 76
2:2	76
2:3	76
2:3–4	72, 76
2:5	76
2:7	76
2:8	76
2:9	72, 76
2:10	76
2:15	76
2:9	76

2 Timothy

1:14	94
2:17	134

Titus

1:15	62

Hebrews

1:4	99
1–2	103
1–12	106
2:1	18
2:3	125
2:14	106
2:16	105, 106
5	114

Hebrews (cont.)

6:3	114
8	96
9:14	94
10:1–2	112
10:17	110
11:6	36
11:7	105, 106
11:32	96
12:3–16	98
12:5–13	98
12:7	98
13	119
13:1	105
13:1–7	105
13:2	105
13:3	96, 110
13:5	97
13:7	105, 175
13:7–18	106
13:9	111, 164
13:9–10	112
13:14	197
13:20	104
13:23	7, 104

James

1:1	15, 35, 178
1:2	178
1:6	89
1:10	89, 178
1:18	178
1:22	29, 41
1:23	41
1:25	38
1:27	89
2	24
2:1	23, 38, 41
2:2	15, 23, 35
2:8	24, 38, 87
2:8–10	25
2:8–13	24
2:9	38
2:14	23
2:14–26	14, 22, 26
2:15–16	23, 89
2:17	23
2:18	23
2:19	21, 23
2:20	23
2:21	23
2:23	23, 28
2:24	23
3:12	23
3:14	23
4:11	23, 38
4:12	89
5:4	38
5:9	38, 89
5:12	38
5:14	15, 23
5:20	38

1 Peter

	167–68
1:1	178
1:4	177
1:6	178
1:8	36
1:12–13	15
1:14	177
1:18	15
1:23	178
1:24	178
2:4–5	177
2:5	177
2:5–12	15
3:19–20	172
4:16	181
5:12	167

2 Peter

	89, 170–71
1:16–19	175
2:3–10	173
2:4	172
2:20	189
3:1	167
3:2	173, 175
3:2–3	174
3:3	174
3:3–4	170
3:15	3, 175
3:16	134, 195

1 John

3:23	36

2 John

1:7	193

Jude

1	14
1:5	36

Revelation

2:14	164
2:20	164
7:4–8	15
11:11	44

APOCRYPHA

1 Maccabees

1:54	77

Ancient Authors Index

Augustine of Hippo, 43n125, 143

Basilides, 194

Chrysostom, John, 48
Cicero, 17–18
Clement of Alexandria, 28, 80n46, 90, 102–3
Clement of Rome, 93n3, 117–18, 123

Eusebius of Caesarea, 18, 103, 179, 193

Ignatius of Antioch, 127, 132, 141, 151, 164, 178, 192, 193
    letter to the Romans, 154
Irenaeus of Lyons, 28, 131n13, 134, 151, 154–55, 164–65, 171, 179, 193, 195

Jerome, 130, 132, 171
John of Damascene (John of Damascus), 58n36
Josephus, 17, 20–21, 53n17, 98, 121, 169–70, 179
Justin Martyr, 189

Marcion of Sinope, 28

Origen of Alexandria, 18, 18n27, 93–94, 103, 171

Philo of Alexandria, 39, 114
    and Hebrews, 95–103
Polycarp of Smyrna, 4, 151, 164, 192, 193, 195

Valentinus, 156, 194

Keywords and Modern Authors Index

Abraham
    justified by faith, 23
    Romans 4's discussion of, 13
Acts, 8–9, 10, 151
    Apollos as Alexandrian Jew, 107
Adam, 138
agapē, 105, 162
Akedah, 23
Alexandrian Judaism, 98, 101, 107
Allen, David, 93n3
Allison, Dale, 17
Ananus, 18
Anderson, Charles, 117
Antiquities of the Jews (Josephus), 20
apokalypsis (Revelation), 159–60
Apollos
    in Acts, 10, 107–8
    as Alexandrian Jew, 107
    as author of Hebrews, 63–64, 92, 107, 124
    as disciple of Paul, 7, 107, 162
    do not forsake gathering, 109–11
    idol food, 111–13
    letter from Italy, 116–20
    meat and maturity, 114–16
    trying, 108–20
Apostles heirs, 191–94
Apostolic Decree, 38, 165, 190
    collection, 54
    as difference maker, 52–64
    fleeing immorality, 61–64
    idol-food, 54–61
    immoral brother and, 47–68
apostolic succession, 192
Aquila, 108, 116
Aquinas, Thomas, 185
Aretas, 53n17
Asia Minor, 162n34, 185, 190, 193
Attridge, Harold, 93–94, 106, 116
authorship of Hebrews, 93n1

Barbaglio, Giuseppe, 85
Barclay, John, 38n102, 44n128
Barrett, C.K., 148
Barth, Karl, 197n45,
Bauckham, Richard, 5, 14, 23–24, 141n37, 146, 170–73, 188–90
Bauer, Bruno, 19
Bauer, Walter, 189, 192–93
Baur, F.C., 3n1, 4, 148–49, 151, 161–62, 181, 197
    reading of early Christianity, 9
Beit Hillel, 79n41
Benedict XVI (Pope), 184
biblical theology, 186
boasting, 25–26
Bockmuehl, Marcus, 146–48, 162, 166–67, 176

Body of Christ, 48
"Bread of Life" discourse, 140–42
"breath of life", 138, 144
brotherly love, 120–21
Brown, Raymond, 188
Bultmann, Rudolf, 27n57, 71n6, 135, 142, 148, 187
Burridge, Richard, 188, 190

Caligula statue, 77
Campbell, Douglas, 14, 29–31, 36n98, 39, 53, 76, 120, 158–61, 179, 196
Campenhausen, Hans von, 148
canon consciousness, 9, 194–96
Carlson, Stephen, 90n79
Case, Brendan, 13, 69, 126, 166n46, 170
Catholicism, early, 4, 149, 186
charisms, 128
charity, 23, 24
Chester Beatty II collection, 93n1
Chesterton, G.K., 1, 196
Cheung, Alex, 163
Childs, Brevard, 9
Christ *see* Jesus Christ
Christian diversity, 188
Christianity
    invention of cultured Seneca, 19
circumcision, 6, 25, 27, 29–30, 32, 36, 39–40, 42, 162
Clark, Alexander, 65n50
Clement, 155, 179, 194
    1 Clement, 117–19, 151, 153, 164, 171
    2 Clement, 171
community purity, 48
conflicted history, 148–50
Congregation purity, 49–52
consciences, 112
Conzelmann, Hans, 48
Corinth, 6, 162–65
Corinthians, 54
cosmos, 50
Cranfield, Charles, 137
Crossan, Dominic, 17, 168
cultus, 112

Davids, Peter, 177
Davies, W.D., 71n6
Dead Sea Scrolls, 39n108, 96

death of Christ, 44n129
Dei verbum, 196
Dibelius, Martin, 15n10, 16n12, 22n41
Didache, 89
dietary laws, 25, 29, 31
dietary regulations, 111–13
divorce, 79–80
Dodd, C.H., 71
Douglass, Frederick, 19–20
Dungan, David, 81n50
Dunn, James, 70n5, 86, 146

early catholicism, 4, 149, 186
early Christianity, 148, 155
    reconstruction of, 192
earthly (*epigeia*) bodies, 140
Ecclesiology, 7, 8, 111, 125, 166
Ehrman, Bart, 16–18, 167–69
Ellingworth, Paul, 97, 99, 110, 120
Engberg-Pedersen, Troels, 129, 135
Enoch
    Book of the Watchers, 172
Ephesus, 107–8
Epictetus, 114
epistemology, 64–65
Epistle of Barnabas, 171
Epistle of James, 5, 17, 22, 26, 29, 41, 87, 89, 178, 183, 196
Epistle to the Hebrews, 18
Epistle to the Smyrneans, 132
Esau tradition, 100
Eucharist (Lord's Supper), 47, 49, 82, 111–12, 141–42
Ezekiel
    Diptych, 136
    vision in "Valley of Dry Bones", 128, 137

faith, 31n78
false brothers, 32, 32n84
false teachers, 164
Fee, Gordon, 128n4, 138
first century church, 146
fornication, 48, 80n46
Fourth Evangelist, 127
Fredriksen, Paula, 131n12

Gabler, J.P., 186
Galatians, 157–62

Keywords and Modern Authors Index 229

Gaston, Lloyd, 42
gentile Christians, 15–16, 122, 163
Glass, William, 1, 47, 93
Gospel communities, 188
Gospel of the Egyptians, The, 194
Gospel of the Hebrews, 130, 132
Goulder, Michael, 82, 148, 162, 188
Great Church, 196
Great Divorce, The, 145
Grebel, Conrad, 191
Griesbach, J.J., 90

halakah, 42, 58
Hart, David Bentley, 133
Hartman, Lars, 74
Hays, Richard, 44n128
heavenly (*epourania*) bodies, 140
"Hebraic" Palestinian Judaism, 16
Hebrews, 7, 93–94
    Christ's death (2:14), 104
    purpose of, 120–24
Hegel, G.W.F., 150
Hellenization, 16, 114, 167, 169
Hengel, Martin, 16–17, 24n49
hermeneutic of continuity, 188–91
hermeneutic of rupture/discontinuity, 184–88
history-of-religions school, 186
Hoegen-Rohls, Christina, 135
Holmes, Michael, 153n19
homophrones, 176–77
House of Shammai, 79
human judgment, 128
Hurd, John, 6, 52, 63
Hurst, Lincoln, 95–96, 99–103, 125
hypodeigma (copy), 95, 101

idol-food/meat, 6, 54–63, 111–13, 163–65, 190
imprisonment, 121
Institution Narrative, 70n4, 78, 82, 89, 130, 141
Italy, 116

Jacobi, Christine, 73, 75
James the Just (brother of Jesus)
    anti-Pauline polemic, 24–29
    Aramaic epistle, 20–22
    as author of the *Epistle of James*, 14–16
    as canon-conscious pseudepigrah, 27
    conception of faith, 23
    justification in Jas 2:14–26, 22–24
    literacy, 16–20
    as originator of Justification Discourse, 12, 22, 24–25, 29, 30–32
    and Paul, 5–6
    and the Teachers, 29–45
Jenson, Robert, 195n38
Jerusalem Council, 54
Jesus Christ, 102
    ascension of, 37, 45, 102, 126, 133
    "Bread of Life" discourse, 140–42
    crucifixion of, 2, 70, 145, 152
    death of, 44n129
    life-giving Spirit, 45
    Moses parallelism, 83–84
    resurrection of, 1, 45, 102
    transfiguration in 2 Corinthians, 83–84
Jewett, Robert, 58n36
Jewish Apocalyptic, 95–96
Jewish Christianity, 15on11, 15, 122
Jewish *cultus*, 112
Jewish *halakhic* discipline, 58, 42
Jewish Messiah
    gentile inclusion in people of, 5, 9
Jewish quasi-sacramental meals, 111
Jewish War, The, 20
John the Evangelist
    account of Christ's resurrection, 144
    and spiritual body, 126–45
    use of 1 Corinthians, 127, 130, 135–36
Johnson, Luke, 94, 105, 114, 116
Judaism
    Alexandrian, 96, 98, 101, 102, 107
    diaspora, 15–16, 111
    first-century, 102, 168
Jude
    and 2 Peter, 173–75
    as author of the *Epistle of Jude*, 173, 196
    and the reception of 2 Peter, 175
Julius, 180

justification, 13–14, 44
  by faith, 23
  in Jas 2:14–26, 22–24
  as Paul's "polemical doctrine", 14n4
  as "subsidiary crater", 14n4

Kant, Immanuel, 191–92
Käsemann, 148
Keith, Chris, 146
Kim, Seyoon, 73
Knox, John, 53n17, 151n15
Kümmel, Werner Georg, 25n57

the Law, 43–44
Lectures on the Doctrine of Justification, 126
LeDonne, Anthony, 146
Lee, Simon, 83
Leithart, Peter, 42, 44
Lewis, C.S., 145
life-giving spirit (*pneuma zōopoioun*), 126, 130, 133
  sōma pneumatikon in debate, 128–30
Lightfoot, J.B., 121–22, 154n20, 180
Lindemann, Andreas, 139n36
Little Apocalypse, 71–77
  in 1–2 Thessalonians, 71–77
Locke, John, 185–86
Lohse, Eduard, 150
"lost tribes" as converted gentiles, 15n7
Lukan Authorship of Hebrews (Allen), 93n3
Luke the Evangelist
  Last Supper, 82
  and spiritual body, 126–45
  use of 1 Corinthians, 127, 130–34
Luther, Martin, 93n3, 192n27

MacIntyre, Alasdair, 101n26
Marcus, Joel, 15n7, 28, 144n43, 189n23
Markan traditions, 69
  Christ's transfiguration in 2 Corinthians, 83–84
  Matthew's "Little Apocalypse" in 1–2 Thessalonians, 71–77
  Petrine primacy as problem in Galatians, 84–85
  in Romans, 85–88

synoptic traditions in 1 Corinthians, 78–82
marriage, 79–80
Martin, Dale, 49–51, 54–55
Martyn, Louis, 64, 161, 14, 29–30, 33, 39
Martyr, Justin, 189
Mary Magdalene, 130
Matson, Joshua, 128, 137
Matthean Apocalypse, 76
Matthew
  Little Apocalypse in 1–2 Thessalonians, 71–77
McGrath, Alister, 13n1
McKnight, Scott, 26n56
Ménégoz, Eugène, 95
Messianic secret, 187
Mishnah, 15n11
Mission Discourse, 80, 89
Mitchell, Margaret, 51n12
mixed marriages, 51
Montefiore, 116
Moo, Douglas, 26n56
Moses-Jesus parallelism, 83–84
Moule, C.F.D., 110, 120

Nag Hammadi scrolls, 134, 156
Najman, Hindy, 102n27
Nanos, Mark, 57–58
neighbor-love, 86–87
Nero, 121–22, 179–80
New Testament (NT), 8
  future theology, 183–97
  heirs of Apostles, 191–94
  hermeneutic of continuity, 188–91
  hermeneutic of rupture, 184–88
  informal discussion of, 1
  problem of Canon, 194–96
  rediscovering homeland, 196–97
New Testament Theology (NTT), 183
Newman, John Henry, 45, 126
Nicodemus, 136
Nienhuis, David, 27–28
Not by Paul Alone (Nienhuis), 27

Orchard, Bernard, 72n10
Orlando, Robert, 2
Orthodoxy and Heresy in Earliest Christianity, 192

Overbeck, Franz, 104, 106
Owen, Paul, 42

Pagels, Elaine, 134
paideia (discipline), 98
Palût in Edessa, 193n30
Papias, 69, 170
Parable of the Ten Virgins, 74–75
Paul of Tarsus, 103–8
   and Barnabas, 151, 159
   and being "in Christ", 14, 31, 135
   chronology, 34, 53n17, 158, 196
   and circumcision, 6, 25, 27, 30, 32, 36, 39–40, 42, 162
   and ethics, 2, 47–67
   and Eucharist/Lord's Supper, 47, 49, 82, 111–12
   evidence for Markan posteriority, 69–90
   excommunication of immoral brother, 5, 49, 51, 62
   and faith, 24–29, 31, 36, 57, 104–5, 114
   gentile mission, 151
   idol-food, 6, 54–63, 111–13, 163–65, 190
   influence on Hebrews, 93–125
   and James, 5–6
   and John, 135–36
   justification, 6, 13–46
   and love, 48, 56, 63, 64–66, 86, 163
   and Luke, 81n50, 82
   Markan traditions in, 71–88
   martyrdom of, 154, 179, 181
   and Matthew, 84–86
   and Peter, 8, 10
   polemical doctrine, 32
   relationships to Judaism, 4
   and sexual immorality, 48–49, 51n13, 55, 59, 61–62, 79–80
   and spiritual body, 8, 126–45
   and synoptic traditions, 69–70, 78–82, 88–90
   warning Corinthians, 49
   and "Works of the Law", 25, 38, 42–43
Paulus und Jakobus (Hengel), 16
Pelagius, 27

Peter, 84–85
   martyrdom of, 179, 181
   and Paul. *see* Peter, and Paul
Peter, and Paul
   conflicted history, 148–50
   Corinth, 162–65
   establishing Petrine voice, 165–75
   Galatians, 157–62
   hearing Peter speak, 175–78
   influence of on NT and early church, 146–82
   Memoriam Apostolorum: Peter and Paul at Rome, 178–81
   Petrine evidence, 165–78
   re-evaluating tradition, 150–56
   rereading Pauline evidence, 157–65
Petrine community, 185
Petrine epistles, 176, 196
philadelphia, 105
Philonic Judaism, 95
pilgrimage, 109
pistis (faith), 31, 36
Pitre, Brant, 141–43
Pliny, 164
Polite Bribe, A, 2
Poppea Sabina, 179–80
porneia, 51n13
Powers, B. Ward, 71
Priscilla, 93n3, 108, 116
prison escape, Peter and Paul, 151
pseudepigraphy, 4, 167, 172
Pseudo-Clementine Recognitions, 148

Q-logion, 81
Qumran community, 95–96

Reasoner, Mark, 58
reconciliation, 67
resurrected body, 8
resurrection, 44, 128, 131–34
   appearance to Mary Magdalene, 130
Richards, Randy (Randolph), 17–18, 169
Riesner, Rainer, 53n17
Riley, Harold, 72n10
ritual practice, 39
Robinson, J.A.T., 13
Roman Christians, 116, 122

Romans, 110–11
Romans 4
    discussion of Abraham, 13
Rothschild, Clare, 104n36, 117n68
Rousseau, Jean-Jacques, 191–92
Rowe, C. Kavin, 183
Runia, David, 102n27

Sabbath, 29
Sadducees, 133
salvation, 31
Sanders, E.P., 25, 149
Schlatter, Adolf, 195
Schleiermacher, Friedrich, 192
Schnelle, Udo, 27n57
Schreiner, 128n4
Schweitzer, Abraham, 14
Schweitzer, Albert, 14n4
second-century church, 8
second marriage, 80n46
Second Temple, 16, 26, 39n108
Semitism, 21
Seneca, 114
sexual immorality, 48–49
    prohibition of, 55
sexual sin, 47
Shema, 23, 26
Shepherd of Hermas, 171
Sim, David, 187n18
Simon of Cyrene, 189n23
sōma psychikon/pneumatikon, 128–30, 137
Sowers, Sidney, 95
Spicq, Ceslaus, 94–95, 96n10, 116
spiritual body, 8
    born of water and spirit, 136–40
    dying seed and new Adam, 143–44
    John in Fourth Gospel, 135–36
    Luke's uneasiness about, 130–34
    man from heaven, 140–43
    Paul's *sōma psychikon/pneumatikon* in debate, 128–30, 137
    solidity of John's, 144–45
Strecker, Georg, 184–85
Suetonius, 122
super-apostles, 33
Synoptic Apocalypse, 77, 89
Synoptic traditions, 69–70, 88–90
    in 1 Corinthians, 78–82

Syria, 10, 190, 193
Syriac (Aramaic) Peshitta version, 22

Tacitus, 122
Teachers (Jewish-Christian missionaries), 29–30
    canonical and hermeneutical implications, 46
    justification as Paul's "polemical doctrine", 30–32
    origins of Paul's justification, 35–40
    Paul response to, 40–45
    Paul's struggles against, 32–35
Tertullian, 28, 134
Thackeray, J., 20
Theissen, Gerd, 76
Theophilus, 171
Thessalonians
    Markan traditions, 71–77
Thiessen, Matthew, 98–99
Thiselton, Anthony, 48, 52, 54n19, 115n57, 128n4
Thompson, A.C.C., 19
Timothy, 7, 123–24
Torah, 5, 111, 128, 151
    Jews to abandon, 61
    free (uncircumcised) gentile mission, 6, 25
    observance, 32, 37, 39
tradition, 195
Trajan, 164
trans-local unity, 8
Transfiguration, 89
Treatise on the Resurrection, The, 134
Troeltsch, Ernst, 186
Tübingen hypothesis, 3n1, 5
Tübingen project, in Germany, 148
Tuckett, Christopher, 73
Two-Document Hypothesis (2DH), 81

Vanhoye, Albert, 106n41
Virgin Mary, 93
Vitellius, 53n17
von Harnack, Adolf, 154n20, 192
Voulgaris, Christos, 120n72

Walsh, Brandon, 131n14
"watertight bulkheads" theory, 188
Watson, Francis, 90n79

"weak" in faith, 57–58
Wenham, David, 74, 76, 85
Weschler, Andreas, 150
wilderness period, 98
Williamson, Ronald, 94n3
Winter, Bruce, 58–59
Witherington, Ben, 115n59
Wittgenstein, Ludwig, 183

Wrede, William, 14, 14n4, 148, 186–87, 194, 197
Wright, N.T., 4, 26, 77, 129, 137n27

Ziesler, John, 56n27
Zwierlein, Otto, 178
Zwingli, Ulrich, 142

www.ingramcontent.com/pod-product-compliance
Lightning Source LLC
Chambersburg PA
CBHW051055230426
43667CB00013B/2301